GREAT LIVES OBSERVED

Gerald Emanuel Stearn, *General Editor*

EACH VOLUME IN THE SERIES VIEWS THE CHARACTER AND ACHIEVE-
MENT OF A GREAT WORLD FIGURE IN THREE PERSPECTIVES—
THROUGH HIS OWN WORDS, THROUGH THE OPINIONS OF HIS CON-
TEMPORARIES, AND THROUGH RETROSPECTIVE JUDGMENTS—THUS
COMBINING THE INTIMACY OF AUTOBIOGRAPHY, THE IMMEDIACY
OF EYEWITNESS OBSERVATION, AND THE OBJECTIVITY OF MODERN
SCHOLARSHIP.

GEORGE H. STEIN (*Ph.D., Columbia University*) *is Associate
Professor of History at the State University of New York at
Binghamton. He is the author of the widely acclaimed book,*
The Waffen SS: Hitler's Elite Guard at War, 1939–1945. *His
articles appear frequently in such professional journals as*
Political Science Quarterly *and* Military Review, *as well as in
popular publications.*

Forthcoming volumes in the Great Lives Observed series

Booker T. Washington, *edited by Emma Lou Thornbrough*

Garibaldi, *edited by Denis Mack Smith*

Huey Long, *edited by Hugh Davis Graham*

John F. Kennedy, *edited by Barton J. Bernstein*

Joseph McCarthy, *edited by Allen Matusow*

Mao, *edited by Jerome Ch'en*

Woodrow Wilson, *edited by John Braeman*

GREAT LIVES OBSERVED

Hitler

Edited by GEORGE H. STEIN

*If it be conceded that evil can be great,
then the quality of greatness cannot,
I think, be denied him.*

—George F. Kennan

A SPECTRUM BOOK

PRENTICE-HALL, INC., ENGLEWOOD CLIFFS, N.J.

All footnotes in this book are by
the editor, unless otherwise indicated.

Contents

PART ONE
HITLER LOOKS AT THE WORLD

1

2

3

54250

14

Introduction

w Intro.

In an age of politicized masses and deterministic systems of thought it is sometimes forgotten how important individuals once were—and still can be. Adolf Hitler's rise from the backwaters of an obscure Austrian border town to absolute mastery over Germany and the better part of Europe reminds us forcefully that an individual who can manipulate the complex forces of the modern mass age can still determine the fate of a people and influence the flow of world history.

#3

In the years between 1933 and 1945 Hitler was the central figure in human events. Even now, more than two decades after his death, his name and something of his reputation are almost everywhere known. His face too—the lank hair slanting across the high forehead, the burning eyes, the toothbrush mustache smudging the upper lip—is instantly recognized by millions of people throughout the world. The most catastrophic events of our century are indissolubly linked with the figure of Adolf Hitler. Indeed, the word *Hitlerism* has become a recognized part of our language, a synonym for the most brutal of totalitarian dictatorships. In a very real sense, moreover, Hitler is still with us, for his deeds and misdeeds have left us a legacy of political and moral problems that have not yet been solved.

Hitler regarded himself as a great man. He was not mistaken. Surely it would be absurd to suggest that anyone who so transfigured the world was of ordinary stature. The expression "great man," however, implies a favorable judgment of quality that most people find impossible to use when referring to the leader of the Third Reich. For in not one major field did he leave the German nation, or any other segment of the earth, better off than he found it. The historian, nonetheless, recognizes both positive and negative greatness; evil men as well as benefactors of mankind may tower above their fellows. Hence, Hitler's greatness, which historically speaking was entirely negative, can be measured only in terms of the ruinous consequences of his policies and the monstrousness of his crimes. During the twelve years he ruled the Third Reich, Hitler raised the German people to dizzying heights of power—making them at one time masters of an empire that stretched from the Atlantic Ocean to the Volga River, from the Arctic Circle to North Africa—and then dropped them into the abyss of desolation that was the price of a lost world war that he had provoked and during which he instituted a program of calculated terror and deliberate human slaughter that surpassed the most bestial excesses previously known to man.

To examine the life and the mind of a person who visited so much misery and destruction on mankind may not be pleasant. But it is necessary. And it will not do to shudder and retreat, or to dismiss Hitler with either pejoratives or oversimplifications. For the combination of political genius and inner compulsion that accounted for so much of Hitler's success, although fortunately rare, is not unique. Nor are the cultural, political, and economic conditions that breed men like Hitler and spawn movements like National Socialism necessarily limited to one place or one time.

This volume is designed to contribute toward an understanding of Adolf Hitler. It attempts to reconstruct his life, illuminate his personality, examine his ideas, and evaluate his role in history by means of a novel three-dimensional presentation. First, through selections from his own spoken and written words, Hitler—speaking, as it were, for himself—reveals not only his points of view but also the workings of his mind. The second part of the book presents a variety of first-hand impressions of Hitler by his contemporaries—friends, followers, journalists, and diplomats—whose diverse observations and opinions shed light on the complex image of the living personality. The historical dimension of time and detachment is represented in the third part, which consists of some recent appraisals, by leading scholars, of Hitler's character, abilities, and role in history. To help the reader correlate these three varying perspectives, the editor has included, immediately following these preliminary remarks, a biographical essay that attempts not only to sketch the principal events of Hitler's life and political career but also to suggest, however tentatively, some of the emotional experiences and inner needs that shaped his thoughts and actions.

The man who was for a decade the most powerful ruler in the world was born on April 20, 1889, in the small Austrian border town of Braunau on the River Inn. If being a child of poverty is one of the prerequisites for a successful career as a totalitarian dictator, Hitler was not fully qualified for the position. For unlike Stalin, who was the son of a poor shoemaker, and Mussolini, who was the son of an impoverished blacksmith, Hitler was the son of an Imperial customs officer whose social status and income placed him comfortably in the middle class.

Neither before his father's death in 1903 nor for some years thereafter was Hitler in financial need—his claim in *Mein Kampf* that his childhood was one of poverty and deprivation arose from an ulterior motive. However, it is doubtless true that young Adolf's home life was not a happy one. He was the fourth child of his father's third marriage;[1] and the elder Hitler—who was twenty-three years older than his wife and fifty-two years older than his son Adolf—was a domineering, unsympathetic, short-tempered man. Under the circumstances it is perhaps not suprising that young Adolf received little of the paternal love and guidance that is so vital to the healthy emotional development of a child. His relationship with his father was certainly not improved by his passive resistance to the elder Hitler's determination to see his son follow a career in the civil service. Adolf did not want to be a civil servant. He wanted to be an artist. The conflict between parental determination and youthful ambition not only had much to do with Adolf's poor performances in high school but also profoundly changed his whole manner of life.

In contrast to his excellent performance throughout his five years in elementary school, Adolf's first year at the technical high school in Linz was a disaster. His teachers found him intelligent but lazy and undisciplined. Although he did reasonably well in drawing, history, and geography, Adolf failed both natural science and mathematics (subjects that require continuous and sustained effort); and he was forced to repeat the entire year. For the next three years he barely managed to slip by in school. Sullen and resentful at home, lazy and uncooperative in school, solitary and lonely in society, Adolf muddled through early adolescence. Neither his father's death in 1903 nor his transfer to another high school in nearby Steyr in 1904 had any appreciable effect on his marginal academic career. Finally, in the fall of 1905, Adolf became a high school drop-out at the age of sixteen. In later years Hitler often made light of his failure to graduate, but in truth it was a failure that disturbed him greatly and found frequent expression in contemptuous remarks about those with diplomas and degrees. The whole experience deeply affected his later development. Its immediate effect was to leave him at once resentful and confused: resentful toward his family and society, confused about himself and his future. Adolf attempted to overcome these problems by withdrawing from the world of hard realities.

For the next two years, Hitler lived comfortably and pleasantly with his widowed mother, of whom he seems to have been genuinely fond. She, in turn, apparently bewildered by her son, left him for the most part to his own devices. These were heady days for the dreamy young man. He refused to seek employment and spent his time reading, drawing, attending the opera, walking in the streets and woods, and dreaming of becoming an artist or an architect. Much as Adolf would have liked to prolong his idleness, his mother's illness, coupled with

[1] Most of the existing accounts label Hitler the third child of this marriage. Recent research, however, has uncovered another child named Otto who died either at birth or in early infancy two years before Adolf was born.

the mounting disapproval of family and neighbors, forced him to put an end to this period of withdrawal.

In September 1907 Hitler—now eighteen years old—set out for Vienna with a portfolio of drawings to seek admission to the Academy of Fine Arts. Much to his surprise, he was unsuccessful. Moreover, neither the School of Architecture nor the School of Construction Technology would have him without a high school diploma. The whole episode was a bitter disappointment. And once again Hitler dealt with the situation by withdrawing into a dream world in which he slept a great deal, read, doodled, went sight-seeing, and visited the opera. His "studies" (as he grandly called his activities) were interrupted by word that his mother was dying of cancer. Hitler reached Linz toward the end of 1907 in time to bury her.

In February 1908 he returned to Vienna to resume his self-imposed moratorium.[2] For the next five years, Hitler lived a lonely, aimless, and obscure life in the teeming capital of the Hapsburg Empire. His stay in Vienna has been the subject of much speculation. In his autobiography, *Mein Kampf*, Hitler portrays himself as a poor, struggling student who diligently earned his meager keep by hard work. In much of the literature, on the other hand, Hitler is pictured during his stay in Vienna as a shiftless tramp who lived in flophouses and worked unwillingly and only occasionally as an unskilled laborer or housepainter. Although much remains unknown, recent studies suggest that neither of these descriptions is accurate. In actual fact there was no reason why Hitler need have suffered from either material deprivation or hunger at any time between 1908 and 1914. The money he inherited from his parents and the income from his orphan's pension assured him of a comfortable existence. Even after his inheritance ran out (perhaps after two years), his pension and the money he earned painting postcards and small pictures were sufficient to sustain him in the bohemian existence he had chosen for himself. There is no evidence that he lived in a flophouse for much longer than a month during the entire five years. Even this brief stay probably had more to do with his desire to avoid the draft than with a lack of money. In 1911, for example, a sizable inheritance from the estate of a deceased aunt, coupled with the income from his picture painting, enabled Hitler to relinquish his orphan's pension in favor of his younger sister. It is difficult to avoid the conclusion that such hardships as Hitler may have experienced in Vienna were largely self-imposed.

At all events, Hitler's stay in Vienna is of historical significance not

---

[2] The concept of psychosocial moratorium ("one possible way of postponing the decision as to what one is and is going to be") is Erik H. Erikson's. See his *Young Man Luther: A Study in Psychoanalysis and History* (New York: W. W. Norton & Company, Inc., 1958), p. 43 and *passim*.

so much for the material conditions in which he lived as for the lessons he learned and the ideas he absorbed. For these were the formative years in which the alienated and resentful young Hitler, searching for an answer to the problems of identity and purpose that had troubled him throughout adolescence, developed the nucleus of the *Weltanschauung*, the philosophy of life, that he carried with him into his political career. Nationalism; racial anti-Semitism; worship of violence; hatred of liberalism, of democracy, of socialism—all these notions were staples of the anti-Semitic and nationalist press and the *völkisch*[3] tracts that seem to have been Hitler's chief literary fare while in Vienna. There, too, he picked up some of the political techniques that would later help him secure power on the basis of these ideas. From the right-radical parties, as well as from the Marxists (whom he despised), Hitler learned the importance both of social problems and of appealing to the masses, the value of discipline and organization, and the techniques of propaganda and showmanship. In short, Hitler was not exaggerating when he wrote in *Mein Kampf* that Vienna had been the "most thorough school" of his life.

Hitler left Vienna permanently late in May 1913 and moved across the border to Munich. The most likely explanation for his move to Germany is that he was trying to evade military service in the Austro-Hungarian Army. And in *Mein Kampf* he deliberately antedated his departure from Vienna by a year in an apparent effort to conceal the reason for his precipitate emigration. The fact is that Hitler should have registered for conscription in 1909, at the age of twenty, which he had deliberately failed to do. He thus became a draft dodger with a possible prison sentence hanging over his head. In Munich he posed as a stateless person; but late in December 1913 the Austrian authorities caught up with him. A month later he was arrested by the German police and turned over to the Austro-Hungarian consulate in Munich. Characteristically, Hitler managed to persuade the authorities not to prosecute him for draft evasion in return for his promise to report for a medical examination in Austria the following month. Early in February 1914 he duly presented himself before an army medical commission in Salzburg, where he was found physically unfit for military service. The incident was closed, and Hitler returned to Munich.

Six months later, World War I broke out. For the twenty-five-year-old expatriate—with no parents, no friends, no profession, and no security—the war offered a welcome solution to the dilemma of his aimless existence. A few days later, the young Austrian who had been

---

[3] The word *völkisch* is untranslatable. Briefly, it was a pseudophilosophical and quasi-scientific doctrine whose principal ingredient (by the time Hitler came into contact with it) was a kind of biological or racial nationalism.

both unwilling and unfit to serve in the army of his native land volunteered and was accepted for service in the German Army.[4] During the years before Hitler became chancellor, and again after his death, his opponents spread rumors designed to destroy the image presented in *Mein Kampf* and elsewhere of Hitler as a war hero. The truth is that Hitler, although perhaps no hero, was a brave and conscientious soldier. Serving a good deal of the time in or near the front lines, he was wounded twice and decorated for bravery or distinguished service five times. His last decoration—awarded shortly before the end of the war—was the Iron Cross First Class, a medal not often conferred on enlisted men in the Imperial Army. Why, despite his excellent service record, Hitler never advanced beyond the rank of private first class,[5] remains one of the minor mysteries of his military career. Temporarily blinded during a gas attack in October 1918, Hitler was sent to a military hospital in northeastern Germany, where news of the armistice reached him early the following month. It was another major turning point in his life.

When we look back from 1918, trying to understand the man who was soon to embark on a political career without parallel in history, we can (ideologically speaking) identify two formative experiences in his life: the years in Vienna and Munich and the years in the army. The period between the beginning of 1908 and the middle of 1914 was a kind of psychic moratorium, a withdrawal from reality, a time of loneliness, frustration, and uncertainty. During these years, as we have already noted, Hitler collected some of the ideas and techniques that subsequently became central to his political career. But he still lacked both the determination and the discipline necessary to make the realization of these ideas and phantasies his life's work. It was the four years in the wartime army that enabled Hitler to transform his romantic escapism into a drive for power and a program of political extremism. In the army he found both a home and a sense of belonging. The comradeship, the excitement, the discipline, and—above all—the sense of purpose inherent in front-line military service helped Hitler to overcome the alienation and rootlessness that had previously warped his existence. The war was a period of emotional awakening for him. It changed Hitler from a frustrated and confused postadolescent into a tough, resolute, and self-reliant man.

It was therefore not surprising that Hitler was shocked by Germany's defeat, and there is little reason to doubt his statement in *Mein Kampf* that it was a decisive experience in his life. The war and

[4] Technically, Hitler enlisted in the Bavarian Army, which in time of war passed under the command of the German Emperor and thus became part of the Imperial German Army.

[5] Hitler's rank of *Gefreiter*, often incorrectly translated as corporal, was the equivalent of British Army lance corporal and United States Army private first class.

Hitler's newly acquired sense of identity—his sense of purpose and his recognized place in society—were inextricably bound together. Germany's defeat meant that his military career would soon be over, and it threatened him with a return to his prewar nothingness. To save his identity Hitler grasped eagerly at the myth that a Jewish-Marxist "stab in the back" had caused Germany's sudden, undeserved collapse, and he resolved to continue the war in the political arena— this time against the internal enemy: the "Jewish-Marxists" whom he had learned to hate in Vienna. In racial anti-Semitism, Hitler found the answer to both his own problems and (so he believed) the problems of postwar Germany.

To be sure, Hitler's first step on the upward path to political power was not simply the result of a sudden and conscious decision on his part. Luck and circumstances also played a considerable role. Unwilling to face the uncertainties of civilian life any sooner than he had to, Hitler returned to his regiment's home base in Munich. In that postwar hotbed of political confusion and violence, Private First Class Adolf Hitler lived through the brief but bloody period of the Soviet Republic. After the communists were ruthlessly crushed by the combined efforts of the regular army and right-wing paramilitary forces, Hitler's evident nationalist and anti-Marxist fervor led his superiors to appoint him a political instructor whose principal task was to combat revolutionary tendencies in the ranks and to indoctrinate his army comrades with right-wing views. This was a stroke of good fortune for Hitler. It gave him not only his start in politics but also the opportunity to discover and employ his special gift: his speaking ability. So, more by accident than by design, Hitler stumbled on his life's work.

In September 1919 Hitler received orders to attend and to report on a meeting of a small political group that called itself the German Workers' Party (*Deutsche Arbeiterpartei,* or DAP). Despite its suspiciously Marxist-sounding name and vaguely anticapitalist program, the DAP turned out to be simply one of the many shabby ultranationalist and anti-Semitic groups that thrived in the hothouse political atmosphere of postwar Munich. Hitler's attendance at the meeting— during which, characteristically unable to keep his mouth shut, he vehemently attacked a speaker who had advocated Bavaria's secession from Germany—earned him (a few days later) an unsolicited invitation to join the DAP. After some hesitation, during which he apparently concluded that this insignificant party might well serve as the perfect vehicle for his political career, Hitler became the fifty-fifth member of the party and the seventh member of the party's executive committee. In *Mein Kampf* he noted, somewhat dramatically that "it was the most decisive resolve of my life. From here there was and could be no turning back." In actual fact, Hitler was far too cautious to burn all his bridges behind him. Although he quickly turned his considerable talents and energies to party affairs, he did not give up his position in the army.

Made responsible for recruitment, Hitler energetically and successfully began to build up the DAP's membership. At the beginning of 1920, he took charge of the party's propaganda activities and immediately laid plans for its first mass meeting. On February 24 nearly 2,000 people gathered in the *Festsaal* of the famous Hofbräuhaus heard Hitler announce for the first time in public the party's new name, National Socialist German Workers' Party (NSDAP), and its twenty-five point program. The program, although it contained elements of originality, was largely an expression of the spirit of the times. Essentially it was a politically expedient mixture of extreme nationalism, virulent anti-Semitism, vague anticapitalism, and a wide-ranging variety of promises to all social classes.

In the smoke-filled beer halls of Munich, Hitler discovered within himself the key that would unlock his special political genius. All of his long-harbored resentments, his accumulated hatreds, his diatribes against the Jews, the Marxists, the Weimar Republic, the Versailles Treaty found an echo in the troubled Munich of the time. At last Hitler was in a position to attempt to settle his personal account on a large scale and in a public arena. He had found his identity.

Thanks to his talents as an organizer and tactician and his effectiveness as a public speaker, the NSDAP grew rapidly in both size and importance. By the end of March 1920 Hitler felt secure enough in his new calling to resign from the army. Little more than a year later, he had become the party's *Führer,* with virtually dictatorial powers. An important stage on his road to power had been reached. Henceforth, the NSDAP became more and more a mass following for one dynamic and charismatic personality: Adolf Hitler. Toward the close of 1921, the NSDAP had some 6,000 registered members, tens of thousands of sympathizers, an office, a newspaper (the *Völkischer Beobachter*), an insignia (the swastika), a flag (red, white, and black), a slogan ("Germany Awake!"), a paramilitary squad of storm troopers (the SA), and a small but growing circle of wealthy and influential supporters.

The NSDAP was the party of misery and despair; five years after the end of the war there was still plenty of both in Germany. By mid-1923, there were over 50,000 card-carrying Nazis in the land. Hitler felt his power and influence growing. He began to see himself as a real force in German politics. When the French occupation of the Ruhr and the inflation of 1923 brought the Weimar Republic to the verge of economic and political disintegration, Hitler thought he saw an opportunity not only to break out of local Bavarian politics but also perhaps to overthrow the regime and seize power in Germany. Impressed by Mussolini's successful "March on Rome" the previous year, Hitler, taking advantage of the unsettled conditions, attempted to unite the nationalist and right-wing forces in Bavaria and to lead them in a "March on Berlin."

The result was the almost comic-opera "Beer Hall *Putsch*" of November 8 and 9, 1923, which ended with a salvo from the rifles of a handful of Bavarian State Police. Sixteen Nazis died, others were wounded. Hitler, who had fled from the scene, went into hiding but was arrested a few days later. He had overreached himself. Ambition, overestimation of his own importance, and misjudgment of the complex political situation in Bavaria had seemingly put an end to his meteoric political career. The NSDAP was suppressed, and in February 1924 Hitler and some of his followers were put on trial for high treason before a special court in Munich.

If there was ever any doubt of Hitler's political and oratorical skill, it was quickly dispelled by the way he transformed his setback into a political victory. The trial, covered by the world press as well as by the leading German newspapers, became a forum in which Hitler not only converted the failure of November 8 and 9 into one of the great propaganda myths of the Nazi movement but also made his name and that of the NSDAP known throughout Germany and much of the western world. In the end, Hitler was given the minimum sentence of five years, of which he served less than nine months before being released. During his imprisonment in Landsberg (for the Nazi leader and his cronies, really more of a spartan resort than a prison), Hitler rested, ate well, and dictated what was to become the first volume of *Mein Kampf*. While he was distilling the ideological refuse of more than two decades of frustration and resentment, the NSDAP fell apart. By the time Hitler left prison in December 1924, the party had become so weak that it was no longer a serious force in politics. Consequently, the authorities lifted the ban on the NSDAP and its newspaper, and Hitler was able to reconstitute his movement. One thing the abortive *Putsch* had taught him was that not violence but legality—or rather a show of legality backed by the threat of violence—offered the best way to achieve power. This would require patience and organization. And it cost Hitler much effort to make this clear to some of his activist followers. There were bitter conflicts and internecine power struggles over the direction in which the party should move. But in the end Hitler once more reigned supreme. His success in intraparty politics, however, was not matched by a similar success in national politics.

Local speaking prohibitions and improved economic conditions in Germany during the second half of the twenties robbed Hitler of his two most effective weapons: discontent and the mass meetings in which his demogogy was employed to best advantage. In 1928, after three years of sustained effort, the NSDAP had managed to attract barely

100,000 dues-paying members and 2.5 per cent of the vote in national elections. The years of Weimar prosperity and stability were lean years for the Nazi movement. But Hitler had learned how to be patient. Never, it seems, did he lose either hope or confidence. Though he was both ignorant of and uninterested in economics, he was certain that Germany's sudden prosperity would not last. He was right. The great depression that spread over much of the industrialized world toward the end of 1929 gave the NSDAP its first opportunity to break into the mainstream of national politics. In Germany the depression caused both an economic crisis of the first magnitude and a political crisis more acute than that suffered by any other western nation. The Weimar Republic, unloved by so many of its citizens, began to disintegrate. The widespread antidemocratic and anti-liberal sentiment that was a legacy from Imperial Germany and the growing economic and social dislocation not only doomed the Republic but also facilitated the rise of Adolf Hitler.

In 1928 the NSDAP had polled only a shade over 800,000 votes, enough to fill a scant twelve seats in the Reichstag. In 1930, under the shadow of the great depression, the Nazi vote rose to nearly six and a half million, and Nazi Reichstag representation leaped to 107 seats. From the smallest party in Parliament, the NSDAP had become the second largest. Economic crisis, political tension, and cultural confusion had catapulted Hitler from political insignificance to the threshold of political power. Soon he began to receive financial support from some of the great industrialists. In the army, too, the feeling grew that Hitler was the man most likely to rebuild Germany's military might. Before long, the NSDAP had established an alliance with the influential German National People's Party.[6] By the end of 1931 Hitler was in direct contact with the men who counted politically.

In order to understand the peculiar way in which Hitler assumed power, it is necessary to know that after the spring of 1930, in the absence of a stable parliamentary majority, Germany was governed by chancellors appointed by the President and dependent for their authority on decrees issued by him on the basis of emergency powers provided for in the Weimar Constitution. In effect, then, political power in Germany was exercised neither by the voters nor by the Reichstag but by a small group of conservative nationalists around the old and ultraconservative president, Field-Marshal von Hindenburg. And yet Hindenburg and his advisors were not satisfied with this situation; they realized that Germany could not be ruled indefinitely by decree. Accordingly, two Reichstag elections were held in 1932 in an effort to

---

[6] Known as the Conservative Party under the Empire, this party of the far right represented Germany's conservative establishment: the aristocracy, the East-Elbian landowners, the officer corps, the great industrialists, and the high-ranking civil servants.

establish a stable government based either on a majority or on a coalition that could command a majority in the legislature. Nothing could have been better calculated to play into Hitler's hands. The elections gave him ample opportunity to employ his extraordinary skill as a public speaker and to capitalize on the superbly organized machinery of the NSDAP and its auxiliary organizations.

The first of the two elections was held in late July 1932; it was a stunning victory for the NSDAP, which now became the largest single party in the nation. With a following of nearly fourteen million voters, a Reichstag representation of 230 seats, a party membership of over one million, and a paramilitary force of 400,000 Storm Troopers, Hitler was clearly the most powerful political figure in Germany. In the face of economic and political anarchy, the members of the conservative camarilla were forced to deal with him. They feared Hitler and his movement; but they feared the left (whose strength had also increased markedly in the elections) even more, and they deluded themselves into believing that they could use the Nazi leader to deliver his mass support into their hands in return for a post in the cabinet. But Hitler wanted the chancellorship, for only as chancellor would he have the opportunity to use the president's emergency power to rule by decree to carry out his revolution. He therefore refused to participate in any coalition not led by himself. In the end Hitler had his way. Although the Nazis had fallen far short of a majority in the last election of 1932 (and indeed had lost some of the votes they had gained the previous July), the conservative nationalists, with the support of key army leaders, engineered the delivery of power to Hitler.

In the Nazi leader they thought they had found a man whom they could manipulate into attaining their goals. They wanted to destroy the Republic, to re-establish an authoritarian regime that would safeguard their economic and social primacy, to undo the consequences of the defeat of 1918, to restore the military power of the nation, and to win for Germany a new place in the sun. These were in part Hitler's aims too. And he brought with him the popular support that the conservative nationalists lacked. Faced with some of Hitler's more radical pronouncements, the conservatives took refuge behind the old saying that "the soup is never served as hot as it is cooked." Responsibility they believed would tame the Nazi leader. In any event, they were certain that their supporters would hold enough posts in the coalition cabinet (eight of eleven) to keep Hitler and his followers in check. It was these arguments that finally overcame President Hindenburg's reluctance to see the "Bohemian Pfc" as head of the German government. On the morning of January 30, 1933, Hitler was appointed chancellor by the President in accordance with the authority vested in him by the Weimar Constitution.

Power may have been delivered to Hitler by the nationalist conservative camarilla; nonetheless, Hitler's regime was not a dictatorship
of a small clique but a political movement that rested on a wide mass
base. It is often pointed out, by way of minimizing Hitler's popularity,
that at most *only* 37.3 per cent of the German electorate voted for
him before his assumption of power. It would perhaps be more significant to stress this fact for just the opposite reason. That the Nazi
Party was able to attract the support of nearly four out of every ten
voters, a cross-section of the nation, was in itself a remarkable feat
under the circumstances (more than a dozen parties ran in the election), and one matched during the preceding twelve years by no other
political party. This popular support, coupled with the passivity or
acquiescence of so many other Germans, was at least as important
to the success of Hitler's revolution as the support of the governing
elite, the civil servants, and the army. The Nazi revolution, however,
did not precede but followed Hitler's assumption of the chancellorship. His rise to power had been legal; it was his exercise of power that
turned out to be revolutionary.

Hitler's domestic policy at the outset was guided by neither an
exact blueprint nor a systematic ideology. He simply wanted to secure
total power. Therefore, the Nazi revolution, in its early stages, was designed not so much to eliminate or to systematically transform all existing institutions as to control them and to make them useful instruments of the Führer's will. This could be accomplished in many
cases by simply altering an organization or institution enough to
destroy its capacity to act independently. This process, called *Gleich-
schaltung* (roughly, coordination) in Nazi jargon, was the principal
instrument used by the National Socialists in carrying out their revolution. It was a means whereby revolutionary power could be exercised
while the outward forms of legality were largely maintained. To be
sure, Hitler did not shun brutal terror and open violations of legality, even during the early days when he was still regarded as the
twenty-second chancellor of the Weimar Republic rather than the
first Führer of the Third Reich, but he preferred to use legal or
pseudolegal methods whenever these would achieve his aims.

At first, Hitler—like his predecessors—ruled with the aid of emergency decrees issued by the President. Unlike his predecessors, however, Hitler used these decrees to undermine the constitution and to
legalize terror. In the wake of the mysterious Reichstag fire, Hitler—
claiming that the event was the beginning of a communist coup—
managed to persuade the aging President to sign an emergency decree
on February 28, 1933, that suspended indefinitely all the basic rights
guaranteed in the Weimar Constitution. Under this decree, which
remained in force until the fall of the Third Reich, any group or
person could be silenced or imprisoned at will by the government

without due process of law. A month later, by a combination of coercion and false promises, Hitler managed to force through the Reichstag a law, the so-called "Enabling Act," that in effect gave him the power both to enact legislation without the Reichstag and to deviate from the constitution whenever he thought it necessary. The passage of this act freed Hitler of any restraint by either the Reichstag or the President. It marked the end of constitutional government in Germany and laid the foundation for Hitler's subsequent dictatorship.

Moving now with lightning rapidity Hitler eliminated first his political opponents and then his political allies. In a series of revolutionary moves that combined infiltration from below, decrees from above, and terror from all sides, the Nazis either destroyed or coordinated Germany's public institutions. The national government, the state governments, the local governments, the trade unions, the political parties, the police, the civil service, the courts, and the schools were either eliminated or brought under Nazi control in short order. In a bloody purge during the summer of 1934, Hitler neutralized the disaffected elements within the Nazi ranks. Finally, the death of President Hindenburg in August 1934 enabled Hitler to add to his already substantial power the prerogatives of Head of State and Commander-in-Chief of the Armed Forces. The Army's acceptance of Hitler as Supreme Commander (formalized by an oath of allegiance to him personally) neutralized the last source of potential opposition to his assumption of total power. The title of president was abolished; Hitler was henceforth to be known by the official title of Führer and Reich Chancellor. Invited to express approval of this step by plebiscite, the German people voted overwhelmingly in favor: 84 per cent of those entitled to vote marked their ballots "Yes." [7] Clearly, no totalitarian dictatorship has been so willingly accepted by so many people as Hitler's was in Germany.

With all power concentrated in his own hands, Hitler now had the means to achieve his two principal goals: the destruction of the Jews and the acquisition of "living space." His domestic policy after 1934 was determined by these goals; it may be summed up as total coordination, institutionalized racial anti-Semitism, and massive rearmament. Although Hitler made little effort to hide his regime's animosity toward the Jews, he was careful not to disclose his foreign policy goals publicly during his first years in power. His protestations of peaceful desires and his seemingly limited aim of revising some of the "injus-

---

[7] The extent to which the plebiscite was "free" is a matter of debate. There is no doubt that the voters were subjected to pressures ranging from intensive propaganda to occasional physical intimidation. But the balloting was, for the most part, secret, and the results were not, as in later elections, systematically falsified. It is this writer's opinion that the announced results of the plebiscite generally, if not precisely, reflected the will of the German people at the time.

tices" of the Versailles Treaty were carefully calculated to win sympathy or support for Germany abroad and to ward off any attempts to interfere with his ultimate designs. In reality, his main objective was neither the restoration of the frontiers of 1914 nor the establishment of a Greater German Reich that would incorporate all of the German-speaking peoples of central Europe. This was merely his minimum program. In the privacy of his own intimate circle—not to mention in *Mein Kampf* and in the countless public speeches he made in the decade before he became chancellor—Hitler never left any doubt that the conquest of non-German land for living space (principally in the east) was the basic aim and purpose of his policies.

From the first military conferences early in 1933 to the invasion of Poland on September 1, 1939, unlimited territorial expansion remained clearly fixed in Hitler's sights; all appearances to the contrary were only tactically motivated temporary departures from a fixed resolve. The agreements and treaties that in the course of the years were made and broken; the fulfillment of limited revisionist goals like the reoccupation of the Rhineland and the annexation of both Austria and the Sudetenland; and finally the promise of peace at Munich in 1938 and the offer of friendship to Great Britain were only means to an end, stepping stones secured without war toward larger conquests that could be secured only by war.

By the middle of 1939, Hitler had overdrawn his bow. Somewhat belatedly, Great Britain and France came to the conclusion that Hitler was not so much interested in reclaiming German territory as he was in using the revision of the Versailles Treaty as a springboard to a general, perhaps limitless, policy of territorial expansion. Consequently, when Hitler turned his attention eastward and began to make territorial demands on Poland, the two western powers announced that they intended to stand by the Poles in the event they were attacked. Hitler, although prepared to fight both the British and the French if necessary, was certain that they were only bluffing. On September 1 he launched the *Wehrmacht* against Poland. Much to his surprise, he discovered that Great Britain and France meant to keep their promise. World War II had begun.

Having succeeded, just prior to the attack, in securing the Soviet Union's benevolent neutrality, Hitler was able to conquer Poland in just three weeks. But the surrender of the Poles in no real sense ended the war in that part of Europe. For with the German occupation came a new kind of war: the racial war. The racial policy that the Nazis had conducted since 1933 had already led to frightful results: the Jews within the Reich had been systematically persecuted, frequently brutalized, sometimes murdered, and fully deprived of both their livelihoods and their civil rights. Now, under the cover of a major war,

Hitler was able to convert his wildest phantasies into a horrible reality. Poland was to become an ideological and racial laboratory, a working model of the Nazi New Order. In this laboratory of horror, the Jews were to be exterminated, and the Poles (as members of an inferior race) were to be reduced to a state of near slavery. So successful were the early stages of the Nazi experiment in Poland that Hitler's racial war was subsequently extended to all of German-occupied Europe as a matter of state policy. In the concentration camps and prisons of the Reich, before the firing squads of the SS execution teams, and in the great extermination camps of the east the Government of the Third Reich, under Hitler's authority, carried out the most enormous program of human slaughter of all time. This stupendous evil—the systematic murder of several million people, Jews as well as other racial or political "undesirables"—was the terrifyingly logical outcome of the irrational ideology that Hitler had developed during his formative years.

While the SS conducted the racial war in Poland, the *Wehrmacht* waged the military war in the west. The technical and strategic superiority of the German forces at first enabled them to win one victory after another. In April 1940 German troops occupied Denmark and Norway. A month later the *Wehrmacht* turned against the western powers. By the end of June the Netherlands, Belgium, Luxembourg, and most of France had been overrun; the British had been swept from the mainland; and France had been forced to her knees. Still, Hitler's plan to invade the British Isles had to be abandoned in the face of Germany's inability either to destroy the Royal Air Force or to win control of the English Channel. The British, however, were temporarily helpless to undertake any offensive action that could conceivably threaten German hegemony on the Continent.

Having avoided the immediate danger of a two-front war, Hitler decided that the time had come to fulfill his crowning ambition in the field of foreign affairs: the destruction of the Soviet Union and the establishment on its territory of a great German colonial empire. A lightning (and unplanned) campaign in the Balkans, undertaken to extricate Hitler's Italian ally from the abyss of defeat, brought Yugoslavia and Greece under German control. Finally, on June 22, 1941, Hitler (ignoring the nonaggression pact of August 1939) launched his armies against Russia. The war, proclaimed by Nazi propaganda as the decisive struggle between the Aryan race and the "Jewish-Bolshevik revolution of subhumans," was waged with a ruthlessness unmatched in modern history. The Germans were spectacularly successful at first; but they were unable to defeat the Russians decisively. The winter of 1941–42 saw the German *Blitzkrieg* effectively halted—just short of Moscow.

Despite further impressive German gains in the south of Russia during the following spring and summer, the tide began to turn in the fall—and not only in Russia but also in Africa. On November 4, 1942, the British forced the Germans and Italians into retreat at the battle of El Alamein; four days later an Anglo-American army under the command of General Eisenhower landed in North Africa; and on November 22 a Russian counteroffensive encircled a German army of a quarter of a million men at Stalingrad. After three years of steady victory and virtually unbroken advance, Hitler's *Wehrmacht* lost the initiative and began its long retreat.

As the course of the war turned ever more sharply against Germany, Hitler began to age rapidly. Not only his health but also his capacities were undermined by adversity. As the memory of past victories was overshadowed by present defeats that even skillful propaganda could no longer hide, many of Hitler's followers realized that he was leading Germany to catastrophe. It was this realization that led a handful of senior Army officers to make an unsuccessful attempt to assassinate their Supreme Commander. The failure of the attempt on Hitler's life inaugurated the last and most terrible period of his rule.

Interpreting his survival as a demonstration of the favor of Providence, Hitler initiated a policy of total war, a last-ditch effort to reverse the course of events. True to his basic ideology, he offered his nation only two alternatives: total victory or total ruin. For the last time the German people responded to their Führer's call, some out of conviction, the rest out of desperation or fear. It was all to no avail. By the beginning of 1945 it was clear to almost everyone that the war was irretrievably lost. Hitler, however, refused to accept the possibility of defeat; he alone still believed in ultimate victory.

The last weeks of the war revealed the bizarre and compulsive character of the man. As Germany crumbled and defeat advanced, Hitler—now by all accounts a physical and mental wreck immured in an underground bunker behind the Reich Chancellery—lost the last vestiges of contact with reality: he issued impossible orders to nonexistent armies; raged incessantly against those he claimed had betrayed him; and, reverting to the inherent nihilism of his ideology, ordered a "scorched earth" policy. Germany was to be made a wasteland. Nothing was to be left to the enemy. Opposed by Albert Speer, Minister for Armaments and Munitions, who had the temerity to point out to his master that nothing could prevent Germany's collapse and that a policy of destruction would deprive those Germans who survived the war of any chance of rebuilding their lives in the future, Hitler replied that if he was to fall, then all should fall with him. For if Germany was to be defeated then the Germans had forfeited their right to survive. In line with his perverted Darwinian view of life, Hitler concluded that if the war was indeed lost, then "the nation

[*Volk*] [8] has proved itself weak, and the future belongs solely to the stronger eastern nation [*Ostvolk*]."

On April 24 the Russians completed the encirclement of Berlin; the following day Russian and American troops met at the Elbe River. The Reich lay in ruins, the *Wehrmacht* had been shattered, and all hope of averting defeat had vanished. Still, it took four more days for Hitler to conclude that the end had at last come. Amid reports that Heinrich Himmler, one of his most trusted lieutenants, had opened negotiations for an armistice and that Russian tanks had broken into the center of the capital, Hitler announced that he intended to take his own life. What followed resembled nothing so much as a shabby imitation of the finale of a Wagnerian melodrama: Hitler's solemn and futile dictation of his personal and political testaments; his distribution of state offices among the faithful; his last-minute marriage to his long-time mistress, Eva Braun; their double suicide; and finally the cremation of their corpses in the garden of the Reich Chancellery amid the bursting shells of Russian artillery.

The creator of the Third Reich, Adolf Hitler, died on April 30, 1945, only ten days after his fifty-sixth birthday. His creation survived him by only one week. Upwards of thirty-five million dead of all nationalities, the devastation of Germany as well as goodly portions of another dozen countries, and the destruction of Europe's position of primacy in the world were the end results of his career.

[8] *Volk* is generally translated as either people or nation. For Hitler, the term also had a racial connotation.

Chronology of the Life of Hitler

1889 (April 20) Born in Braunau am Inn, Austria, son of Alois Hitler (born Alois Schicklgruber), a customs official.

1900–1905 In high school (*Realschule*); first in Linz, then in Steyr.

1903 Father dies.

1905 Drops out of high school before graduation.

1907 (September) Fails to gain admission to Academy of Fine Arts in Vienna.

(December) Mother dies

1907–1913 Aimless existence in Vienna; absorbs ideas and techniques that later become central elements in his political ideology.

1913 Moves to Munich, Germany, probably to avoid military service in the Austrian Army.

1914–1918 Volunteers for service in the German Army and serves with distinction as a courier until incapacitated by poison gas shortly before the end of the war.

1919 In Munich as political instructor in the postwar German Army (*Reichswehr*).

1919 (September) Joins the German Workers' Party, or DAP (later NSDAP).

1920 (February 24) Announces the twenty-five point program of the NSDAP at a mass meeting in a Munich beer hall.

(March 31) Resigns from the *Reichswehr* to devote all his time to politics.

1921 Becomes *Führer* of the NSDAP with almost unlimited authority in party affairs.

1923 (November 8–9) Leads abortive "Beer-Hall *Putsch*" in Munich.

1924 (February–March) Tried for high treason; convicted and sentenced to five years imprisonment at Landsberg.

Writes first volume of *Mein Kampf*.

(December) Pardoned and released from prison.

1925 (February) Formally reconstitutes NSDAP in Munich.

1929 World-wide economic depression.

1930 (September) National election raises Reichstag representation of NSDAP from 12 to 107 seats.

1932	Runs for presidency; receives one-third of votes but loses to incumbent, Hindenburg.
1933	(January 30) Appointed Reich Chancellor by President Hindenburg.
	(February 27) Reichstag fire; Hitler blames Communists.
	(February 28) Prevails on President Hindenburg to sign an emergency decree "for the Protection of the People and the State" suspending those sections of the constitution guaranteeing individual and civil liberties.
	(March 5) NSDAP receives 44 per cent of the vote in Reichstag election.
	(March 24) Reichstag passes the so-called "Enabling Act," which in effect gives Hitler authority to enact laws and to deviate from the constitution.
	(July 14) All political parties except the NSDAP outlawed.
1934	(June 30) Purges SA; Röhm and other Storm Troop leaders as well as a number of non-Nazi enemies of Hitler shot.
	(August 2) Hindenburg dies. Hitler abolishes office of president and takes title of "Führer and Reich Chancellor." Armed Forces take personal oath to Hitler as Supreme Commander.
1935	(March 16) Announces build-up of Armed Forces and reintroduces general military conscription—all in violation of the Versailles Treaty.
	(September) Passage of the anti-Jewish "Nuremberg Laws."
1936	(March 7) Repudiates the Locarno Treaty and sends German troops into the Rhineland.
1937	(November 5) Outlines to highest ranking military and civilian leaders his plans for territorial aggrandizement and war. ("Hossbach Memorandum").
1938	(February 4) Takes direct command of the German Armed Forces (Wehrmacht) in wake of the Blomberg-Fritsch affair. Also appoints Ribbentrop foreign minister in place of Neurath.
	(March 13) Annexes Austria ("Anschluss").
	(September-October) Sudetenland crisis; Munich agreement; German occupation of the Sudetenland.
	(November 9) Organized pogrom against the Jews of Germany ("Kristallnacht").
1939	(March 15) German troops occupy Czechoslovakia.
	(August 23) Nonaggression pact between Germany and USSR.
	(September 1) German invasion of Poland; World War II begins.
	(September 3) Great Britain and France declare war on Germany.

1940	(April) German conquest of Denmark and Norway.
	(May–June) German conquest of Belgium, Luxembourg, and the Netherlands. France militarily defeated and largely occupied by *Wehrmacht*. British Expeditionary Force driven from Continent.
1941	(April) German conquest of Yugoslavia and Greece.
	(June 22) German invasion of the USSR. Systematic extermination of eastern European Jewry begins.
	(December) Germany declares war on the United States. German advance grinds to halt short of Moscow. Hitler takes personal command of Army operations.
1942	(January) "Final Solution" (physical extermination of the Jews) extended to all areas under German control.
	(Summer) Hitler's empire at its peak.
	(Autumn) Tide of war turns against Germany and her allies.
1943	(January–February) Catastrophic German defeat at Stalingrad.
	(July) Allied invasion of Sicily and collapse of Mussolini's fascist regime in Italy.
1944	(June 6) Allied invasion of France ("D-Day").
	(July 20) Hitler survives assassination attempt by handful of German army officers.
	(September) British and American troops reach Germany's western frontier.
	(December) Hitler launches major counteroffensive in the West in an unsuccessful effort to reverse the course of the war.
1945	(January) Red Army breaks through German defense and advances rapidly through eastern Germany.
	(March) American troops cross the Rhine. Hitler issues "scorched earth" directive.
	(April 15) Issues last Order of the Day to German forces on the eastern front.
	(April 25) Berlin completely encircled.
	(April 29) Marries Eva Braun and prepares private and political testaments.
	(April 30) Commits suicide.

- Hitler pocecced qualities of a leader.

HITLER LOOKS AT THE WORLD

It may well be true that no man can tell the whole truth about himself. Yet a man's words, in the aggregate, are the man himself—and through them a discerning reader can form a definite impression of the author's style, personality, and points of view. This part of the book presents selections from the rich storehouse of public and personal materials in which Adolf Hitler reveals himself in his own words.

1

The Foundations of Hitlerism

Hitler's well-deserved reputation as a cynical, cunning, and unscrupulous political opportunist often serves to obscure the fact that he was equally an ideological dogmatist. Indeed, in the sense that he was intensely concerned with ideas, lived by them, and built his movement on them, Hitler must be regarded not only as a man of action but also as an ideologist and an intellectual.

Like so many other Europeans, especially Germans, of his day, Hitler was a casualty of the moral and spiritual crisis, the breakdown of traditional culture and society, that was the by-product of rapid industrialization and urbanization. Unable to cope with the stresses and strains of life in an evolving industrial society, Hitler, while still a young man, was gripped by the terrible frustration, the corrosive rootlessness, the deep-seated disaffection, and the agonizing anxiety of the alienated intellectual in the modern world. In Hitler's case this generalized anxiety, sparked by a childhood detrimental to psychological stability and reinforced by an adolescence and early adulthood of almost unrelieved personal failure, deteriorated into a neurotic fear of becoming nothing, a dread of nonexistence. In seeking to overcome this fear, to find his own identity and give meaning to his own life—in short, to meet his own spiritual and psychological needs—Hitler fashioned an ideology that was at once the expres-

sion of a personal need and a program for political action and national salvation.

The basic outlines of Hitler's Weltanschauung, his philosophy of life, were acquired during his Vienna days. By the time he wrote Mein Kampf, *little more than a decade later, Hitler had committed himself to certain fixed and clearly defined ideological assumptions to which he adhered with remarkable consistency for the remainder of his life.*

That Hitler's ideas were superficial, crude, unoriginal, and based on false premises is undeniable. But to dismiss them on these grounds as unworthy of serious attention would be to miss the very essence of their appeal. Ideas are expressed by individuals but they are social products, and they reflect social realities. Hitler was nothing if not the product of his time and environment, and the attractiveness of his ideas and the impact of his rhetoric lay precisely in the fact that millions of Germans—most of them respectable and many of them well-educated—shared both his mood and his ideological presuppositions.

Therefore, if we are to understand Hitler and the success of the movement he led, it is important to examine not only the techniques he employed but also the ideas he purveyed.

STRUGGLE IS THE FATHER OF ALL THINGS [1]

The fundamental presupposition that shaped Hitler's Weltanschauung was that life is a struggle in which the strong survive and the weak perish. For Hitler struggle was the eternal law of nature, the basic rule of existence, that at once prevented universal decay and ensured further achievement. This perverted Darwinian view of life led Hitler to conclude that force and power were the sole determinants in the cosmic struggle for survival and greatness.

The following selection—excerpts from three speeches made by Hitler some five years before he became chancellor—presents an uninhibited exposition of the doctrine that might makes right.

The idea of struggle is as old as life itself, for life is only preserved because other living things perish through struggle. . . . In this struggle, the stronger, the more able win, while the less able, the

---

[1] From Gordon W. Prange, ed., *Hitler's Words, 1923–1943* (Washington, D.C.: American Council on Public Affairs, 1944), pp. 7–9. Reprinted by permission of Public Affairs Press.

weak lose. Struggle is the father of all things. Only through struggle has man raised himself above the animal world. Even today it is not by the principles of humanity that man lives or is able to preserve himself above the animal world, but solely by means of the most brutal struggle. As it is with the individual so it is in the destiny of nations. Only by struggle are the strong able to raise themselves above the weak. And every people that loses out in this eternally shifting struggle has, according to the laws of nature, received its just desert. A *Weltanschauung* that denies the idea of struggle is contrary to nature and will lead a people that is guided by it to destruction. The road that must be traveled by a people which wishes to develop itself still higher is not the road of comfort and ease, but the road of relentless struggle. For if you do not fight for life, then life will never be won.[2]

There is no achievement without breaking down resistance. Every new deed of mankind signifies the conquest of a previous one. . . . Force determines the way of life. Right exists only when it is created and protected by power and force.[3]

The first fundamental of any rational *Weltanschauung* is the fact that on earth and in the universe force alone is decisive. Whatever goal man has reached is due to his originality plus his brutality. . . . There will never be a solution to the German problem until we return to the three fundamental principles which control the existence of every nation: The concept of struggle, the purity of blood, and the ingenuity of the individual.[4]

BLOOD AND RACE [5]

In Hitler's concept of eternal struggle, the protagonists were not so much people and nations as races and racial communities (Völker). Drawing heavily on the ideas of nineteenth- and early twentieth-century racial theorists, Hitler regarded race (which he defined in biological terms as a factor transmitted through the blood that distinguished a group of people from all other groups not only physically but also mentally and spiritually) as the key element that governs and explains all of history and all of human experience. For Hitler, one race—the "Aryan" race, to which

[2] Speech at Kulmbach, February 5, 1928.

[3] Speech at Neustadt an der Aisch, January 15, 1928.

[4] Speech at Chemnitz, April 2, 1928.

[5] From Adolf Hitler, *Mein Kampf*, trans. Ralph Manheim (Boston: Houghton Mifflin Company, 1943), pp. 285–86, 288–90, 296, 338–39. Copyright © 1943 by Houghton Mifflin Company. Copyright © 1927 by Verlag Frz. Eher Nachf. G.m.b.H. All extracts from *Mein Kampf* are from this edition and are reprinted by permission of the publisher.

most Germans belonged—was inherently superior to all others; to protect it, to perserve the purity of its blood, and to assure its triumph over the inferior races, the cosmic struggle must be waged.

Racial thought was the core of Hitler's ideology, and it is the key to an understanding of Hitlerism. Here, in a passage from Mein Kampf, *Hitler holds forth on blood and race.*

All great questions of the day are questions of the moment and represent only consequences of definite causes. Only one among all of them, however, possesses causal importance, and that is the question of the racial preservation of the nation. In the blood alone resides the strength as well as the weakness of man. As long as peoples do not recognize and give heed to the importance of their racial foundation, they are like men who would like to teach poodles the qualities of greyhounds, failing to realize that the speed of the greyhound like the docility of the poodle are not learned, but are qualities inherent in the race. Peoples which renounce the preservation of their racial purity renounce with it the unity of their soul in all its expressions. The divided state of their nature is the natural consequence of the divided state of their blood, and the change in their intellectual and creative force is only the effect of the change in their racial foundations. . . .

Any crossing of two beings not at exactly the same level produces a medium between the level of the two parents. This means: the offspring will probably stand higher than the racially lower parent, but not as high as the higher one. Consequently, it will later succumb in the struggle against the higher level. Such mating is contrary to the will of Nature for a higher breeding of all life. The precondition for this does not lie in associating superior and inferior, but in the total victory of the former. The stronger must dominate and not blend with the weaker, thus sacrificing his own greatness. Only the born weakling can view this as cruel, but he after all is only a weak and limited man; for if this law did not prevail, any conceivable higher development of organic living beings would be unthinkable. . . . In the struggle for daily bread all those who are weak and sickly or less determined succumb, while the struggle of the males for the female grants the right or opportunity to propagate only to the healthiest. And struggle is always a means for improving a species' health and power of resistance and, therefore, a cause of its higher development.

If the process were different, all further and higher development would cease and the opposite would occur. For, since the inferior always predominates numerically over the best, if both had the same possibility of preserving life and propagating, the inferior would multiply so much more rapidly that in the end the best would inevitably be driven into the background, unless a correction of this state of affairs were undertaken. . . .

Historical experience offers countless proofs of this. It shows with terrifying clarity that in every mingling of Aryan blood with that of lower peoples the result was the end of the cultured people. North America, whose population consists in by far the largest part of Germanic elements who mixed but little with the lower colored peoples, shows a different humanity and culture from Central and South America, where the predominantly Latin immigrants often mixed with the aborigines on a large scale. By this one example, we can clearly and distinctly recognize the effect of racial mixture. The Germanic inhabitant of the American continent, who has remained racially pure and unmixed, rose to be master of the continent; he will remain the master as long as he does not fall a victim to defilement of the blood.

The result of all racial crossing is therefore in brief always the following:

(a) Lowering of the level of the higher race;

(b) Physical and intellectual regression and hence the beginning of a slowly but surely progressing sickness.

To bring about such a development is, then, nothing else but to sin against the will of the eternal creator. . . .

Everything we admire on this earth today—science and art, technology and inventions—is only the creative product of a few peoples and originally perhaps of *one* race. On them depends the existence of this whole culture. If they perish, the beauty of this earth will sink into the grave with them. . . .

All great cultures of the past perished only because the originally creative race died out from blood poisoning.

The ultimate cause of such a decline was their forgetting that all culture depends on men and not conversely; hence that to preserve a certain culture the man who creates it must be preserved. This preservation is bound up with the rigid law of necessity and the right to victory of the best and stronger in this world.

Those who want to live, let them fight, and those who do not want to fight in this world of eternal struggle do not deserve to live. . . .

All the human culture, all the results of art, science, and technology that we see before us today, are almost exclusively the creative product of the Aryan. This very fact admits of the not unfounded inference that he alone was the founder of all higher humanity, therefore representing the prototype of all that we understand by the word "man." He is the Prometheus of mankind from whose bright forehead the divine spark of genius has sprung at all times, forever kindling anew that fire of knowledge which illumined the night of silent mysteries and thus caused man to climb the path to mastery over the other beings of this earth. Exclude him—and perhaps after a few thousand years darkness will again descend on the earth, human culture will pass, and the world turn to a desert. . . .

Blood mixture and the resultant drop in the racial level is the sole cause of the dying out of old cultures; for men do not perish as a result of lost wars, but by the loss of that force of resistance which is contained only in pure blood.

All who are not of good race in this world are chaff.

And all occurrences in world history are only the expression of the races' instinct of self-preservation, in the good or bad sense. . . .

Anyone who wants to free the German blood from the manifestations and vices of today, which were originally alien to its nature, will first have to redeem it from the foreign virus of these manifestations.

Without the clearest knowledge of the racial problem and hence of the Jewish problem there will never be a resurrection of the German nation.

The racial question gives the key not only to world history, but to all human culture.

THE "RACIAL" JEW [6]

Anyone that has the stamina to wade through the many volumes of Hitler's speeches, writings, and table talk cannot but conclude that the cement which bound together the whole of his Weltanschauung was an obsessive anti-Semitism. For Hitler, the Jew was the cause and incarnation of all that he hated and feared: capitalism, Social Democracy, parliamentarianism, Bolshevism, antimilitarism, class warfare, pacifism, internationalism, modern art—and much more. There can be no doubt that Hitler firmly believed what he said about the Jews. Indeed, his expressed anti-Semitism was merely the visible aspect of a deeper, far more implacable, and totally irrational hatred, whose explication must be left to the psychiatrists.

In Hitler's ideology, anti-Semitism provided the nexus between the concepts of struggle and race. For Hitler regarded the Jews not as adherents of a religious faith but as members of a race; a race, moreover, that possessed all the qualities that stood in opposition to the qualities of the Aryan race.

[6] From *Mein Kampf*, pp. 300, 302–3, 305–7, 325–26, 623. All italics in the original.

In Hitler's view, the Jew was not only the Aryan's antithesis but also his mortal enemy in the racial struggle. Hence, there was no evil, no crime, no perversion that Hitler did not attribute to the Jews, as part of their satanic effort to weaken and then to enslave the Aryan race. The following selection from Mein Kampf, *although somewhat less virulent than many of his spoken diatribes, illustrates Hitler's view of the Jews.*

The mightiest counterpart to the Aryan is represented by the Jew. In hardly any people in the world is the instinct of self-preservation developed more strongly than in the so-called "chosen." Of this, the mere fact of the survival of this race may be considered the best proof. Where is the people which in the last two thousand years has been exposed to so slight changes of inner disposition, character, etc., as the Jewish people? What people, finally, has gone through greater upheavals than this one—and nevertheless issued from the mightiest catastrophes of mankind unchanged? What an infinitely tough will to live and preserve the species speaks from these facts! . . .

The Jewish people, despite all apparent intellectual qualities, is without any true culture, and especially without any culture of its own. For what sham culture the Jew today possesses is the property of other peoples, and for the most part it is ruined in his hands. . . .

Thus, the Jew lacks those qualities which distinguish the races that are creative and hence culturally blessed. . . .

No, the Jew possesses no culture-creating force of any sort, since the idealism, without which there is no true higher development of man, is not present in him and never was present. Hence his intellect will never have a constructive effect, but will be destructive, and in very rare cases perhaps will at most be stimulating, but then as the prototype of the "force which always wants evil and nevertheless creates good." [7] Not through him does any progress of mankind occur, but in spite of him. . . .

The Jew never possessed a state with definite territorial limits and therefore never called a culture his own. . . .

He is and remains the typical parasite, a sponger who like a noxious bacillus keeps spreading as soon as a favorable medium invites him. And the effect of his existence is also like that of spongers: wherever he appears, the host people dies out after a shorter or longer period.

Thus, the Jew of all times has lived in the states of other peoples, and there formed his own state, which, to be sure, habitually sailed under the disguise of "religious community" as long as outward cir-

[7] Goethe's *Faust*, lines 1336–1337: Mephistopheles to Faust. [Translator's note—ED.]

cumstances made a complete revelation of his nature seem inadvisable. But as soon as he felt strong enough to do without the protective cloak, he always dropped the veil and suddenly became what so many of the others previously did not want to believe and see: the Jew.

The Jew's life as a parasite in the body of other nations and states explains a characteristic which once caused Schopenhauer . . . to call him the "great master in lying." Existence impels the Jew to lie, and to lie perpetually, just as it compels the inhabitants of the northern countries to wear warm clothing.

His life within other peoples can only endure for any length of time if he succeeds in arousing the opinion that he is not a people but a "religious community," though of a special sort.

And this is the first great lie.

In order to carry on his existence as a parasite on other peoples, he is forced to deny his inner nature. The more intelligent the individual Jew is, the more he will succeed in this deception. Indeed, things can go so far that large parts of the host people will end by seriously believing that the Jew is really a Frenchman or an Englishman, a German or an Italian, though of a special religious faith. . . .

On this first and greatest lie, that the Jews are not a race but a religion, more and more lies are based in necessary consequence. Among them is the lie with regard to the language of the Jew. For him it is not a means for expressing his thoughts, but a means for concealing them. When he speaks French, he thinks Jewish, and while he turns out German verses, in his life he only expresses the nature of his nationality. As long as the Jew has not become the master of the other peoples, he must speak their languages whether he likes it or not, but as soon as they became his slaves, they would all have to learn a universal language (Esperanto, for instance!), so that by this additional means the Jews could more easily dominate them! . . .

How close they see approaching victory can be seen by the hideous aspect which their relations with the members of other peoples takes on.

With satanic joy in his face, the black-haired Jewish youth lurks in wait for the unsuspecting girl whom he defiles with his blood, thus stealing her from her people. With every means he tries to destroy the racial foundations of the people he has set out to subjugate. Just as he himself systematically ruins women and girls, he does not shrink back from pulling down the blood barriers for others, even on a large scale. It was and it is Jews who bring the Negroes into the Rhineland, always with the same secret thought and clear aim of ruining the hated white race by the necessarily resulting bastardization, throwing it down from its cultural and political height, and himself rising to be its master.

For a racially pure people which is conscious of its blood can never be enslaved by the Jew. In this world he will forever be master over bastards and bastards alone.

And so he tries systematically to lower the racial level by a continuous poisoning of individuals.

And in politics he begins to replace the idea of democracy by the dictatorship of the proletariat.

In the organized mass of Marxism he has found the weapon which lets him dispense with democracy and in its stead allows him to subjugate and govern the peoples with a dictatorial and brutal fist.

He works systematically for revolutionization in a twofold sense: economic and political.

Around peoples who offer too violent a resistance to attack from within he weaves a net of enemies, thanks to his international influence, incites them to war, and finally, if necessary, plants the flag of revolution on the very battlefields.

In economics he undermines the states until the social enterprises which have become unprofitable are taken from the state and subjected to his financial control.

In the political field he refuses the state the means for its self-preservation, destroys the foundations of all national self-maintenance and defense, destroys faith in the leadership, scoffs at its history and past, and drags everything that is truly great into the gutter.

Culturally he contaminates art, literature, the theater, makes a mockery of natural feeling, overthrows all concepts of beauty and sublimity, of the noble and the good, and instead drags men down into the sphere of his own base nature.

Religion is ridiculed, ethics and morality represented as outmoded, until the last props of a nation in its struggle for existence in this world have fallen. . . .

And so the Jew today is the great agitator for the complete destruction of Germany. Wherever in the world we read of attacks against Germany, Jews are their fabricators, just as in peacetime and during the War the press of the Jewish stock exchange and Marxists systematically stirred up hatred against Germany until state after state abandoned neutrality and, renouncing the true interests of the peoples, entered the service of the World War coalition.

The Jewish train of thought in all this is clear. The Bolshevization of Germany—that is, the extermination of the national folkish German[8] intelligentsia to make possible the sweating of the German working class under the yoke of Jewish world finance—is conceived only as a preliminary to the further extension of this Jewish tendency of world conquest. As often in history, Germany is the great pivot in the

---

[8] The English translation from which this passage has been reprinted (p. 623) erroneously renders this word as *Jewish*. The German edition of *Mein Kampf* (p. 703) reads *deutschen* (German).

mighty struggle. If our people and our state become the victim of these bloodthirsty and avaricious Jewish tyrants of nations, the whole earth will sink into the snares of this octopus; if Germany frees herself from this embrace, this greatest of dangers to nations may be regarded as broken for the whole world.

LEADERSHIP IS PRIMARY AND DECISIVE [9]

Hitler insisted that in order to wage the racial struggle Germany had first to be welded into a racial, or völkisch, *community, in which citizenship would be based not upon territorial considerations or geographic residence but upon blood and race. Such a* Volksstaat, *he believed, could be neither realized nor maintained under a system of majority rule in which the mass counted more than the individual. For just as Hitler believed in the inequality of races, so he believed in the inequality of individuals. Hence, even within the Aryan racial community some people were better than others. And the best minds, the strongest personalities, the most able individuals—those who had been sifted by the struggle for daily life—must form a hierarchy of authoritative and responsible leadership that could compel unity, end domestic conflict, and impose the discipline necessary to create the* Volksstaat *and to lead it to victory in the struggle for racial survival. At the top of the hierarchical pyramid would stand the* Führer, *the supreme leader, who (according to the Nazi cosmology) was to be neither a dictator nor a representative but a medium or interpreter, who sensed and sought to actualize the mystical will of the* Volk.

"All life," Hitler declared in 1928, "is bound up in three theses: Struggle is the father of all things, virtue lies in blood, leadership is primary and decisive." In this one brief statement, Hitler expressed the quintessence of his Weltanschauung.

The preceding selections have set forth Hitler's concepts of struggle and race, as well as the anti-Semitism that bound the two together; the present passage, taken from Mein Kampf, *illustrates the* Führerprinzip, *the leadership principle, which was at once a rationalization of dictatorship and an expression of Hitler's belief in the role of the individual, especially of the historical personality.*

The folkish[10] National Socialist state sees its chief task in *educating and preserving the bearer of the state.* It is not sufficient to encour-

[9] From *Mein Kampf,* pp. 442–43, 446, 449–50. All italics in the original.

[10] This is the translator's literal rendering of *völkisch,* which can perhaps be most meaningfully translated in this context as "racial."

age the racial elements as such, to educate them and finally instruct them in the needs of practical life; the state must also adjust its own organization to this task.

It would be lunacy to try to estimate the value of man according to his race, thus declaring war on the Marxist idea that men are equal, unless we are determined to draw the ultimate consequences. And the ultimate consequence of recognizing the importance of blood—that is, of the racial foundation in general—is the transference of this estimation to the individual person. In general, I must evaluate peoples differently on the basis of the race they belong to, and the same applies to the individual men within a national community. The realization that peoples are not equal transfers itself to the individual man within a national community, in the sense that men's minds cannot be equal, since here, too, the blood components, though equal in their broad outlines, are, in particular cases, subject to thousands of the finest differentiations.

The first consequence of this realization might at the same time be called the cruder one: an attempt to promote in the most exemplary way those elements within the national community that have been recognized as especially valuable from the racial viewpoint and to provide for their special increase.

This task is cruder because it can be recognized and solved almost mechanically. It is more difficult to recognize among the whole people the minds that are most valuable in the intellectual and ideal sense, and to gain for them that influence which not only is the due of these superior minds, but which above all is beneficial to the nation. This sifting according to capacity and ability cannot be undertaken mechanically; it is a task which the struggle of daily life unceasingly performs.

A philosophy of life which endeavors to reject the democratic mass idea and give this earth to the best people—that is, the highest humanity—must logically obey the same aristocratic principle within this people and make sure that the leadership and the highest influence in this people fall to the best minds. Thus, it builds, not upon the idea of the majority, but upon the idea of personality. . . .

It is not the mass that invents and not the majority that organizes or thinks, but in all things only and always the individual man, the person.

A human community appears well organized only if it facilitates the labors of these creative forces in the most helpful way and applies them in a manner beneficial to all. The most valuable thing about the invention itself, whether it lie in the material field or in the world of ideas, is primarily the inventor as a personality. Therefore, to employ him in a way benefiting the totality is the first and highest task in the organization of a national community. Indeed, the organization itself must be a realization of this principle. Thus, also, it is redeemed from the curse of mechanism and becomes a living thing. *It must itself be an embodiment of the endeavor to place thinking individuals above the masses, thus subordinating the latter to the former.*

Consequently, the organization must not only not prevent the emergence of thinking individuals from the mass; on the contrary, it must in the highest degree make this possible and easy by the nature of its own being. In this it must proceed from the principle that the salvation of mankind has never lain in the masses, but in its creative minds, which must therefore really be regarded as benefactors of the human race. To assure them of the most decisive influence and facilitate their work is in the interest of the totality. Assuredly this interest is not satisfied, and is not served by the domination of the unintelligent or incompetent, in any case uninspired masses, but solely by the leadership of those to whom Nature has given special gifts for this purpose.

The selection of these minds, as said before, is primarily accomplished by the hard struggle for existence. Many break and perish, thus showing that they are not destined for the ultimate, and in the end only a few appear to be chosen. . . .

The folkish state must care for the welfare of its citizens by recognizing in all and everything the importance of the value of personality, thus in all fields preparing the way for that highest measure of productive performance which grants to the individual the highest measure of participation.

And accordingly, the folkish state must free all leadership and especially the highest—that is, the political leadership—entirely from the parliamentary principle of majority rule—in other words, mass rule—and instead absolutely guarantee the right of the personality.

From this the following realization results:

The best state constitution and state form is that which, with the most unquestioned certainty, raises the best minds in the national community to leading position and leading influence.

But as, in economic life, the able men cannot be appointed from above, but must struggle through for themselves, and just as here the endless schooling, ranging from the smallest business to the largest enterprise, occurs spontaneously, with life alone giving the examinations, obviously political minds cannot be "discovered." Extraordinary geniuses permit of no consideration for normal mankind.

From the smallest community cell to the highest leadership of the entire Reich, the state must have the personality principle anchored in its organization.

There must be no majority decisions, but only responsible persons, and the word "council" must be restored to its original meaning. Surely every man will have advisors by his side, but *the decision will be made by one man.*

The principle which made the Prussian army in its time into the most wonderful instrument of the German people must someday, in a transferred sense, become the principle of the construction of our whole state conception: *authority of every leader downward and responsibility upward.*

Even then it will not be possible to dispense with those corporations which today we designate as parliaments. But their councillors will then actually give counsel; responsibility, however, can and may be borne only by *one* man, and therefore only he alone may possess the authority and right to command.

2
Autobiographical Memories

Despite the recent flood of literature on Hitler, the autobiographical portions of Mein Kampf *remain an important source of information on his life in the years before he achieved prominence. Although self-serving, distorted, and in places fictitious, Hitler's romanticized account of his past not only illuminates his personality and early experience but also illustrates his style of expression and mode of thought.*

The following autobiographical selections from Mein Kampf *highlight the story of Hitler's political development from the formative years in Vienna (1908–13) to the first major success of his political career (1920).*

YEARS OF STUDY AND SUFFERING IN VIENNA (1908–1913)[1]

When my mother died, Fate, at least in one respect, had made its decisions. . . .

After the death of my mother I went to Vienna for the third time, to remain for many years. . . . I wanted to become an architect, and obstacles do not exist to be surrendered to, but only to be broken. I was determined to overcome these obstacles, keeping before my eyes the image of my father, who had started out as the child of a village shoemaker, and risen by his own efforts to be a government official. I had a better foundation to build on, and hence my possibilities in the struggle were easier, and what then seemed to be the harshness of Fate, I praise today as wisdom and Providence. While the Goddess of Suffering took me in her arms, often threatening to crush me, my will to resistance grew, and in the end this will was victorious.

I owe it to that period that I grew hard and am still capable of being hard. And even more, I exalt it for tearing me away from the hollowness of comfortable life; for drawing the mother's darling out of his soft downy bed and giving him "Dame Care" for a new mother; for hurling me, despite all resistance, into a world of misery and poverty, thus making me acquainted with those for whom I was later to fight.

[1] From *Mein Kampf,* pp. 19–22, 122–25.

In this period my eyes were opened to two menaces of which I had previously scarcely known the names, and whose terrible importance for the existence of the German people I certainly did not understand: Marxism and Jewry.

To me Vienna, the city which, to so many, is the epitome of innocent pleasure, a festive playground for merrymakers, represents, I am sorry to say, merely the living memory of the saddest period in my life.

Even today this city can arouse in me nothing but the most dismal thoughts. For me the name of this Phaeacian city[2] represents five years of hardship and misery. Five years in which I was forced to earn a living, first as a day laborer, then as a small painter; a truly meager living which never sufficed to appease even my daily hunger. Hunger was then my faithful bodyguard; he never left me for a moment and partook of all I had, share and share alike. Every book I acquired aroused his interest; a visit to the Opera prompted his attentions for days at a time; my life was a continuous struggle with this pitiless friend. And yet during this time I studied as never before. Aside from my architecture and my rare visits to the Opera, paid for in hunger, I had but one pleasure: my books.

At that time I read enormously and thoroughly. All the free time my work left me was employed in my studies. In this way I forged in a few years' time the foundations of a knowledge from which I still draw nourishment today.

And even more than this:

In this period there took shape within me a world picture and a philosophy which became the granite foundation of all my acts. In addition to what I then created, I have had to learn little; and I have had to alter nothing. . . .

In this period my inner revulsion toward the Habsburg state steadily grew.

The more particularly I concerned myself with questions of foreign policy, the more my conviction rose and took root that this political formation could result in nothing but the misfortune of Germanism. More and more clearly I saw at last that the fate of the German nation would no longer be decided here, but in the Reich itself. This was true, not only of political questions, but no less for all manifestations of cultural life in general. . . .

Thus more and more I began to lead a double life; reason and reality told me to complete a school as bitter as it was beneficial in Austria, but my heart dwelt elsewhere.

An oppressive discontent had seized possession of me, the more I

[2] Phaeacian city. The allusion to the happy isle of the Phaeacians is more popular in Germany than in English-speaking countries. Hitler's use of it does not mean that he has read the *Odyssey*. [Translator's note—ED.]

recognized the inner hollowness of this state and the impossibility of saving it, and felt that in all things it could be nothing but the misfortune of the German people.

I was convinced that this state inevitably oppressed and handicapped any really great German as, conversely, it would help every un-German figure.

I was repelled by the conglomeration of races which the capital showed me, repelled by this whole mixture of Czechs, Poles, Hungarians, Ruthenians, Serbs, and Croats, and everywhere, the eternal mushroom of humanity—Jews and more Jews.

To me the giant city seemed the embodiment of racial desecration.

The German of my youth was the dialect of Lower Bavaria; I could neither forget it nor learn the Viennese jargon. The longer I lived in this city, the more my hatred grew for the foreign mixture of peoples which had begun to corrode this old site of German culture.

The idea that this state could be maintained much longer seemed to me positively ridiculous. . . .

Since my heart had never beaten for an Austrian monarchy, but only for a German Reich, the hour of this state's downfall could only seem to me the beginning of the redemption of the German nation.

For all these reasons a longing rose stronger and stronger in me, to go at last whither since my childhood secret desires and secret love had drawn me. . . .

I wanted to enjoy the happiness of living and working in the place which some day would inevitably bring about the fulfillment of my most ardent and heartfelt wish: the union of my beloved homeland with the common fatherland, the German Reich.

Even today many would be unable to comprehend the greatness of such a longing, but I address myself to those to whom Fate has either hitherto denied this, or from whom in harsh cruelty it has taken it away; I address myself to all those who, detached from their mother country, have to fight even for the holy treasure of their language, who are persecuted and tortured for their loyalty to the fatherland, and who now, with poignant emotion, long for the hour which will permit them to return to the heart of their faithful mother; I address myself to all these, and I know that they will understand me!

Only he who has felt in his own skin what it means to be a German, deprived of the right to belong to his cherished fatherland, can measure the deep longing which burns at all times in the hearts of children separated from their mother country. It torments those whom it fills and denies them contentment and happiness until the gates of their father's house open, and in the common Reich, common blood gains peace and tranquillity.

Yet Vienna was and remained for me the hardest, though most thorough, school of my life. I had set foot in this town while still half a boy and I left it a man, grown quiet and grave. In it I obtained the foundations for a philosophy in general and a political view in particular which later I only needed to supplement in detail, but which never left me. But not until today have I been able to estimate at their full value those years of study.

That is why I have dealt with this period at some length, because it gave me my first visual instruction in precisely those questions which belonged to the foundations of a party which, arising from smallest beginnings, after scarcely five years is beginning to develop into a great mass movement. I do not know what my attitude toward the Jews, Social Democracy, or rather Marxism as a whole, the social question, etc., would be today if at such an early time the pressure of destiny—and my own study—had not built up a basic stock of personal opinions within me.

For if the misery of the fatherland can stimulate thousands and thousands of men to thought on the inner reasons for this collapse, this can never lead to that thoroughness and deep insight which are disclosed to the man who has himself mastered Fate only after years of struggle.

TRANSFORMATION INTO AN ANTI-SEMITE [3]

Today it is difficult, if not impossible, for me to say when the word "Jew" first gave me ground for special thoughts. . . .

Not until my fourteenth or fifteenth year did I begin to come across the word "Jew," with any frequency. . . .

Then I came to Vienna. . . .

Once, as I was strolling through the Inner City, I suddenly encountered an apparition in a black caftan and black hair locks. Is this a Jew? was my first thought.

For, to be sure, they had not looked like that in Linz. I observed the man furtively and cautiously, but the longer I stared at this foreign face, scrutinizing feature for feature, the more my first question assumed a new form:

Is this a German?

As always in such cases, I now began to try to relieve my doubts by books. For a few hellers I bought the first anti-Semitic pamphlets of my life. Unfortunately, they all proceeded from the supposition that in principle the reader knew or even understood the Jewish question to a certain degree. Besides, the tone for the most part was such that doubts again arose in me, due in part to the dull and amazingly unscientific arguments favoring the thesis.

I relapsed for weeks at a time, once even for months.

[3] From *Mein Kampf*, pp. 51–52, 56–57, 60, 64–65. All italics in the original.

The whole thing seemed to me so monstrous, the accusations so boundless, that, tormented by the fear of doing injustice, I again became anxious and uncertain.

Yet I could no longer very well doubt that the objects of my study were not Germans of a special religion, but a people in themselves; for since I had begun to concern myself with this question and to take cognizance of the Jews, Vienna appeared to me in a different light than before. Wherever I went, I began to see Jews, and the more I saw, the more sharply they became distinguished in my eyes from the rest of humanity. Particularly the Inner City and the districts north of the Danube Canal swarmed with a people which even outwardly had lost all resemblance to Germans. . . .

The cleanliness of this people, moral and otherwise, I must say, is a point in itself. By their very exterior you could tell that these were no lovers of water, and, to your distress, you often knew it with your eyes closed. Later I often grew sick to my stomach from the smell of these caftan-wearers. Added to this, there was their unclean dress and their generally unheroic appearance.

All this could scarcely be called very attractive; but it became positively repulsive when, in addition to their physical uncleanliness, you discovered the moral stains on this "chosen people."

In a short time I was made more thoughtful than ever by my slowly rising insight into the type of activity carried on by the Jews in certain fields.

Was there any form of filth or profligacy, particularly in cultural life, without at least one Jew involved in it?

If you cut even cautiously into such an abscess, you found, like a maggot in a rotting body, often dazzled by the sudden light—a kike!

What had to be reckoned heavily against the Jews in my eyes was when I became acquainted with their activity in the press, art, literature, and the theater. . . .

I no longer avoided discussion of the Jewish question; no, now I sought it. And when I learned to look for the Jew in all branches of cultural and artistic life and its various manifestations, I suddenly encountered him in a place where I would least have expected to find him.

When I recognized the Jew as the leader of the Social Democracy, the scales dropped from my eyes. A long soul struggle had reached its conclusion. . . .

For me this was the time of the greatest spiritual upheaval I have ever had to go through.

I had ceased to be a weak-kneed cosmopolitan and become an anti-Semite. . . .

If, with the help of this Marxist creed, the Jew is victorious over the other peoples of the world, his crown will be the funeral wreath of humanity and this planet will, as it did thousands of years ago, move through the ether devoid of men.

Eternal Nature inexorably avenges the infringement of her commands.

Hence today I believe that I am acting in accordance with the will of the Almighty Creator: *by defending myself against the Jew, I am fighting for the work of the Lord.*

THE YOUNG WAR VOLUNTEER (1914) [4]

To me those hours seemed like a release from the painful feelings of my youth. Even today I am not ashamed to say that, overpowered by stormy enthusiasm, I fell down on my knees and thanked Heaven from an overflowing heart for granting me the good fortune of being permitted to live at this time.

A fight for freedom had begun, mightier than the earth had ever seen; for once Destiny had begun its course, the conviction dawned on even the broad masses that this time not the fate of Serbia or Austria was involved, but whether the German nation was to be or not to be. . . .

My own position on the conflict was likewise very simple and clear; for me it was not that Austria was fighting for some Serbian satisfaction, but that Germany was fighting for her existence, the German nation for life or death, freedom and future. . . . If the struggle were carried through to victory, our nation would enter the circle of great nations from the standpoint of external power, and only then could the German Reich maintain itself as a mighty haven of peace without having, for the sake of peace, to cut down on the daily bread of her children.

As a boy and young man I had so often felt the desire to prove at least once by deeds that for me national enthusiasm was no empty whim. . . . Thus my heart, like that of a million others, overflowed with proud joy that at last I would be able to redeem myself from this paralyzing feeling. I had so often sung *"Deutschland über Alles"* and shouted *"Heil"* at the top of my lungs, that it seemed to me almost a belated act of grace to be allowed to stand as a witness in the divine court of the eternal judge and proclaim the sincerity of this conviction. . . . I . . . was ready at any time to die for my people and for the Reich which embodied it.

On the third of August, I submitted a personal petition to His Majesty, King Ludwig III, with a request for permission to enter a

[4] From *Mein Kampf*, pp. 161–65.

Bavarian regiment. The cabinet office certainly had plenty to do in those days; so much the greater was my joy to receive an answer to my request the very next day. With trembling hands I opened the document; my request had been approved and I was summoned to report to a Bavarian regiment. My joy and gratitude knew no bounds. A few days later I was wearing the tunic which I was not to doff until nearly six years later.

For me, as for every German, there now began the greatest and most unforgettable time of my earthly existence. Compared to the events of this gigantic struggle, everything past receded to shallow nothingness. . . . I think back with proud sadness on those first weeks of our people's heroic struggle, in which Fate graciously allowed me to take part.

As though it were yesterday, image after image passes before my eyes. I see myself donning the uniform in the circle of my dear comrades, turning out for the first time, drilling, etc., until the day came for us to march off.

A single worry tormented me at that time, me, as so many others: would we not reach the front too late? Time and time again this alone banished all my calm. Thus, in every cause for rejoicing at a new, heroic victory, a slight drop of bitterness was hidden, for every new victory seemed to increase the danger of our coming too late.

At last the day came when we left Munich to begin the fulfillment of our duty. For the first time I saw the Rhine as we rode westward along its quiet waters to defend it, the German stream of streams, from the greed of the old enemy. When through the tender veil of the early morning mist the Niederwald Monument gleamed down upon us in the gentle first rays of the sun, the old *Watch on the Rhine* roared out of the endless transport train into the morning sky, and I felt as though my heart would burst.

And then came a damp, cold night in Flanders, through which we marched in silence, and when the day began to emerge from the mists, suddenly an iron greeting came whizzing at us over our heads, and with a sharp report sent the little pellets flying between our ranks, ripping up the wet ground; but even before the little cloud had passed, from two hundred throats the first hurrah rose to meet the first messenger of death. Then a crackling and a roaring, a singing and a howling began, and with feverish eyes each one of us was drawn forward, faster and faster, until suddenly past turnip fields and hedges the fight began, the fight of man against man. And from the distance the strains of a song reached our ears, coming closer and closer, leaping from company to company, and just as Death plunged a busy hand into our ranks, the song reached us too and we passed it along: *"Deutschland, Deutschland über Alles, über Alles in der Welt!"*

DECISION TO ENTER POLITICS (1918)[5]

On a hill south of Wervick, we came on the evening of October 13 [1918] into several hours of drumfire with gas shells which continued all night more or less violently. As early as midnight, a number of us passed out, a few of our comrades forever. Toward morning I, too, was seized with pain which grew worse with every quarter hour, and at seven in the morning I stumbled and tottered back with burning eyes; taking with me my last report of the War.

A few hours later, my eyes had turned into glowing coals; it had grown dark around me.

Thus I came to the hospital at Pasewalk in Pomerania, and there I was fated to experience—the greatest villainy of the century.

For a long time there had been something indefinite but repulsive in the air. . . . Even in the hospital, people were discussing the end of the War which they hoped would come soon, but no one counted on anything immediate. I was unable to read the papers.

In November the general tension increased.

And then one day, suddenly and unexpectedly, the calamity descended. Sailors arrived in trucks and proclaimed the revolution; a few Jewish youths were the "leaders" in this struggle for the "freedom, beauty, and dignity" of our national existence. . . .

My first hope was still that this high treason might still be a more or less local affair. . . .

The next few days came and with them the most terrible certainty of my life. The rumors became more and more oppressive. What I had taken for a local affair was now said to be a general revolution. To this was added the disgraceful news from the front. They wanted to capitulate. Was such a thing really possible?

On November 10, the pastor came to the hospital for a short address: now we learned everything.

In extreme agitation, I, too, was present at the short speech. The dignified old gentleman seemed all atremble as he informed us that the House of Hohenzollern should no longer bear the German imperial crown; that the fatherland had become a "republic"; that we must pray to the Almighty not to refuse His blessing to this change and not to abandon our people in the times to come. . . . But when the old gentleman tried to go on, and began to tell us that we must now end the long War, yes, that now that it was lost and we were throwing ourselves upon the mercy of the victors, our fatherland would for the future be exposed to dire oppression, that the armistice

[5] From *Mein Kampf*, pp. 202–6.

should be accepted with confidence in the magnanimity of our previous enemies—I could stand it no longer. It became impossible for me to sit still one minute more. Again everything went black before my eyes; I tottered and groped my way back to the dormitory, threw myself on my bunk, and dug my burning head into my blanket and pillow. . . .

And so it had been in vain. In vain all the sacrifices and privations; in vain the hunger and thirst of months which were often endless; in vain the hours in which, with mortal fear clutching at our hearts, we nevertheless did our duty; and in vain the death of two millions who died. Would not the graves of all the hundreds of thousands open, the graves of those who with faith in the fatherland had marched forth never to return? Would they not open and send the silent mud- and blood-covered heroes back as spirits of vengeance to the homeland which had cheated them with such mockery of the highest sacrifice which a man can make to his people in this world? Had they died for this, the soldiers of August and September, 1914? Was it for this that in the autumn of the same year the volunteer regiments marched after their old comrades? Was it for this that these boys of seventeen sank into the earth of Flanders? Was this the meaning of the sacrifice which the German mother made to the fatherland when with sore heart she let her best-loved boys march off, never to see them again? Did all this happen only so that a gang of wretched criminals could lay hands on the fatherland?

Was it for this that the German soldier had stood fast in the sun's heat and in snowstorms, hungry, thirsty, and freezing, weary from sleepless nights and endless marches? Was it for this that he had lain in the hell of the drumfire and in the fever of gas attacks without wavering, always thoughtful of his one duty to preserve the fatherland from the enemy peril? . . .

And yet, was it only our own sacrifice that we had to weigh in the balance? Was the Germany of the past less precious? Was there no obligation toward our own history? Were we still worthy to relate the glory of the past to ourselves? And how could this deed be justified to future generations?

Miserable and degenerate criminals!

The more I tried to achieve clarity on the monstrous event in this hour, the more the shame of indignation and disgrace burned my brow. What was all the pain in my eyes compared to this misery?

There followed terrible days and even worse nights—I knew that all was lost. Only fools, liars, and criminals could hope in the mercy of the enemy. In these nights hatred grew in me, hatred for those responsible for this deed.

In the days that followed, my own fate became known to me. . . .

At last it became clear to me that what had happened was what I had so often feared but had never been able to believe with my emotions.

Kaiser William II was the first German Emperor to hold out a conciliatory hand to the leaders of Marxism, without suspecting that scoundrels have no honor. While they still held the imperial hand in theirs, their other hand was reaching for the dagger.

There is no making pacts with Jews; there can only be the hard: either–or.

I, for my part, decided to go into politics.

THE NATIONAL SOCIALIST PARTY'S FIRST MASS MEETING (1920) [6]

On February 24, 1920, in the Munich Hofbräuhaus, Hitler presented the twenty-five points of the Nazi Party's new program to an audience of some 2,000 people.

The meeting was to be opened at 7:30. At 7:15 I entered the Festsaal of the Hofbräuhaus on the Platzl in Munich, and my heart nearly burst for joy. The gigantic hall—for at that time it still seemed to me gigantic—was overcrowded with people, shoulder to shoulder, a mass numbering almost two thousand people. And above all—those people to whom we wanted to appeal had come. Far more than half the hall seemed to be occupied by Communists and Independents.[7] They had resolved that our first demonstration would come to a speedy end.

But it turned out differently. After the first speaker had finished, I took the floor. A few minutes later there was a hail of shouts, there were violent clashes in the hall, a handful of the most faithful war comrades and other supporters battled with the disturbers, and only little by little were able to restore order.

I was able to go on speaking. After half an hour the applause slowly began to drown out the screaming and shouting.

I now took up the program and began to explain it for the first time.

From minute to minute the interruptions were increasingly drowned out by shouts of applause. And when I finally submitted the twenty-five theses, point for point, to the masses and asked them personally to pronounce judgment on them, one after another was accepted with steadily mounting joy, unanimously and again unanimously, and when the last thesis had found its way to the heart of the masses, there stood

[6] From *Mein Kampf*, pp. 369–70.

[7] In April 1917 a group of Socialists opposing the war left the party and founded the Independent Social Democratic Party under the leadership of Haase and Kautsky. [Translator's note—ED.]

before me a hall full of people united by a new conviction, a new faith, a new will.

When after nearly four hours the hall began to empty and the crowd, shoulder to shoulder, began to move, shove, press toward the exit like a slow stream, I knew that now the principles of a movement which could no longer be forgotten were moving out among the German people.

A fire was kindled from whose flame one day the sword must come which would regain freedom for the Germanic Siegfried and life for the German nation.

And side by side with the coming resurrection. I sensed that the goddess of inexorable vengeance for the perjured deed of November 9, 1918,[8] was striding forth.

Thus slowly the hall emptied.

The movement took its course.

[8] The English edition from which this passage is taken incorrectly gives this date as 1919. Hitler is referring to the outbreak of massive demonstrations in Berlin, the abdication of the Kaiser, and the proclamation of a democratic republic.

3
Tactics and Techniques

The methods Hitler used to build a mass movement and to secure power were essentially no more original than his political philosophy; he simply combined and varied known techniques. But these techniques had never been so skillfully and consistently employed. Hitler's political genius, therefore, lay in his recognition of the sources of power in a modern mass-society and his unequalled grasp of the means to manipulate them.

In Mein Kampf, *Hitler set down clearly and systematically his principles for political action. The extracts in this section spell out the most important of these principles: the use of propaganda, the value of organization, the importance of the spoken word, the efficacy of terror in winning the masses, the employment of naked force against political opponents, and the necessity of the mass meeting.*

PROPAGANDA [1]

Ever since I have been scrutinizing political events, I have taken a tremendous interest in propagandist activity. . . .

But it was not until the War that it became evident what immense results could be obtained by a correct application of propaganda. . . .

Is propaganda a means or an end?

It is a means and must therefore be judged with regard to its end. It must consequently take a form calculated to support the aim which it serves. It is also obvious that its aim can vary in importance from the standpoint of general need, and that the inner value of the propaganda will vary accordingly. . . .

When the nations on this planet fight for existence—when the question of destiny, "to be or not to be," cries out for a solution—then all considerations of humanitarianism or aesthetics crumble into nothingness. . . .

And since these criteria of humanitarianism and beauty must be eliminated from the struggle, they are also inapplicable to propaganda. . . .

[1] From *Mein Kampf,* pp. 176–82.

To whom should propaganda be addressed? To the scientifically trained intelligentsia or to the less educated masses?

It must be addressed always and exclusively to the masses.

What the intelligentsia—or those who today unfortunately often go by that name—what they need is not propaganda but scientific instruction. The content of propaganda is not science any more than the object represented in a poster is art. The art of the poster lies in the designer's ability to attract the attention of the crowd by form and color. A poster advertising an art exhibit must direct the attention of the public to the art being exhibited; the better it succeeds in this, the greater is the art of the poster itself. The poster should give the masses an idea of the significance of the exhibition, it should not be a substitute for the art on display. Anyone who wants to concern himself with the art itself must do more than study the poster; and it will not be enough for him just to saunter through the exhibition. We may expect him to examine and immerse himself in the individual works, and thus little by little form a fair opinion.

A similar situation prevails with what we today call propaganda.

The function of propaganda does not lie in the scientific training of the individual, but in calling the masses' attention to certain facts, processes, necessities, etc., whose significance is thus for the first time placed within their field of vision.

The whole art consists in doing this so skillfully that everyone will be convinced that the fact is real, the process necessary, the necessity correct, etc. But since propaganda is not and cannot be the necessity in itself, since its function, like the poster, consists in attracting the attention of the crowd, and not in educating those who are already educated or who are striving after education and knowledge, its effect for the most part must be aimed at the emotions and only to a very limited degree at the so-called intellect.

All propaganda must be popular and its intellectual level must be adjusted to the most limited intelligence among those it is addressed to. Consequently, the greater the mass it is intended to reach, the lower its purely intellectual level will have to be. . . .

The more modest its intellectual ballast, the more exclusively it takes into consideration the emotions of the masses, the more effective it will be. And this is the best proof of the soundness or unsoundness of a propaganda campaign, and not success in pleasing a few scholars or young aesthetes.

The art of propaganda lies in understanding the emotional ideas of the great masses and finding, through a psychologically correct form, the way to the attention and thence to the heart of the broad masses. . . .

Once we understand how necessary it is for propaganda to be adjusted to the broad mass, the following rule results:

It is a mistake to make propaganda many-sided, like scientific instruction, for instance.

The receptivity of the great masses is very limited, their intelligence is small, but their power of forgetting is enormous. In consequences of these facts, all effective propaganda must be limited to a very few points and must harp on these in slogans until the last member of the public understands what you want him to understand by your slogan. As soon as you sacrifice this slogan and try to be many-sided, the effect will piddle away, for the crowd can neither digest nor retain the material offered. In this way the result is weakened and in the end entirely cancelled out.

Thus we see that propaganda must follow a simple line and correspondingly the basic tactics must be psychologically sound. . . .

The function of propaganda is, for example, not to weigh and ponder the rights of different people, but exclusively to emphasize the one right which it has set out to argue for. Its task is not to make an objective study of the truth, in so far as it favors the enemy, and then set it before the masses with academic fairness; its task is to serve our own right, always and unflinchingly.

ORGANIZATION [2]

As I have already remarked, I devoted myself to propaganda in the first period of my activity in the movement. What it had to do was gradually to fill a small nucleus of men with the new doctrine, and so prepare the material which could later furnish the first elements of an organization.

When a movement harbors the purpose of tearing down a world and building another in its place, complete clarity must reign in the ranks of its own leadership with regard to the following principles:

Every movement will first have to sift the human material it wins into two large groups: supporters and members.

The function of propaganda is to attract supporters, the function of organization to win members.

A supporter of a movement is one who declares himself to be in agreement with its aims, a member is one who fights for them.

The supporter is made amenable to the movement by propaganda. The member is induced by the organization to participate personally in the recruiting of new supporters, from whom in turn members can be developed.

Since being a supporter requires only a passive recognition of an idea, while membership demands active advocacy and defense, to ten supporters there will at most be one or two members.

[2] From *Mein Kampf*, pp. 581–83. All italics in the original.

Being a supporter is rooted only in understanding, membership in the courage personally to advocate and disseminate what has been understood.

Understanding in its passive form corresponds to the majority of mankind which is lazy and cowardly. Membership requires an activistic frame of mind and thus corresponds only to the minority of men.

Propaganda will consequently have to see that an idea wins supporters, while the organization must take the greatest care only to make the most valuable elements among the supporters into members. Propaganda does not, therefore, need to rack its brains with regard to the importance of every individual instructed by it, with regard to his ability, capacity, and understanding, or character, while the organization must carefully gather from the mass of these elements those which really make possible the victory of the movement.

*   *   *

Propaganda tries to force a doctrine on the whole people; the organization embraces within its scope only those who do not threaten on psychological grounds to become a brake on the further dissemination of the idea.

*   *   *

Propaganda works on the general public from the standpoint of an idea and makes them ripe for the victory of this idea, while the organization achieves victory by the persistent, organic, and militant union of those supporters who seem willing and able to carry on the fight for victory.

*   *   *

The victory of an idea will be possible the sooner, the more comprehensively propaganda has prepared people as a whole and the more exclusive, rigid, and firm the organization which carries out the fight in practice.

From this it results that the number of supporters cannot be too large, but that the number of members can more readily be too large than too small.

*   *   *

If propaganda has imbued a whole people with an idea, the organization can draw the consequences with a handful of men. Propaganda and organization, in other words, supporters and members, thus stand in a certain mutual relation. The better the propaganda has worked, the smaller the organization can be; and the larger the number of supporters, the more modest the number of members can be; and vice versa: the poorer the propaganda is, the larger the organization must be, and the smaller the host of followers of a movement remains, the more extensive the number of its members must be, if it still hopes to count on any success at all.

* * *

The first task of propaganda is to win people for subsequent organization; the first task of organization is to win men for the continuation of propaganda. The second task of propaganda is the disruption of the existing state of affairs and the permeation of this state of affairs with the new doctrine, while the second task of organization must be the struggle for power, thus to achieve the final success of the doctrine.

* * *

The most striking success of a revolution based on a philosophy of life will always have been achieved when the new philosophy of life as far as possible has been taught to all men, and, if necessary, later forced upon them, while the organization of the idea, in other words, the movement, should embrace only as many as are absolutely required for occupying the nerve centers of the state in question.

POWER OF THE SPOKEN WORD [8]

The greatest revolutions in this world have never been directed by a goose-quill!

No, to the pen it has always been reserved to provide their theoretical foundations.

But the power which has always started the greatest religious and political avalanches in history rolling has from time immemorial been the magic power of the spoken word, and that alone.

Particularly the broad masses of the people can be moved only by the power of speech. And all great movements are popular movements, volcanic eruptions of human passions and emotional sentiments, stirred either by the cruel Goddess of Distress or by the firebrand of the word hurled among the masses; they are not the lemonade-like outpourings of literary aesthetes and drawing-room heroes.

Only a storm of hot passion can turn the destinies of peoples, and he alone can arouse passion who bears it within himself.

It alone gives its chosen one the words which like hammer blows can open the gates to the heart of a people.

But the man whom passion fails and whose lips are sealed—he has not been chosen by Heaven to proclaim its will.

Therefore, let the writer remain by his ink-well, engaging in "the-

[8] From *Mein Kampf,* pp. 106–7.

oretical" activity, if his intelligence and ability are equal to it; for leadership he is neither born nor chosen.

A movement with great aims must therefore be anxiously on its guard not to lose contact with the broad masses.

It must examine every question primarily from this standpoint and make its decisions accordingly.

It must, furthermore, avoid everything which might diminish or even weaken its ability to move the masses, not for "demagogic" reasons, but in the simple knowledge that without the mighty force of the mass of a people, no great idea, however lofty and noble it may seem, can be realized.

WINNING THE MASSES [4]

The nationalization of the broad masses can never be achieved by half-measures, by weakly emphasizing a so-called objective standpoint, but only by a ruthless and fanatically one-sided orientation toward the goal to be achieved. . . .

The broad masses of a people consist neither of professors nor of diplomats. The scantiness of the abstract knowledge they possess directs their sentiments more to the world of feeling. That is where their positive or negative attitude lies. It is receptive only to an expression of force in one of these two directions and never to a half-measure hovering between the two. Their emotional attitude at the same time conditions their extraordinary stability. Faith is harder to shake than knowledge, love succumbs less to change than respect, hate is more enduring than aversion, and the impetus to the mightiest upheavals on this earth has at all times consisted less in a scientific knowledge dominating the masses than in a fanaticism which inspired them and sometimes in a hysteria which drove them forward.

Anyone who wants to win the broad masses must know the key that opens the door to their heart. Its name is not objectivity (read weakness), but will and power.

The soul of the people can only be won if along with carrying on a positive struggle for our own aims, we destroy the opponent of these aims.

The people at all times see the proof of their own right in ruthless attack on a foe, and to them renouncing the destruction of the adversary seems like uncertainty with regard to their own right if not a sign of their own unright.

The broad masses are only a piece of Nature and their sentiment does not understand the mutual handshake of people who claim that they want the opposite things. What they desire is the victory of the

[4] From *Mein Kampf*, pp. 337–38, 42–44. All italics in the original.

stronger and the destruction of the weak or his unconditional subjection.

The nationalization of our masses will succeed only when, aside from all the positive struggle for the soul of our people, their international poisoners are exterminated. . . .

The psyche of the great masses is not receptive to anything that is half-hearted and weak.

Like the woman, whose psychic state is determined less by grounds of abstract reason than by an indefinable emotional longing for a force which will complement her nature, and who, consequently, would rather bow to a strong man than dominate a weakling, likewise the masses love a commander more than a petitioner and feel inwardly more satisfied by a doctrine, tolerating no other beside itself, than by the granting of liberalistic freedom with which, as a rule, they can do little, and are prone to feel that they have been abandoned. . . .

I achieved an equal understanding of the importance of physical terror toward the individual and the masses.

Here, too, the psychological effect can be calculated with precision.

Terror at the place of employment, in the factory, in the meeting hall, and on the occasion of mass demonstrations will always be successful unless opposed by equal terror.

USE OF NAKED FORCE [5]

Can spiritual ideas be exterminated by the sword? Can "philosophies" be combated by the use of brute force? . . .

If we ponder analogous cases, particularly on a religious basis, which can be found in history, the following fundamental principle emerges:

Conceptions and ideas, as well as movements with a definite spiritual foundation, regardless whether the latter is false or true, can, after a certain point in their development, only be broken with technical instruments of power if these physical weapons are at the same time the support of a new kindling thought, idea, or philosophy.

The application of force alone, without the impetus of a basic spiritual idea as a starting point, can never lead to the destruction of an idea and its dissemination, except in the form of a complete extermination of even the very last exponent of the idea and the destruction of the last tradition. This, however, usually means the disappearance of such a state from the sphere of political importance, often for an indefinite time and sometimes forever; for experience shows that such a blood sacrifice strikes the best part of the people, since every persecution which occurs without a spiritual basis seems morally un-

[5] From *Mein Kampf*, pp. 170–72.

justified and whips up precisely the more valuable parts of a people in protest, which results in an adoption of the spiritual content of the unjustly persecuted movement. In many this occurs simply through a feeling of opposition against the attempt to bludgeon down an idea by brute force.

As a result, the number of inward supporters grows in proportion as the persecution increases. Consequently, the complete annihilation of the new doctrine can be carried out only through a process of extermination so great and constantly increasing that in the end all the truly valuable blood is drawn out of the people or state in question. The consequence is that, though a so-called "inner" purge can now take place, it will only be at the cost of total impotence. . . .

The very first requirement for a mode of struggle with the weapons of naked force is and remains persistence. In other words: only the continuous and steady application of the methods for repressing a doctrine, etc., makes it possible for a plan to succeed. . . .

This persistence, however, can always and only arise from a definite spiritual conviction. Any violence which does not spring from a firm, spiritual base, will be wavering and uncertain. It lacks the stability which can only rest in a fanatical outlook. It emanates from the momentary energy and brutal determination of an individual, and is therefore subject to the change of personalities and to their nature and strength. . . .

Thus, in summing up, we can establish the following:

Any attempt to combat a philosophy with methods of violence will fail in the end, unless the fight takes the form of attack for a new spiritual attitude. Only in the struggle between two philosophies can the weapon of brutal force, persistently and ruthlessly applied, lead to a decision for the side it supports.

THE MASS MEETING [*]

The mass meeting is . . . necessary for the reason that in it the individual, who at first, while becoming a supporter of a young movement, feels lonely and easily succumbs to the fear of being alone, for the first time gets the picture of a larger community, which in most people has a strengthening, encouraging effect. The same man, within a company or a battalion, surrounded by all his comrades, would set out on an attack with a lighter heart than if left entirely on his own. In the crowd he always feels somewhat sheltered, even if a thousand reasons actually argue against it.

But the community of the great demonstration not only strengthens the individual, it also unites and helps to create an *esprit de corps.*

[*] From *Mein Kampf,* pp. 478–79. All italics in the original.

The man who is exposed to grave tribulations, as the first advocate of a new doctrine in his factory or workshop, absolutely needs that strengthening which lies in the conviction of being a member and fighter in a great comprehensive body. And he obtains an impression of this body for the first time in the mass demonstration. When from his little workshop or big factory, in which he feels very small, he steps for the first time into a mass meeting and has thousands and thousands of people of the same opinions around him, when, as a seeker, he is swept away by three or four thousand others into the mighty effect of suggestive intoxication and enthusiasm, when the visible success and agreement of thousands confirm to him the rightness of the new doctrine and for the first time arouse doubt in the truth of his previous conviction—then he himself has succumbed to the magic influence of what we designate as "mass suggestion." The will, the longing, and also the power of thousands are accumulated in every individual. The man who enters such a meeting doubting and wavering leaves it inwardly reinforced: he has become a link in the community.

4

Public Poses

*Although there is no doubt that both Hitler's basic
beliefs and his true character are revealed in* Mein Kampf, *the*
Secret Conversations,[1] *and his early speeches, these sources alone
do not do full justice to the complexity of the man. Nor does*
Mein Kampf, *that primer of totalitarian tactics and techniques,
disclose all of the political and demogogic methods that Hitler
employed in his quest for power. The fact is that Hitler was a
man of many faces. Just as he had the ability to change his character to fit his surroundings, so he had the political shrewdness
to tailor his words to fit his audience. The two speeches excerpted
in this section illustrate two of Hitler's most effective—though
entirely different—public poses.*

CHAMPION OF PRIVATE ENTERPRISE (1932)[2]

*On January 27, 1932, little more than a year before he became
chancellor, Hitler traveled to Düsseldorf, capital of the German
steel industry, to address a gathering of west Germany's leading
industrial magnates. Many of these men shared at least some of
Hitler's views, particularly his nationalism, his authoritarianism,
and his hostility to communism. But they were suspicious of the
anticapitalist elements in the Nazi movement and they were
somewhat uneasy about the crude and strident tone of much of
Hitler's rhetoric. Their reception of the Nazi leader was therefore something less than enthusiastic. Hitler, however, was unin-
timidated. Dressed for the occasion in a dark blue double-breasted
suit and black tie, he spoke for two and a half hours with all the
political astuteness and oratorical skill he possessed. During the
entire time, the word "Jew" never once passed his lips. Missing
also was his usual vulgarity of expression. Nevertheless, Hitler
managed to ring up, in specially tailored form, nearly all of his*

[1] See Chapter 5.

[2] From Norman H. Baynes, ed., *The Speeches of Adolf Hitler* (London: Oxford
University Press, 1942), I, 777–78, 780, 786–88, 790, 804–5, 808–10, 813, 821–26. Reprinted by permission of the publisher.

*basic ideas and stock propaganda phrases. The speech, represen-
tative portions of which are reproduced here, was remarkably
effective. Long before Hitler stopped speaking, the captains of
German industry, men of relative reason and prudence, had been
won over. When the Nazi leader sat down, the audience gave
him a long and tumultuous ovation. They were convinced that
they had found their champion—the man who would defend
their economic interests, destroy the radicals of the left, and establish an authoritarian regime under which big business could
prosper. As a result of the deep impression Hitler made on this
occasion, the industrial concerns of the Rhenish-Westphalian
region contributed heavily to the coffers of the Nazi Party.*

If today the National Socialist Movement is regarded amongst
widespread circles in Germany as being hostile to our business life, I
believe the reason for this view is to be found in the fact that we
adopted . . . an attitude which differed from that of all the other organizations which are of any importance in our public life. . . . It
is not true that our distress has its final cause in a world-crisis, in a
world-catastrophe:[3] the true view is that we have reached a state of
general crisis, because from the first certain mistakes were made. . . .
I am of the opinion that there is nothing which has been produced by
the will of man which cannot in its turn be altered by another human
will. . . . Neither foreign policy nor economic policy is of primary
significance. Of course a people needs the business world in order to
live. But business is but one of the functions of this body-politic
whereby its existence is assured. But primarily the essential thing is
the starting-point and that is the people itself.

You maintain, gentlemen, that German business life must be constructed on a basis of private property. . . . And then I am bound to
say that private property can be morally and ethically justified only if I
admit that men's achievements are different. . . . And once this is admitted it is madness to say: in the economic sphere there are undoubtedly differences in value, but that is not true in the political sphere.
It is absurd to build up economic life on the conceptions of achievement, of the value of personality, and therefore in practice on the
authority of personality, but in the political sphere to deny the authority of personality and to thrust into its place the law of the greater
number—democracy. . . . In the economic sphere Communism is analogous to democracy in the political sphere. . . . In the last resort
political decisions are decisive and determine achievement in the single
sphere. . . .

[3] The world-wide economic crisis of 1931–32.

In my view it is to put the cart before the horse when today people believe that by business methods they can, for instance, recover Germany's power-position instead of realizing that the power-position is also the condition for the improvement of the economic situation. . . . There can be no flourishing economic life which has not before it and behind it the flourishing powerful State as its protection. . . . There can be no economic life unless behind this economic life there stands the determined political will of the nation absolutely ready to strike—and to strike hard. . . .

In the life of peoples the strength which can be turned outwards depends upon the strength of a nation's internal organization, and that in its turn is dependent upon the stability of views held in common on certain fundamental questions. What use is it for a Government to publish a decree with the aim of saving the people's economic life, when the nation as the living object of that purpose has itself two completely different attitudes towards economics? One section says: the pre-condition for economics is private property; the other section maintains that private property is theft: fifty per cent declare for one principle and fifty per cent for the other. . . . Fifty per cent see in the State a necessity, but another fifty per cent wish only to smash the State in pieces: they feel themselves to be the vanguard not only of an alien attitude towards the State and of an alien conception of the State, but also the vanguard of a will which is hostile to the State. . . .

Gentlemen, these conflicts strike at the power and strength of the nation as a whole. How is a people still to count for anything abroad when in the last resort fifty per cent are inclined to Bolshevism and fifty per cent are Nationalists or anti-Bolshevists. It is quite conceivable to turn Germany into a Bolshevist State—it would be a catastrophe, but it is conceivable. It is also conceivable to build up Germany as a national State. But it is inconceivable that one should create a strong and sound Germany if fifty per cent of its citizens are Bolshevist and fifty per cent nationally minded. From the solution of this problem we cannot escape! . . . Unless Germany can master this internal division in *Weltanschauungen,* no measures of the legislature can stop the decline of the German nation. . . .

Even today there are many in Germany who believe that we National Socialists would not be capable of constructive work—they deceive themselves! If we were not, already today there would be no more *bourgeoisie* alive in Germany: the question Bolshevism or not Bolshevism would long ago have been decided. . . . And I am convinced that for all those who still believe in a future for Germany it is clear what their attitude must be. For here they see before them an organization which does not preach as mere theory the views which earlier in my speech I characterized as essential, but puts them into practice, an organization inspired to the highest degree by national sentiment, constructed on the conception of an absolute authority in the leadership in all spheres, at every stage—the solitary party which amongst its members has completely overcome not only the conception of internationalism but also the idea of democracy, which in its entire organization acknowledges only the principles of Responsibility, Command, and Obedience, and which besides all this for the first time has introduced into the political life of Germany a body numbering millions which is built up on the principle of achievement. Here is an organization which is filled with an indomitable aggressive spirit, an organization which when a political opponent says "your behavior we regard as a provocation" for the first time does not see fit immediately to retire from the scene but brutally enforces its own will and hurls against the opponent the retort, "We fight today! We fight to-morrow! And if you regard our meeting today as a provocation we shall hold yet another next week—until you have learned that it is no povocation when *German* Germany also professes its belief!" . . . And when people cast in our teeth our intolerance, we proudly acknowledge it—yes, we have formed the inexorable decision to destroy Marxism in Germany down to its very last root. . . .

Today we stand at the turning-point of Germany's destiny. . . . Either we shall succeed in working out a body-politic hard as iron from this conglomerate of parties, associations, unions, and conceptions of the world, from this pride of rank and madness of class, or else, lacking this internal consolidation, Germany will fall in final ruin. . . .

If I speak to you today it is not to ask for your votes or to induce you on my account to do this or that for the Party. No, I am here to expound a point of view, and I am convinced that the victory of this point of view would mean the only possible starting-point for a German recovery.

MAN OF THE PEOPLE (1933)[4]

Much of National Socialism's appeal to the masses lay in its promise to eliminate the differences in class and status that had so long divided Germany into mutually hostile social and political factions. Although there was in actual fact no real social change in the Third Reich, the Nazi social revolution, such as it was, did manage to abolish, at least outwardly, some class distinctions and to increase the opportunities for social mobility. That so many Germans were influenced by this aspect of the Nazi siren

[4] From Gordon W. Prange, ed., *Hitler's Words, 1923–1943* (Washington, D.C.: American Council on Public Affairs, 1944), pp. 105–6. Reprinted by permission of Public Affairs Press.

call was due in no small measure to the fact that Hitler, the Führer, styled himself as a man who had risen from the lower orders of society to the leadership of a great nation. With this went a policy of glorification of the worker and the farmer. On November 10, 1933, toward the end of his first year in power, Hitler spoke to the assembled workers of the Siemens electric plant in Berlin. His speech on this occasion, a portion of which is excerpted below, was in sharp contrast to the one he delivered before the Ruhr industrialists in 1932. Standing on a platform used in assembling dynamos, wearing a civilian jacket, uniform breeches, and black jackboots, addressing his audience with the intimate plural form Ihr, Hitler adopted one of his favorite public poses: Man of the People.

When I speak to you today and thus to millions of other German workers, I have more right to do this than anyone else. I have grown out of you yourselves; once I myself stood among you, I was among you in the war for four and one-half years and now I speak to you to whom I belong, with whom I feel myself to be bound still today, and for whom in the final analysis I carry on the struggle. As far as I was concerned the struggle was not necessary. Nor would I wage it for a class or any certain stratum of society. I lead the struggle for the masses of millions of our honest, industriously working, and creative people. . . .

In my youth I was a worker like you, and then I worked my way up by industry, by study, and, I can say, by starving. In my innermost being, however, I have always remained what I was before. When, after the war, I entered political life, I did so with the conviction that our people was poorly advised by its political leadership, that a horrible future awaited the German people as a result of this bad leadership. I acted then with the most sincere self-justification because I did not belong to those who were in any way responsible for the war. I was just as little responsible for the war as anyone among you, for at that time I was, just like you, an unknown person, whom fate passed over in the order of the day. In any case I have not counted myself among those who set themselves against their own nation at the time.

I was convinced that one had to enter the struggle for the destiny of the nation, if sooner or later the entire people was not to suffer a terrible ordeal. That is what separated me from the others who turned against Germany. When the war was over I, as a front soldier, assumed the right to represent that which I had recognized to be right. Before this I had not made any speeches, nor had I engaged in any activity. I was simply a man who earned his daily bread. Not until I saw after the conclusion of the war that the political leadership did not live up to what it had promised the nation, but that the contrary was true, did I go among the people and work with six other quite insignificant workers and found a Movement. . . .

I began with six or seven men. Today it is the greatest German Movement; this is so not by chance and not because the way was made easy for me, but because the ideas upon which I built are right. It was only for this reason that they could be carried through. For you can imagine, my workers, that when a man in your station in life begins a Movement, success does not just fly to him. That is self-understood. One needs great tenacity and a tremendous will to begin such an enterprise at all. And I should like to say this to you: If I had this faith, I had it only because I knew the people and because I had no doubts as to the quality of the German people. The intellectual groups did not give me the courage to begin this gigantic work; I took courage only because I knew the German worker and the German peasant. I knew that these two classes would one day become the bearers of the new Reich and that the group of intellectual workers would also join them of itself. A gigantic program! When I was called on January 30th, after a bitter struggle of fourteen years, I had only one wish and that was to fulfill this great task. What does a title mean to me? I do not need a title. My name, which I achieved with my own strength, is my title. I only wish that posterity would sometime confirm the fact that I have striven to achieve my program decently and honestly. . . .

In Germany I am the guarantor that this community will not work out to the advantage of any element of our German people. You can look upon me as the man who belongs to no class, who belongs to no group, who is above all such considerations. I have nothing but my connection with the German people. To me everyone is entirely equal. What interest do the intellectuals have for me, the middle class, or the proletariat? I am interested only in the German people. I belong exclusively to the German people and I struggle for the German people.

5
Visions of the Future

In Mein Kampf *and its sequel,*[1] *as well as in the count-less public utterances he made in the years before the Nazi as-sumption of power, Hitler laid bare not only his* Weltanschauung *but also the methods and aims of his struggle. It was not until after the beginning of World War II, however, that he was in a position to project his ideas to their logical conclusion. In his war-time table conversations, stenographically recorded and subse-quently published,*[2] *Hitler made plain what he had in mind for those he regarded as his enemies. In the following selections, largely drawn from his informal table talk, Hitler expounds on Germany's need for* Lebensraum *(living space) in the East, his plans for a great German land-empire at Russia's expense, the extirpation of Christianity, and the "Final Solution" of the Jew-ish problem.*

LEBENSRAUM IN THE EAST [3]

Hitler's concept of racial struggle led him to conclude that the existence and future growth of the Aryan (read German) racial community could be assured only by the acquisition of adequate Lebensraum, *living space. This territorial expansion, Hitler as-serted, must be directed not across the seas but toward eastern Europe, especially Russia. It was clear that such a policy could not be fulfilled without a large and bloody war of conquest.*

---

[1] Written in 1928 but not discovered until 1958, it was first published in Germany as *Hitlers zweites Buch,* ed. Gerhard L. Weinberg (Stuttgart: Deutsche Verlags-Anstalt, 1961). The English translation is entitled *Hitler's Secret Book* (New York: Grove Press, 1961).

[2] An abbreviated German edition, edited by one of the stenographers, Dr. Henry Picker, was published under the title *Hitlers Tischgespräche* (Bonn: Athenäum-Verlag, 1951). A more comprehensive English version is *Hitler's Secret Conversa-tions, 1941–1944* (New York: Farrar, Straus and Young, Inc., 1953); also published in a paperbound edition by Signet Books, 1961.

[3] From *Mein Kampf,* pp. 131, 134, 138–39, 646, 649, 652–55, 664. All italics in the original.

But in Hitler's view, the goal—a great colonial empire that would make the German Volk dominant in Europe—was worth the price. As this extract shows, Hitler laid out clearly in Mein Kampf his plans for territorial aggrandizement—a goal which required German rearmament and which made a general European war likely, if not inevitable. It is unfortunate that European statesmen did not take more seriously Hitler's expressed intentions, for the foreign policy he conducted in the thirties and forties was in no significant point different from the one he had outlined earlier in Mein Kampf.

Germany has an annual increase in population of nearly nine hundred thousand souls. The difficulty of feeding this army of new citizens must grow greater from year to year and ultimately end in catastrophe, unless ways and means are found to forestall the danger of starvation and misery in time. . . .

Today only those races are stricken with such suffering which no longer possess the force and strength to secure for themselves the necessary territories in this world. For as matters stand there are at the present time on this earth immense areas of unused soil, only waiting for the men to till them. But it is equally true that Nature as such has not reserved this soil for the future possession of any particular nation or race; on the contrary, this soil exists for the people which possesses the force to take it and the industry to cultivate it. . . .

It must be said that such a territorial policy cannot be fulfilled in the Cameroons, but today almost exclusively in Europe. We must, therefore, coolly and objectively adopt the standpoint that it can certainly not be the intention of Heaven to give one people fifty times as much land and soil in this world as another. In this case we must not let political boundaries obscure for us the boundaries of eternal justice. If this earth really has room for all to live in, let us be given the soil we need for our livelihood.

True, they will not willingly do this. But then the law of self-preservation goes into effect; and what is refused to amicable methods, it is up to the fist to take. . . .

The National Socialist movement must strive to eliminate the disproportion between our population and our area—viewing this latter as a source of food as well as a basis for power politics—between our historical past and the hopelessness of our present impotence. . . .

The demand for restoration of the frontiers of 1914 is a political absurdity of such proportions and consequences as to make it seem a crime. Quite aside from the fact that the Reich's frontiers in 1914 were anything but logical. For in reality they were neither complete in the sense of embracing the people of German nationality, nor sensible with regard to geo-military expediency. . . .

As opposed to this, we National Socialists must hold unflinchingly to our aim in foreign policy, namely, *to secure for the German people the land and soil to which they are entitled on this earth.* And this action is the only one which, before God and our German posterity, would make any sacrifice of blood seem justified: before God, since we have been put on this earth with the mission of eternal struggle for our daily bread, beings who receive nothing as a gift, and who owe their position as lords of the earth only to the genius and the courage with which they can conquer and defend it; and before our German posterity in so far as we have shed no citizen's blood out of which a thousand others are not bequeathed to posterity. The soil on which some day German generations of peasants can beget powerful sons will sanction the investment of the sons of today, and will some day acquit the responsible statesmen of blood-guilt and sacrifice of the people, even if they are persecuted by their contemporaries. . . .

For no people on this earth possesses so much as a square yard of territory on the strength of a higher will or superior right. Just as Germany's frontiers are fortuitous frontiers, momentary frontiers in the current political struggle of any period, so are the boundaries of other nations' living space. And just as the shape of our earth's surface can seem immutable as granite only to the thoughtless soft-head, but in reality only represents at each period an apparent pause in a continuous development, created by the mighty forces of Nature in a process of continuous growth, only to be transformed or destroyed tomorrow by greater forces, likewise the boundaries of living spaces in the life of nations.

State boundaries are made by man and changed by man.

The fact that a nation has succeeded in acquiring an undue amount of soil constitutes no higher obligation that it should be recognized eternally. At most it proves the strength of the conquerors and the weakness of the nations. And in this case, right lies in this strength alone. . . . Just as our ancestors did not receive the soil on which we live today as a gift from Heaven, but had to fight for it at the risk of their lives, in the future no folkish grace will win soil for us and hence life for our people, but only the might of a victorious sword.

Much as all of us today recognize the necessity of a reckoning with France, it would remain ineffectual in the long run if it represented the whole of our aim in foreign policy. It can and will achieve meaning only if it offers the rear cover for an enlargement of our people's living space in Europe. . . .

If we speak of soil in Europe today, we can primarily have in mind only *Russia* and her vassal border states.

Here Fate itself seems desirous of giving us a sign. By handing

Russia to Bolshevism, it robbed the Russian nation of that intelligentsia which previously brought about and guaranteed its existence as a state. For the organization of a Russian state formation was not the result of the political abilities of the Slavs in Russia, but only a wonderful example of the state-forming efficacity of the German element in an inferior race. . . . For centuries Russia drew nourishment from this Germanic nucleus of its upper leading strata. Today it can be regarded as almost totally exterminated and extinguished. It has been replaced by the Jew. . . . He himself is no element of organization, but a ferment of decomposition. The Persian[4] empire in the east is ripe for collapse. And the end of Jewish rule in Russia will also be the end of Russia as a state. . . . The political testament of the German nation to govern its outward activity for all time should and must be:

Never suffer the rise of two continental powers in Europe. Regard any attempt to organize a second military power on the German frontiers, even if only in the form of creating a state capable of military strength, as an attack on Germany, and in it see not only the right, but also the duty, to employ all means up to armed force to prevent the rise of such a state, or, if one has already arisen, to smash it again.—See to it that the strength of our nation is founded, not on colonies, but on the soil of our European homeland. Never regard the Reich as secure unless for centuries to come it can give every scion of our people his own parcel of soil. Never forget that the most sacred right on this earth is a man's right to have earth to till with his own hands, and the most sacred sacrifice the blood that a man sheds for this earth.

RUSSIA: GERMANY'S INDIA [5]

Less than two decades after he had outlined in Mein Kampf *the doctrine of eastern* Lebensraum, *Hitler was within sight of his goal: the conquest of Russia and the establishment on her soil of a German colonial empire that (in Hitler's words) would be "what India was for England." During the victorious months of 1941–42, Hitler regularly subjected his intimate table companions to passionate monologues in which he set forth his grandiose plans for the future German empire in the East. The following extracts from Hitler's table talk offer a vivid picture*

---

[4] Second edition has "giant" instead of "Persian." [Translator's note—ED.]

[5] From *Hitler's Secret Conversations, 1941–1944,* trans. Norman Cameron and R. H. Stevens (New York: Farrar, Straus and Young, Inc., 1953), pp. 13–14, 20, 27–29, 56–57, 501. Copyright © 1953 by Farrar, Straus and Young, Inc. Reprinted by permission of Farrar, Straus & Giroux, Inc., and Weidenfeld & Nicolson, Ltd.

of what a Nazi victory in World War II might have meant for eastern Europe.

July 27, 1941

It should be possible for us to control this region to the East with two hundred and fifty thousand men plus a cadre of good administrators. Let's learn from the English, who, with two hundred and fifty thousand men in all, including fifty thousand soldiers, govern four hundred million Indians. This space in Russia must always be dominated by Germans. . . .

We'll take the southern part of the Ukraine, especially the Crimea, and make it an exclusively German colony. There'll be no harm in pushing out the population that's there now. The German colonist will be the soldier-peasant, and for that I'll take professional soldiers, whatever their line may have been previously. . . . The Reich will put at their disposal a completely equipped farm. The soil costs us nothing, we have only the house to build. . . . These soldier-peasants will be given arms, so that at the slightest danger they can be at their posts when we summon them. That's how the ancient Austria used to keep its Eastern peoples under control.

August 8–11, 1941

The German colonists ought to live on handsome, spacious farms. The German services will be lodged in marvelous buildings, the governors in palaces. Beneath the shelter of the administrative services, we shall gradually organize all that is indispensable to the maintenance of a certain standard of living. Around the city, to a depth of thirty to forty kilometers, we shall have a belt of handsome villages connected by the best roads. What exists beyond that will be another world, in which we mean to let the Russians live as they like. It is merely necessary that we should rule them. In the event of a revolution, we shall only have to drop a few bombs on their cities, and the affair will be liquidated. Once a year we shall lead a troop of Kirghizes through the capital of the Reich, in order to strike their imaginations with the size of our monuments.

What India was for England, the territories of Russia will be for us.

September 17–18, 1941

The struggle for the hegemony of the world will be decided in favor of Europe by the possession of the Russian space. Thus Europe will be an impregnable fortress, safe from all threat of blockade. All this opens up economic vistas which, one might think, will incline the most liberal of the Western democrats towards the New Order.

The essential thing, for the moment, is to conquer. After that everything will be simply a question of organization.

When one contemplates this primitive world, one is convinced that nothing will drag it out of its indolence unless one compels the people to work. The Slavs are a mass of born slaves, who feel the need of a master. . . . If left to himself, the Slav would never have emerged from the narrowest of family communities. . . . The Slav peoples are not destined to live a cleanly life. They know it, and we would be wrong to persuade them of the contrary. It was we who, in 1918, created the Baltic countries and the Ukraine. But nowadays we have no interest in maintaining Baltic States, any more than in creating an independent Ukraine. We must likewise prevent them from returning to Christianity. That would be a grave fault, for it would be giving them a form of organization.

I am not a partisan, either, of a university at Kiev. It's better not to teach them to read. They won't love us for tormenting them with schools. Even to give them a locomotive to drive would be a mistake. And what stupidity it would be on our part to proceed to a distribution of land! In spite of that, we'll see to it that the natives live better than they've lived hitherto. We'll find among them the human material that's indispensable for tilling the soil.

We'll supply grain to all in Europe who need it. The Crimea will give us its citrus fruits, cotton and rubber (100,000 acres of plantation would be enough to insure our independence).

The Pripet marshes will keep us supplied with reeds.

We'll supply the Ukrainians with scarves, glass beads and everything that colonial peoples like.

The Germans—this is essential—will have to constitute amongst themselves a closed society, like a fortress. The least of our stable-lads must be superior to any native.

For German youth, this will be a magnificent field of experiment. We'll attract to the Ukraine Danes, Dutch, Norwegians, Swedes. The army will find areas for maneuvers there, and our aviation will have the space it needs.

October 17, 1941

In comparison with the beauties accumulated in Central Germany, the new territories in the East seem to us like a desert. Flanders, too, is only a plain—but of what beauty! This Russian desert, we shall populate it. The immense spaces of the Eastern Front will have been the field of the greatest battles in history. We'll give this country a past.

We'll take away its character of an Asiatic steppe, we'll Europeanize it. With this object, we have undertaken the construction of roads that will lead to the southernmost point of the Crimea and to the Caucasus. These roads will be studded along their whole length with German towns, and around these towns our colonists will settle.

As for the two or three million men whom we need to accomplish this task, we'll find them quicker than we think. They'll come from Germany, Scandinavia, the Western countries and America. I shall no longer be here to see all that but in twenty years the Ukraine will already be a home for twenty milion inhabitants besides the natives. In three hundred years, the country will be one of the loveliest gardens in the world.

As for the natives, we'll have to screen them carefully. The Jew, that destroyer, we shall drive out. As far as the population is concerned, I get a better impression in White Russia than in the Ukraine.

We shan't settle in the Russian towns, and we'll let them fall to pieces without intervening. And, above all, no remorse on this subject! We're not going to play at children's nurses; we're absolutely without obligations as far as these people are concerned. To struggle against the hovels, chase away the fleas, provide German teachers, bring out newspapers—very little of that for us! We'll confine ourselves, perhaps, to setting up a radio transmitter, under our control. For the rest, let them know just enough to understand our highway signs, so that they won't get themselves run over by our vehicles!

For them the word "liberty" means the right to wash on feast-days. If we arrive bringing soap, we'll obtain no sympathy. These are views that will have to be completely readjusted. There's only one duty: to Germanize this country by the immigration of Germans, and to look upon the natives as Redskins. If these people had defeated us, Heaven have mercy! But we don't hate them. That sentiment is unknown to us. We are guided only by reason. They, on the other hand, have an inferiority complex. They have a real hatred towards a conqueror whose crushing superiority they can feel. The *intelligentsia?* We have too many of them at home.

All those who have the feeling for Europe can join in our work.

In this business I shall go straight ahead, cold-bloodedly. What they may think about me, at this juncture, is to me a matter of complete indifference. I don't see why a German who eats a piece of bread should torment himself with the idea that the soil that produces this bread has been won by the sword. When we eat wheat from Canada, we don't think about the despoiled Indians.

The precept that it's men's duty to love one another is theory—and the Christians are the last to practice it!

August 6, 1942

The foundation of St. Petersburg by Peter the Great was a fatal event in the history of Europe; and St. Petersburg must therefore disappear utterly from the earth's surface. Moscow, too. Then the Russians will retire into Siberia.

It is not by taking over the miserable Russian hovels that we shall establish ourselves as masters in the East. The German colonies must be organized on an altogether higher plane. . . . As for the ridiculous hundred million Slavs, we will mold the best of them to the shape that suits us, and we will isolate the rest of them in their own pig-sties; and anyone who talks about cherishing the local inhabitant and civilizing him, goes straight off into a concentration camp!

CHRISTIANITY: A DISEASE [6]

Although Hitler was clearly both anticlerical and anti-Christian, he was not an arrant atheist. Reared as a Roman Catholic, he became early in his youth a rationalist (at least in matters of religion), who believed that God was "the dominion of natural laws throughout the whole universe." [7] Hitler's reading of these natural laws, however, was diametrically opposed to the teachings of the Christian churches. In his view, Christianity, like Bolshevism, was a Jewish invention, designed to enslave humanity. To be sure, political considerations forced him to restrain his violent anticlericalism, but in private Hitler made plain both his detestation of Christianity and his determination to settle accounts with the churches after the war.

July 11–12, 1941

When National Socialism has ruled long enough, it will no longer be possible to conceive of a form of life different from ours.

In the long run, National Socialism and religion will no longer be able to exist together. . . .

The heaviest blow that ever struck humanity was the coming of Christianity. Bolshevism is Christianity's illegitimate child. Both are inventions of the Jew. The deliberate lie in the matter of religion was introduced into the world by Christianity. Bolshevism practises a lie of the same nature, when it claims to bring liberty to men, whereas in reality it seeks only to enslave them. In the ancient world, the relations between men and gods were founded on an instinctive respect. It was a world enlightened by the idea of tolerance. Christianity was the first creed in the world to exterminate its adversaries in the name of love. Its key-note is intolerance. . . .

October 14, 1941

I've always kept the Party aloof from religious questions. . . . The main thing is to be clever in this matter and not to look for a struggle where it can be avoided.

[6] From *Hitler's Secret Conversations*, pp. 6, 49–52, 247, 261, 264, 279.

[7] *Ibid.*, p. 36.

Being weighed down by a superstitious past, men are afraid of things that can't, or can't yet, be explained—that is to say, of the unknown. If anyone has needs of a metaphysical nature, I can't satisfy them with the Party's program. Time will go by until the moment when science can answer all the questions.

So it's not opportune to hurl ourselves now into a struggle with the Churches. The best thing is to let Christianity die a natural death. A slow death has something comforting about it. The dogma of Christianity gets worn away before the advances of science. Religion will have to make more and more concessions. Gradually the myths crumble. All that's left is to prove that in nature there is no frontier between the organic and the inorganic. When understanding of the universe has become widespread, when the majority of men know that the stars are not sources of light but worlds, perhaps inhabited worlds like ours, then the Christian doctrine will be convicted of absurdity.

Originally, religion was merely a prop for human communities. It was a means, not an end in itself. It's only gradually that it became transformed in this direction, with the object of maintaining the rule of the priests, who can live only to the detriment of society collectively.

The instructions of a hygienic nature that most religions gave, contributed to the foundation of organized communities. The precepts ordering people to wash, to avoid certain drinks, to fast at appointed dates, to take exercise, to rise with the sun, to climb to the top of the minaret—all these were obligations invented by intelligent people. The exhortation to fight courageously is also self-explanatory. Observe, by the way, that, as a corollary, the Mussulman was promised a paradise peopled with houris, where wine flowed in streams—a real earthly paradise. The Christians, on the other hand, declare themselves satisfied if after their death they are allowed to sing Hallelujahs! All these elements contributed to form human communities. It is to these private customs that peoples owe their present characters.

Christianity, of course, has reached the peak of absurdity in this respect. And that's why one day its structure will collapse. Science has already impregnated humanity. Consequently, the more Christianity clings to its dogmas, the quicker it will decline.

But one must continue to pay attention to another aspect of the problem. It's possible to satisfy the needs of the inner life by an intimate communion with nature, or by knowledge of the past. Only a minority, however, at the present stage of the mind's development, can feel the respect inspired by the unknown, and thus satisfy the metaphysical needs of the soul. The average human being has the same needs, but can satisfy them only by elementary means. That's particularly true of women, as also of peasants who impotently watch the destruction of their crops. The person whose life tends to simplification is thirsty for belief, and he dimly clings to it with all his strength.

Nobody has the right to deprive simple people of their childish certainties until they've acquired others that are more reasonable. Indeed, it's most important that the higher belief should be well established in them before the lower belief has been removed. We must finally achieve this. But it would serve no purpose to replace an old belief by a new one that would merely fill the place left vacant by its predecessor.

It seems to me that nothing would be more foolish than to re-establish the worship of Wotan. Our old mythology had ceased to be viable when Christianity implanted itself. Nothing dies unless it is moribund. At that period the ancient world was divided between the systems of philosophy and the worship of idols. It's not desirable that the whole of humanity should be stultified—and the only way of getting rid of Christianity is to allow it to die little by little.

A movement like ours mustn't let itself be drawn into metaphysical digressions. It must stick to the spirit of exact science. It's not the Party's function to be a counterfeit for religion.

If, in the course of a thousand or two thousand years, science arrives at the necessity of renewing its points of view, that will not mean that science is a liar. Science cannot lie, for it's always striving, according to the momentary state of knowledge, to deduce what is true. When it makes a mistake, it does so in good faith. It's Christianity that's the liar. It's in perpetual conflict with itself.

One may ask whether the disappearance of Christianity would entail the disappearance of belief in God. That's not to be desired. The notion of divinity gives most men the opportunity to concretize the feeling they have of supernatural realities. Why should we destroy this wonderful power they have of incarnating the feeling for the divine that is within them?

The man who lives in communion with nature necessarily finds himself in opposition to the Churches. And that's why they're heading for ruin—for science is bound to win.

I especially wouldn't want our movement to acquire a religious character and institute a form of worship. It would be appalling for me, and I would wish I'd never lived, if I were to end up in the skin of a Buddha!

If at this moment we were to eliminate the religions by force, the people would unanimously beseech us for a new form of worship. You can imagine our Gauleiters giving up their pranks to play at being saints! As for our Minister for Religion, according to his own coreligionists, God himself would turn away from his family!

I envisage the future, therefore as follows: First of all, to each man his private creed. Superstition shall not lose its rights. The Party is sheltered from the danger of competing with the religions. These latter must simply be forbidden from interfering in future with temporal matters. From the tenderest age, education will be imparted in such a way that each child will know all that is important to the maintenance of the State. As for the men close to me, who, like me, have escaped from the clutches of dogma, I've no reason to fear that the Church will get its hooks on them.

We'll see to it that the Churches cannot spread abroad teachings in conflict with the interests of the State. We shall continue to preach the doctrine of National Socialism, and the young will no longer be taught anything but the truth.

February 8, 1942

The evil that's gnawing our vitals is our priests, of both creeds. I can't at present give them the answer they've been asking for, but it will cost them nothing to wait. It's all written down in my big book. The time will come when I'll settle my accounts with them, and I'll go straight to the point. . . . I shan't let myself be hampered by juridical scruples. Only necessity has legal force. In less than ten years from now, things will have quite another look. I can promise them.

We shan't be able to go on evading the religious problem much longer. If anyone thinks it's really essential to build the life of human society on a foundation of lies, well, in my estimation, such a society is not worth preserving. If, on the other hand, one believes that truth is the indispensable foundation, then conscience bids one intervene in the name of truth, and exterminate the lie.

Periods that have endured such affronts without protesting will be condemned by people of the coming generations. Just as the pyres for heretics have been suppressed, so all these by-products of ignorance and bad faith will have to be eliminated in their turn.

February 20–21, 1942

The biretta!

The mere sight of one of these abortions in cassocks makes me wild! Man has been given his brain to think with. But if he has the misfortune to make use of it, he finds a swarm of black bugs on his heels. The mind is doomed to the auto-da-fé. . . .

Since my fourteenth year I have felt liberated from the superstition that the priests used to teach. Apart from a few Holy Joes, I can say that none of my comrades went on believing in the miracle of the eucharist.

The only difference between then and now is that in those days I was convinced one must blow up the whole show with dynamite.

February 27, 1942

Our epoch will certainly see the end of the disease of Christianity. It will last another hundred years, two hundred years perhaps. My regret will have been that I couldn't, like whoever the prophet was, behold the promised land from afar. . . .

"THE JEWS MUST DISAPPEAR FROM EUROPE"

None of Hitler's many visions of the future came closer to realization than that of a Europe free of Jews. Of the approximately eight million Jews who at the outbreak of World War II lived in what was to become Hitler's Europe, barely two million survived their oppressor. The planned, cold-blooded slaughter of millions of Jewish men, women, and children was the final, shattering consequence of Hitler's racial anti-Semitism. "History," in the words of Justice Robert M. Jackson,[8] "does not record a crime ever perpetrated against so many victims or one ever carried out with such calculated cruelty." By the beginning of the war the number of Jews in Germany had declined markedly: tens of thousands had been driven into exile, thousands had been killed or imprisoned, and those that remained had been stripped of most of their civil rights. Before long, however, German conquests brought millions of foreign Jews under Nazi rule. During 1940 and the first half of 1941, the Nazis attempted to deal with this new state of affairs by deporting large numbers of Jews to ghettos, reservations, and concentration camps in German-occupied Poland. Although thousands died of maltreatment or were indiscriminately murdered during these mass deportations, the Nazis had not yet adopted a policy of total extermination. The German invasion of the Soviet Union, however, brought a radical shift in the Nazi treatment of the Jewish question: special SS Einsatzgruppen began to conduct mass shootings of Jews in areas newly conquered by the advancing German armies. By 1942, the fate of much of European Jewry was sealed; the decision had been made to apply the "Final Solution" to the Jewish problem. In the course of the next three years, the bulk of the Jews in Hitler's Europe were systematically exterminated by shooting or gassing. The following statements—two public, two private—show the progressive radicalization of Hitler's views on the Jewish question.

[8] U.S. chief counsel at the Nuremberg war-crimes trial.

January 30, 1939 [9]

In the course of my life I have very often been a prophet, and I have usually been ridiculed for it. During the time of my struggle for power, it was in the first instance the Jewish race which received my prophecies with laughter when I said that I would one day take over the leadership of the state, and with it that of the whole nation, and that I would then, among many other things, settle the Jewish problem. . . . Today I will once more be a prophet. If the international Jewish financiers in and outside Europe should succeed in plunging the nations once more into a world war, then the result will not be the Bolshevization of the earth and thus the victory of Jewry, but the annihilation of the Jewish race in Europe! . . .

January 23, 1942 [10]

One must act radically. When one pulls out a tooth, one does it with a single tug, and the pain quickly goes away. The Jew must clear out of Europe. Otherwise no understanding will be possible between Europeans. It's the Jew who prevents everything. When I think about it, I realize that I'm extraordinarily humane. . . . I restrict myself to telling them they must go away. If they break their pipes on the journey, I can't do anything about it. But if they refuse to go voluntarily, I see no other solution but extermination.[11]

January 27, 1942 [12]

The Jews must pack up, disappear from Europe. Let them go to Russia. Where the Jews are concerned, I'm devoid of all sense of pity. They'll always be the ferment that moves peoples one against the other. They sow discord everywhere, as much between individuals as between peoples.

They'll also have to clear out of Switzerland and Sweden. It's where they're to be found in small numbers that they're most dangerous. Put five thousand Jews in Sweden—soon they'll be holding all the posts there. Obviously, that makes them all the easier to spot.

It's entirely natural that we should concern ourselves with the question on the European level. It's clearly not enough to expel them

[9] From Hitler's speech before the Reichstag, *Hitler's Words*, p. 82.

[10] From *Hitler's Secret Conversations*, p. 193.

[11] At the time Hitler made this statement, no further possibility of emigrating from Europe remained to the Jews in Nazi-occupied areas; moreover, the mass shootings of eastern Jews which characterized the first stage of the "Final Solution" had already been going on for more than six months.

[12] From *Hitler's Secret Conversations*, p. 212–13.

from Germany. We cannot allow them to retain bases of withdrawal at our doors. We want to be out of danger of all kinds of infiltration.

January 30, 1942 [18]

The war will not end as the Jews imagine it will, namely, with the uprooting of the Aryan peoples of Europe. On the contrary, the result of this war will be the complete annihilation of the Jews. Now for the first time they will not bleed other people to death; rather, for the first time the genuine old Jewish law of "an eye for an eye, a tooth for a tooth," will be applied. . . . And the hour will come when the most evil world-enemy of all times, or at least of the last thousand years, will have played his part to the end.

[18] From Hitler's speech in the Berlin *Sportpalast*, Foreign Broadcast Monitoring Service, Federal Communications Commission. The FCC translation has been compared to the German text published by the official German news agency (*Deutsches Nachrichtenbüro*), and a number of minor corrections have been made by the editor. It is interesting to note that the published German version of the speech omitted the phrase "Now for the first time they will not bleed other people to death. . . ."

6
In Victory and in Defeat

On September 1, 1939, while German bombs and shells falling on Polish soil signaled the opening of World War II, Hitler appeared before his Reichstag *wearing a uniform of* Wehrmacht *field-gray. "From now on," he declared, "I am just the first soldier of the German Reich. I have once more put on that coat that was the most sacred and dear to me. I will not take it off again until victory is secured—or I will not survive the outcome." Thus began a new, and final, chapter in the career of Adolf Hitler: that of military commander and war leader. Although the* Wehrmacht, *under Hitler's leadership, at first reaped a series of spectacular and unprecedented successes, it failed to win final victory. True to his word, Hitler chose not to survive the outcome. On April 29, 1945, he dictated both his private will and his political testament. The next day, in the face of Germany's imminent defeat and with Russian troops only blocks away from the bunker in which he had sought refuge, Hitler committed suicide. The following selections present Hitler in his role as war leader and illustrate his wartime rhetoric in both victory and defeat. The section concludes with Hitler's political testament, in which he reiterates the old lies and distortions and, maniacally consistent to the end, calls upon his followers to continue the racial struggle against "the universal poisoner of all peoples, International Jewry."*

DECISION FOR WAR: TWO VERSIONS

Private Truths: To the Commanders in Chief of the Wehrmacht, August 22, 1939 [1]

I have called you together to give you a picture of the political situation, in order that you may have some insight into the individual

[1] Hitler met with his senior military commanders at the Berghof, his retreat on the Obersalzberg, near Berchtesgaden. He addressed his guests twice: once in the morning, again in the afternoon. The minutes of the meeting were captured by American troops at the end of the war and were submitted to the International Military Tribunal at Nuremberg as Documents 798-PS and 1014-PS. The translation

factors on which I have based my decision to act and in order to strengthen your confidence.

After this we shall discuss military details.

It was clear to me that a conflict with Poland had to come sooner or later. I had already made this decision in the spring, but I thought that I would first turn against the West in a few years, and only after that against the East. . . . But this plan, which appealed to me, could not be executed, as fundamental points had changed. It became clear to me that . . . in certain circumstances a conflict with Poland might come at an inopportune moment. I give as reasons for this conclusion:

First of all two personal factors:

My own personality and that of Mussolini.

Essentially all depends on me, on my existence, because of my political talents. Furthermore, the fact that probably no one will ever again have the confidence of the whole German people as I have. There will probably never again in the future be a man with more authority than I have. My existence is therefore a factor of great value. But I can be eliminated at any time by a criminal or a lunatic.

The second personal factor is the Duce. His existence is also decisive. If anything happens to him, Italy's loyalty to the alliance will no longer be certain.

The other side presents a negative picture as far as authoritative persons are concerned. There is no outstanding personality in England and France.

It is easy for us to make decisions. We have nothing to lose; we have everything to gain. Because of our restrictions [*Einschränkungen*] our economic situation is such that we can only hold out for a few more years. Göring can confirm this. We have no other choice, we must act. Our opponents will be risking a great deal and can gain only a little. . . .

All these favorable circumstances will no longer prevail in two or three years' time. No one knows how much longer I shall live. Therefore, better a conflict now. . . . The probability is still great that the West will not intervene. We must take the risk with ruthless determination. The politician must take a risk just as much as the general. We are faced with the harsh alternatives of striking or of certain annihilation sooner or later. . . .

We will hold our position in the West until we have conquered Poland. We must bear in mind our great production capacity. It is much greater than in 1914–1918.

The enemy had another hope, that Russia would become our enemy

from which this selection has been excerpted may be found in U.S. Department of State, *Documents on German Foreign Policy, 1918–1945*, Series D (Washington, D.C.: U.S. Government Printing Office, 1956), VII, 200–6.

after the conquest of Poland. The enemy did not reckon with my great strength of purpose. Our enemies are small fry. I saw them in Munich.

I was convinced that Stalin would never accept the English offer. Four days ago I took a special step, which led to Russia replying yesterday that she is prepared to sign. Personal contact with Stalin is established. The day after tomorrow von Ribbentrop will conclude the treaty.[2] Now Poland is in the position in which I wanted her. . . .

I am only afraid that at the last moment some swine or other will yet submit to me a plan for mediation. . . .

The destruction of Poland has priority.[3] The aim is to eliminate active forces, not to reach a definite line. Even if war breaks out in the West, the destruction of Poland remains the priority. A quick decision in view of the season.

I shall give a propagandist reason for starting the war, no matter whether it is plausible or not. The victor will not be asked afterwards whether he told the truth or not. When starting and waging a war it is not right that matters, but victory.

Close your hearts to pity. Act brutally. Eighty million people must obtain what is their right. Their existence must be made secure. . . .

Public Lies: To the Reichstag and the World, September 1, 1939 [4]

Members of the German Reichstag:

For months we have been tormented by a problem once imposed upon us by the Dictate of Versailles and which, in its deterioration and corruption, has now become utterly intolerable. Danzig was and is a German City! The Corridor was and is German! All these territories owe their cultural development exclusively to the German people, without whom absolute barbarism would reign in these Eastern territories. Danzig was separated from us! The Corridor was annexed by Poland! The German minorities living there were mistreated in the most appalling manner. . . . As usual, I have tried to change this intolerable state of affairs through proposals for a peaceful revision. . . .

Those proposals were rejected! But not only that! They were answered by mobilization, by increased terrorism, by intensified pres-

---

[2] The Russo-German Nonaggression Pact, signed in Moscow on August 23, 1939, assured Hitler that the Soviet Union would not intervene in the event the invasion of Poland resulted in a war between Germany and the western powers.

[3] The last three paragraphs of this selection are from the second (afternoon) speech by Hitler on August 22, 1939.

[4] From Nuremberg Document 2322-PS, Office of United States Chief Counsel for Prosecution of Axis Criminality, *Nazi Conspiracy and Aggression* (Washington, D.C.: U.S. Government Printing Office, 1946), IV, 1026–32. The hasty Nuremberg translation of this speech has been checked against the original German text, and a number of changes and corrections have been made by the editor.

sure on the people of German blood living in these territories, and by a gradual economic, political and, during the past few weeks, even military strangulation and blockade of the Free City of Danzig. . . .

These are our aims; I am determined to solve them:

First, the question of Danzig;

Second, the question of the Corridor;

Third, to see to it that change shall take place in Germany's relations to Poland, which will insure a peaceful coexistence of the two powers.

I am determined to fight until either the present Polish Government is willing to effect this change or another Polish Government is prepared to do so.

I am determined to eliminate from the German frontiers the element of insecurity, the atmosphere which permanently resembles civil war. I shall see to it that peace on the Eastern frontier shall be the same as it is on our other frontiers. . . .

I will not wage war against women and children. I have instructed my air force to limit their attacks to military objectives. However, if the enemy should conclude from this that he might get away with waging war in a different manner he will receive such an answer that he'll be knocked out of his wits!

Last night for the first time regular soldiers of the Polish Army fired shots on our territory. Since 5:45 a.m. we have been returning their fire! From now on, every bomb will be answered by another bomb. Whoever fights with poison gas will be fought with poison gas. Whoever disregards the rules of humane warfare can but expect us to do the same.

I will carry on this fight, no matter against whom, until such time as the safety of the Reich and its rights are secured!

For more than six years now I have been engaged in building up the German armed forces. During this period more than ninety billion Reichsmark were spent building up the Wehrmacht. Today, ours are the best equipped armed forces in the world and they are far superior to those of 1914. My confidence in them can never be shaken!

If I call upon the Wehrmacht and if I ask sacrifices of the German people and, if necessary, unlimited sacrifices, then I have the right to do so, for I myself am just as ready today as I was in the past to make every personal sacrifice. I don't ask anything of any German which I myself was not prepared to do at any moment for more than four years. There shall not be any deprivations for Germans in which I myself will not immediately share. From this moment on my whole life belongs more than ever to my people. . . .

As a National Socialist and a German soldier I enter upon this fight with a stout heart! My whole life has been but one continuous struggle for my people, for its resurrection, for Germany, and this whole struggle has been inspired by one single conviction: faith in this people!

One word I have never known: capitulation. And if there is anyone who thinks that hard times lie ahead of us I'd like him not to forget the fact that at one time a Prussian king with a ridiculously small state confronted one of the greatest coalitions ever known and came forth victoriously after three campaigns because he possessed that strong and firm faith which is required of us in these times. As for the rest of the world, I can only assure them that a November 1918 shall never occur again in German history!

I ask of every German what I myself am prepared to do at any moment: to be ready to lay down his life for his people and for his country. Whoever thinks he can, directly or indirectly, evade this patriotic duty shall perish! We will not tolerate traitors!

We all are acting only in accordance with our old principle: our own life matters nothing, all that matters is that our people, that Germany shall live! . . .

I conclude with the words with which I once started my fight for power in the Reich. At that time I said: "If our will is so strong that it cannot be broken by any adversity, then our will and our German state will be able to smash and overcome adversity."

Germany—Sieg Heil!

AT THE HEIGHT OF VICTORY:
PROCLAMATION TO THE GERMAN PEOPLE,
OCTOBER 3, 1941 [5]

German men and women! . . .

Since June 22 a battle of decisive importance for the entire world has been raging.[6] Only posterity will clearly recognize both the magnitude and the implications of this event. Only posterity will realize that it marked the beginning of a new era. But even this struggle was not desired by me. . . .

The conspiracy of Democrats, Jews, and Free Masons was responsible for plunging Europe into war two years ago. Arms had to decide.

Since then a struggle has been taking place between truth and lies; and, as always, this war will end in victory for truth. In other words,

---

[5] From the *Völkischer Beobachter*, October 5, 1941; trans. G. H. Stein. Hitler had not addressed the German people for many months. He used the occasion presented by the launching of the annual "Wartime Winter Assistance Program" (*Kriegswinterhilfswerk*) not only to make a brief appeal in support of the program but also to issue a major proclamation on the course of the war. The speech, delivered at the *Sportpalast* in Berlin, was broadcast to the entire German nation.

[6] The German invasion of the Soviet Union.

no matter what lies British propaganda, international world Jewry, and their democratic accomplices may concoct, historical facts will not be changed. And the historical facts are not that the English are in Germany, not that other states have occupied Berlin, not that they have advanced in either the East or the West. Rather, the historical truth is that for the past two years Germany has been defeating one opponent after another. . . .

But in August and September of last year one thing was becoming clear: A showdown with England, which would have tied down the entire German Air Force, was no longer possible; for in my rear stood a state that was daily increasing its preparations for an attack against Germany at such a moment. . . . I finally decided to take the first step myself. When I see an enemy pointing his rifle at me I am not going to wait until he pulls the trigger. I would prefer to be the first to let loose.

Today I can tell you that it was the most difficult decision of my entire life, for such a step always involves risk, and only posterity will know the exact outcome. Thus one can rely only on one's conscience, on the confidence in one's people, on the strength of one's weapons, and, finally—as I have often said—on an appeal to Almighty God that He bless him who is himself ready and willing to fight and make sacrifices for his right to exist.

On the morning of June 22, the greatest battle in the history of the world began. Since then something like three and a half months have elapsed, and I can confirm one thing here today: Everything has gone according to plan. . . . Never during the entire period did we lose the initiative for even one second. On the contrary, right up to the present moment every action has developed just as much according to plan as was formerly the case in the East against Poland, then against Norway, and finally both against the West and in the Balkans. There is one more point I must make in this connection: We have not been mistaken either about the effectiveness of our plans or the efficiency and bravery of our soldiers. Nor have we been mistaken about the quality of our weapons.

We have not been mistaken about the smooth working of all the operations at the front and of the occupation process that controls the vast area in the rear. Nor have we been mistaken about the German homeland. We have, however, been mistaken about one thing. We had no idea how gigantic were this enemy's preparations against Germany and Europe, how immeasurably great was the danger, and how narrowly we have escaped the destruction not only of Germany but also of Europe. This I can reveal here today. I reveal it today only because I can also say that this enemy is already beaten and will never rise again. . . .

The course of this unique event is more or less known to you in outline. Two large army groups thrust forward to break open the center. One of the two flanking groups had the task of advancing against Leningrad; the other to occupy the Ukraine. These first tasks have been substantially completed. During this period of great and decisive struggle, the enemy often asked, "Why is nothing happening?" [7] Well, something was happening all the time. It was precisely because something was happening that we could not speak.

If I were the British Prime Minister today, I would, under the circumstances, also imagine that peace reigned; for in fact nothing is happening over there. And that is precisely the difference. . . . We could not counter the enemy's claims, not because we did not sufficiently appreciate the constantly outstanding achievements of our soldiers, but because we did not want to give the enemy information which he—with his miserable intelligence service—would only find out about days, or even weeks, later. . . .

A German Armed Forces communiqué is a truthful report, even if some stupid British newspaper jerk [Lümmel] declares that it must first be confirmed. German Armed Forces communiqués have been thoroughly confirmed in the past.

There is after all no doubt that it was not the Poles but we who were victorious in Poland, although the British press reported it the other way around. There is also no doubt that we are sitting in Norway, and not the English. Nor is there any doubt that we were successful in Belgium and Holland, and not the British. There is also no doubt that Germany defeated France, and not the other way around. And finally, there is no doubt that we are in Greece, and once again not the British or the New Zealanders. And not they, but we are the victors. Thus the German army communiqués spoke the truth. . . .

And it is not different in the East now. According to the British version we have suffered one defeat after another for the last three months; yet we are 1,000 kilometers beyond our own frontiers; we are east of Smolensk; we are before Leningrad; we are on the Black Sea; we are near the Crimea—and the Russians are nowhere near the Rhine. Therefore, if the Russians have been continuously victorious they have made poor use of their victories, for after each of their victories they immediately marched back 100 or 200 kilometers—evidently to lure us deep into the area.

In addition, the following figures attest to the magnitude of this battle. . . . The number of Russian prisoners has now risen to roughly 2,500,000. The number of captured or destroyed artillery pieces in our hands is around 22,000. The number of captured or destroyed tanks in our possession amounts to over 18,000. The number of aircraft destroyed on the ground or shot down is over 14,500. And behind our

[7] Hitler is referring to the British; the Russians, of course, were well aware of what was happening.

troops lies an area of Russian territory twice as large as the German Reich at the time I took over its leadership in 1933, or four times as large as Great Britain.

German soldiers have covered 800 to 1,000 kilometers. This is as the crow flies! The distance they had to march on the ground is often one and a half or two times as great. All this on a fighting front of gigantic length, and against an enemy that, I must say, consists not of human beings but of animals or beasts. . . . And against this cruel, bestial, and animal-like opponent, armed with powerful weapons, our soldiers have won mighty victories. I cannot think of any words that would do justice to their performance. What they are continually achieving by their boldness, bravery, and immeasurable efforts cannot even be imagined. . . .

What is being accomplished behind this front is, in its own way, just as impressive as the achievements at the front. Over 25,000 kilometers of Russian railways are in operation again. Over 15,000 kilometers of Russian railways have again [sic] been converted to the German gauge. . . . Behind this front a new administration is already being built to ensure that if the war lasts much longer this gigantic area will be of use to Germany and her allies. Its exploitation will be of immense value, and no one need doubt that we know how to organize it. . . .

Behind this front of sacrifice, courage, and bravery in the face of death stands the home front, a front created by both city and country. Millions of German farmers . . . [and] millions of German workers labor without respite. . . . We can really say that for the first time in history an entire people [Volk] is engaged in the struggle. . . .

The events that I have spoken to you about here today have led me, an old National Socialist, to one inescapable conclusion. We are confronted by two extreme systems. One consists of the capitalist states, who by lies and trickery deny their people their natural rights, and who care only about their financial interests—for the preservation of which they are always prepared to sacrifice the lives of millions of human beings. On the other hand we have the communist extreme: a state that has brought indescribable misery to millions and a doctrine that would sacrifice everyone else to the same fate. In my opinion this imposes on us only one duty: to strive more than ever to fulfill our National Socialist ideals. For we must be clear on one point: When this war is finally over, it will be the German soldier who has won it; the German soldier who has come from the farm and factory, who really represents the masses of our nation.

It will have been won by the German homeland, with millions of male and female workers and farmers; it will have been won by the creative people in the offices and in the professions. All these millions of creative German people will have won it. And it is exclusively on these people that this state must be aligned in the future.

When this war is over I will return to the people [*Volk*] as an even more fanatical National Socialist than I was before. It will be the same in all those appointed to positions of leadership. . . . The German people can be proud today. They have the best political leaders, the best military leaders, the best engineers, the best economic leaders, and the best administrators. They also have the best workers and the best farmers. To weld all these people into one indissoluble community was the task we set ourselves as National Socialists. This task confronts us more clearly today than ever before. . . .

Only when the entire German people becomes a single community of sacrifice [*Opfergemeinschaft*] can we hope and expect that Providence will stand by us in the future.

Almighty God has never helped a lazy man. Nor does he help a coward. Under no circumstances does he help those who do not help themselves. This principle applies here: German people, help yourselves and Almighty God will not deny you his assistance.

ON THE THRESHOLD OF DEFEAT:
ORDER OF THE DAY TO THE GERMAN TROOPS
ON THE EASTERN FRONT, APRIL 15, 1945 [8]

Soldiers of the German Eastern Front!

For the last time our mortal enemies, the Jewish Bolsheviks and their hordes, have gone over to the attack. They are attempting to reduce Germany to ruins and to exterminate our people. Most of you soldiers of the East already know at first hand the fate that threatens, above all, German women, girls, and children. While the old men and children will be murdered, the women and girls will be reduced to barrack-whores. The rest will be marched off to Siberia.

We have anticipated this hour; and since last January everything possible has been done to build up a strong front. A massive concentration of artillery awaits the enemy. Gaps in our infantry have been replaced by countless new units. Our front is strengthened by stand-by units, newly established units, and Volkssturm. This time the Bolshevik will meet the old fate of Asia: he must and will bleed to death before the capital of the German Reich.

Whoever fails in his duty at this moment acts as a traitor to our people. The regiment or the division that abandons its position behaves so disgracefully that it must be ashamed before the women and children who are withstanding the terror of bombing in our cities.

Above all, watch out for the few treacherous officers and soldiers who, in order to insure their own miserable lives, will fight against us

[8] From Deutsches Nachrichtenbüro-Text, April 16, 1945, reprinted in Max Domarus, ed., *Hitler: Reden und Proklamation, 1932–1945* (Munich: Süddeutscher Verlag, 1965), II, 2223–24; trans. G. H. Stein.

in the pay of the Russians, perhaps even in German uniforms. Anyone not positively known to you who orders you to retreat is to be arrested immediately and, if necessary, killed instantly, regardless of his rank.

If every soldier on the Eastern front does his duty in the days and weeks that lie ahead, the last assault of Asia will shatter, just as the breakthrough by our enemies in the West will, in spite of everything, fail in the end.

Berlin remains German. Vienna will be German again, and Europe will never be Russian.

Fashion a sworn brotherhood to defend not the empty idea of a Fatherland but your homes, your wives, your children—and therewith your future.

In this hour, the whole German nation has its eye on you, my warriors in the East, and only hopes that—through your resolution and fanaticism, through your weapons and under your leadership—the Bolshevik assault will be drowned in a bath of blood. At this moment, when fate has removed from the earth the greatest war criminal of all time,[9] the turning-point of this war will be determined.

signed: Adolf Hitler

PRIVATE WILL AND POLITICAL TESTAMENT, APRIL 29, 1945 [10]

My Private Will

Since I did not feel that I could accept the responsibility of marriage during the years of struggle, I have decided now, before the end of my earthly career, to take as my wife the girl [*Mädchen*] who, after many years of loyal friendship, came of her own free will to this city, already almost besieged, in order to share my fate with me. At her own request she goes to her death with me as my wife. Death will compensate us for what we were both deprived of by my labors in the service of my people.

What I possess—in so far as it has any value—belongs to the Party; or if it no longer exists, to the State. If the State too is destroyed, no further decision on my part is necessary.

The paintings in the collections that I bought during the course of the years were never collected for private purposes; they were intended

---

[9] This is a reference to the death (on April 12) of President Franklin D. Roosevelt.

[10] From the German text of Nuremberg Document 3569-PS; trans. G. H. Stein. An execrable English translation of this document is printed in *Nazi Conspiracy and Aggression,* VI, 259–63. The original German text has recently been reprinted in Max Domarus, ed., *Hitler: Reden und Proklamationen, 1932–1945* (Munich: Süddeutscher Verlag, 1965), II, 2236–41.

solely for the establishment of a gallery in my home town of Linz on the Danube.

It is my most heartfelt wish that this bequest be duly executed.

As executor of this will, I appoint my most faithful Party comrade, Martin Bormann. He is given full legal authority to make all decisions. He is permitted to take out for my brothers and sisters whatever has any value as a personal memento or is necessary to maintain a modest standard of living [*zur Erhaltung eines kleinen bürgerlichen Lebens*]; the same applies also to my wife's mother and to my male and female secretaries, to Frau Winter, and to the others, who for many years supported me through their labors, and who are all well known to him.

My wife and I choose to die in order to escape the shame of deposition or capitulation. It is our wish that our bodies be burned immediately, here where I have performed the greater part of my daily work during the twelve years I served my people.

Given in Berlin, April 29, 1945, 4:00 a.m.

Adolf Hitler

Witnesses:
Martin Bormann
Dr. Joseph Goebbels
Nicolaus von Below

My Political Testament

More than thirty years have passed since I made my modest contribution in 1914 as a volunteer in the First World War, a war which was forced upon the Reich.

In these three decades, all my thoughts, all my deeds, and all other aspects of my life were motivated only by my love of my people and by my loyalty to them. They gave me the strength to make the most difficult decisions that have ever confronted mortal man. In these three decades I have exhausted my time, my working strength, and my health.

It is not true that I or anybody else in Germany, wanted war in 1939. It was wanted and provoked exclusively by those international statesmen who either were of Jewish origin or worked for Jewish interests. I have made too many offers for the restriction and control of armaments—which posterity will not be able to ignore forever—for responsibility for the outbreak of this war to be placed on me. Moreover, I have never wished that the first terrible world war should be followed by a second one against England, let alone America. Centuries will pass, but from the ruins of our towns and monuments hatred of those ultimately responsible will always grow anew, those whom we have to thank for all this: International Jewry and its helpers!

Only three days before the outbreak of the German-Polish war I proposed to the British ambassador in Berlin a solution to the German-Polish problem, a solution similar to the one that was applied in the case of the Saar district when it was placed under international control. This offer also cannot be denied. It was rejected only because leading circles in English politics wanted war, partly because they anticipated an increase in business, partly because they were influenced by propaganda disseminated by International Jewry.

I also left no doubt that if the peoples of Europe were once more to be treated as mere shares to be bought and sold by these international monetary and financial conspirators, then the responsibility would be shared by that people [Volk] which is the real guilty party in this murderous struggle: Jewry! Further, I left no one in doubt that this time millions of grown men were not going to suffer death, and hundreds of thousands of women and children were not going to be burned and bombed to death in the cities, without the guilty ones having to pay, even if by more humane means, for their guilt.

After a six-year struggle, which in spite of all setbacks will one day go down in history as the most glorious and heroic manifestation of a people's will to live, I cannot forsake the city that is the capital of this Reich. Since our forces are too small to hold out any longer against the enemy's assualt on this place, and since our resistance is gradually being undermined by creatures who are as deluded as they are lacking in strength of character,[11] I wish to share the fate that millions of others have accepted by staying here in this city. Besides, I do not wish to fall into the hands of an enemy who requires a new spectacle, staged by the Jews, to amuse his frenzied masses.

I have therefore decided to remain in Berlin and there to choose death voluntarily at the moment when I believe that the residence of the Führer and Chancellor can no longer be held. I die with a happy heart in view of my knowledge of the immeasurable deeds and accomplishments of our soldiers at the front, our women at home, the achievements of our farmers and workers, and the military efforts—unique in history—of our youth which bears my name.[12]

That I express my thanks to all of you from the bottom of my heart is just as self-evident as my wish that you will therefore under no circumstances give up the struggle but will carry it on against the enemies of the Fatherland, no matter where, according to the principles

[11] This is a reference to those members of Hitler's entourage, like Göring and Himmler, who had betrayed their Führer by entering into negotiations with the western allies.

[12] Hitler is referring to the *Hitlerjugend,* or Hitler Youth organization, whose members, teen-aged boys, often fought fanatically during the last days of the Third Reich.

of the great Clausewitz.[13] The sacrifices of our soldiers and my own bond with them unto death has sown a seed that will, in one way or another, once again blossom into a glorious rebirth of the National Socialist movement and therewith the realization of a genuine racial community.

Many of the most courageous men and women have decided to tie their lives to mine right to the end. I have begged and finally ordered them not to do this, but rather to take part in the nation's continuing struggle. I ask the leaders of the Armies, the Navy, and the Air Force to strengthen with every possible means the spirit of resistance of our soldiers in the National Socialist sense, with special emphasis on the fact that also I myself, as the founder and creator of this movement, have preferred death to cowardly abdication or even to capitulation.

In the future may it be a point of honor with German officers—as it already is in our Navy—that the surrender of a district or a town is out of the question and that, above all, the commanders must set a shining example of faithful devotion to duty unto death.

Before my death, I expel from the Party the former Reich Marshal, Hermann Göring, and I withdraw from him all the rights conferred on him by the Decree of June 29, 1941 and by my Reichstag speech of September 1, 1939. In his place I appoint Grand Admiral Dönitz as President of the Reich and Supreme Commander of the Armed Forces.

Before my death, I expel from the Party and from all his official positions the former Reichsführer SS and Reich Minister of the Interior, Heinrich Himmler. In his place, I appoint Gauleiter Karl Hanke as Reichsführer SS and Chief of the German Police, and Gauleiter Paul Giesler as Reich Minister of the Interior.

Göring and Himmler, by their secret negotiations with the enemy, which they conducted without my knowledge and against my wishes, and by their illegal attempt to seize control of the state, have—quite apart from their disloyalty to my person—done incalculable harm to the country and to the whole people.

In order to give the German people a government composed of honorable men, a government that will continue the war by every possible means, I appoint as leaders of the nation the following members of the new cabinet:

[list omitted]

A number of these men, such as Martin Bormann, Dr. Goebbels, and others, including their wives, have voluntarily joined me here. They did not wish to leave the capital of the Reich under any cir-

---

[13] Karl von Clausewitz (1780–1831) was a Prussian general and military writer whose doctrines, including that of total war, had an enormous effect on military strategy and tactics.

cumstances; they were willing to die with me. Nevertheless, I must ask them to obey my request, and in this case to put the interests of the nation above their own feelings. By their work and loyalty as associates they will be just as close to me in death as I hope my spirit will be to them; may it linger among them and accompany them always. Let them be hard, but never unjust; above all, let them never allow fear to influence their actions, and let them put the honor of the nation above all else on Earth. Finally, let them be conscious of the fact that our task for the coming centuries is the continuing construction of a National Socialist state, and this places every single person under an obligation always to serve the common interest and to subordinate his own advantage to this end. I demand of all Germans, all National Socialists, men, women, and all soldiers of the Armed Forces, that they be faithful and obedient unto death to the new government and to its president.

Above all, I enjoin the leaders of the nation and those under them to uphold the racial laws to their full extent and to oppose mercilessly the universal poisoner of all peoples [*Völker*], International Jewry.

Given in Berlin, April 29, 1945, 4:00 a.m.

Adolf Hitler

Witnesses:
Dr. Joseph Goebbels
Martin Bormann
Wilhelm Burgdorf
Hans Krebs

THE WORLD LOOKS AT HITLER

"Next to a man himself," it has been said, "the persons who know most about him are likely to be found among his contemporaries." [1] *And yet it is also true that the more famous (or infamous) the person is, the more likely that his contemporaries will offer all kinds of conflicting statements about him. And so it is in the case of Adolf Hitler. In the literature and memoirs of the period, Hitler emerges as a man of many faces. We are told that he was personally charming, even endearing; that he laughed easily and joked readily; that he was sensitive and capable of deep and genuine feeling; and that he displayed great idealism and often spoke from the heart. But as Shakespeare noted in Hamlet, "one may smile, and smile, and be a villain." In other accounts (and not infrequently in the same accounts), his eyes flashing, the spittle spraying from his lips, Hitler appears at best a fanatic and at worst a madman. To some he appeared a brilliant statesman; to others a cheap demagogue. Some observers were overpowered by his personal magnetism; others wondered what anyone could find attractive in such an uninteresting, even vulgar person. Not a few of those who met him were impressed by the breadth of his intellect, while others were dismayed or repulsed by his coarse and narrow mind. In short, Hitler—like so many men of historical importance—has evoked from his contemporaries a whole range of characterizations from saintliness to devilishness—and nearly all of them have an unquestionable basis in fact. For Hitler was an accomplished actor who not only cast himself into many roles, but played all of them with the conviction born of an extraordinary capacity for self-delusion. This part of the book presents a variety of firsthand views of Hitler by those who knew him: a boyhood friend, some of his followers, and a number of foreign diplomats and journalists.*

[1] Dumas Malone, "Biography and History," in *The Interpretation of History*, ed. Joseph R. Strayer (Princeton: Princeton University Press, 1943), p. 124.

7

Adolf: The Young Hitler as Seen by a Boyhood Friend[1]

Although Hitler's public life is now well-known, his early years—especially the formative years between the time he left school and the beginning of World War I—are relatively undocumented. One of the few accounts that goes beyond Mein Kampf *to shed light on Hitler's life and character during this crucial period is the retrospective memoir by August Kubizek, who was Hitler's closest associate in Linz and Vienna between 1904 and 1908. Kubizek's reminiscences—written some forty years after the events they describe—are not only somewhat romanticized but also occasionally inaccurate in details. Nevertheless, the main contours of Hitler's life and character during the period Kubizek knew him are plausibly recorded. In this selection, Kubizek presents an intimate and generally sympathetic portrait of Hitler at a stage in his development when he had not yet become the totally alienated and largely dehumanized Hitler known to history.*

Adolf was of middle height and slender, at that time already taller than his mother. His physique was far from sturdy, rather too thin for its height, and he was not at all strong. His health, in fact, was rather poor, which he was the first to regret. He had to take special care of himself during the foggy and damp winters which prevailed in Linz. He was ill from time to time during that period and coughed a lot. In short, he had weak lungs.

His nose was quite straight and well-proportioned, but in no way remarkable. His forehead was high and receded a little. I was always sorry that even in those days he had the habit of combing his hair straight down over his forehead. Yet this traditional forehead-nose-mouth description seems rather ridiculous to me. For in this countenance the eyes were so outstanding that one didn't notice anything else. Never in my life have I seen any other person whose appearance —how shall I put it—was so completely dominated by the eyes. They

[1] From August Kubizek, *The Young Hitler I Knew,* trans. E. V. Anderson (Boston: Houghton Mifflin Company, 1955), pp. 15–19, 22–23. Published in England under the title of *Young Hitler* by The Hamlyn Publishing Group Ltd. Reprinted by permission of Houghton Mifflin Company and The Hamlyn Publishing Group Ltd.

were the light eyes of his mother, but her somewhat staring, penetrating gaze was even more marked in the son and had even more force and expressiveness. It was uncanny how these eyes could change their expression, especially when Adolf was speaking. To me his sonorous voice meant much less than the expression of his eyes. In fact, Adolf spoke with his eyes, and even when his lips were silent one knew what he wanted to say. When he first came to our house and I introduced him to my mother, she said to me in the evening, "What eyes your friend has!" And I remember quite distinctly that there was more fear than admiration in her words. If I am asked where one could perceive, in his youth, this man's exceptional qualities, I can only answer "In the eyes."

Naturally his extraordinary eloquence, too, was striking. But I was then too inexperienced to attach to it any special significance for the future. I, for one, was certain that Hitler one day would be a great artist, a poet I thought at first, then a great painter, until later, in Vienna, he convinced me that his real talent was in the field of architecture. But for these artistic ambitions his eloquence was of no use, rather a hindrance. Nevertheless, I always liked to listen to him. His language was very refined. He disliked dialect, in particular Viennese, the soft melodiousness of which was utterly repulsive to him. To be sure, Hitler did not speak Austrian in the true sense. It was rather that in his diction, especially in the rhythm of his speech, there was something Bavarian. Perhaps this was due to the fact that, from his third to his sixth year, the real formative years for speech, he lived in Passau, where his father was then a Customs official.

There is no doubt that my friend Adolf had shown a gift for oratory from his earliest youth. And he knew it. He liked to talk, and talked without pause. Sometimes when he soared too high in his fantasies I couldn't help suspecting that all this was nothing but an exercise in oratory. But then again I thought otherwise. Did I not take everything for Gospel that he said? Sometimes Adolf would try out his powers of oratory on me or on others. It always stuck in my memory how, when not yet eighteen, he convinced my father that he should release me from his workshop and send me to Vienna to the Conservatoire. In view of the awkward and unforthcoming nature of my father this was a considerable achievement. From the moment I had this proof of his talent—for me so decisive—I considered that there was nothing that Hitler could not achieve by a convincing speech.

He was in the habit of emphasizing his words by measured and studied gestures. Now and then, when he was speaking on one of his favorite subjects, such as the bridge over the Danube, the rebuilding of the Museum or even the subterranean railway station which he had planned for Linz, I would interrupt him and ask him how he imagined he would ever carry out these projects—we were only poor devils.

Then he would throw at me a strange and hostile glance as though he had not understood my question at all. I never got an answer; at the most he would shut me up with a wave of his hand. Later I got used to it and ceased to find it ridiculous that the sixteen or seventeen-year-old boy should develop gigantic projects and expound them to me down to the last detail. If I had listened only to his words the whole thing would have appeared to be either idle fantasy or sheer lunacy; but the eyes convinced me that he was in deadly earnest.

Adolf set great store by good manners and correct behavior. He observed with painstaking punctiliousness the rules of social conduct, however little he thought of society itself. He always emphasized the position of his father, who as a Customs official ranked more or less with a captain in the army. Hearing him speak of his father, one would never have imagined how violently he disliked the idea of being a Civil Servant. Nevertheless, there was in his bearing something very precise. He would never forget to send regards to my people, and every postcard bore greetings to my "esteemed parents."

When we lodged together in Vienna, I discovered that every evening he would put his trousers carefully under the mattress so that the next morning he could rejoice in a faultless crease. Adolf realized the value of a good appearance, and, in spite of his lack of vanity, knew how to make the best of himself. He made excellent use of his un-doubted histrionic talents, which he cleverly combined with his gift for oratory. I used to ask myself why Adolf, in spite of all these pro-nounced capabilities, did not get on better in Vienna; only later did I realize that professional success was not at all his ambition. People who knew him in Vienna could not understand the contradiction be-tween his well-groomed appearance, his educated speech and his self-assured bearing on the one hand, and the starveling existence that he led on the other, and judged him either haughty or pretentious. He was neither. He just didn't fit into any bourgeois order.

Adolf had brought starvation to a fine art, though he ate very well when occasion offered. To be sure, in Vienna he generally lacked the money for food. But even if he had it, he would prefer to starve and spend it on a theatre seat. He had no comprehension of enjoyment of life as others knew it. He did not smoke, he did not drink, and in Vienna, for instance, he lived for days on milk and bread only.

With his contempt for everything pertaining to the body, sport, which was then coming into fashion, meant nothing to him. I read somewhere of how audaciously the young Hitler had swum across the Danube. I do not recollect anything of the sort; the most swim-ming we did was an occasional dip in the Rodel stream. He showed some interest in the bicycle club, mainly because they ran an ice-rink in the winter. And this, only because the girl he adored used to prac-tice skating there.

Walking was the only exercise that really appealed to Adolf. He walked always and everywhere and, even in my workshop and in my room, he would stride up and down. I recall him always on the go. He could walk for hours without getting tired. We used to explore the surroundings of Linz in all directions. His love of nature was pronounced, but in a very personal way. Unlike other subjects, nature never attracted him as a matter for study; I hardly ever remember seeing him with a book on the subject. Here was the limit of his thirst for knowledge. Details did not interest him, but only nature as a whole. . . .

Being in the open had an extraordinary effect upon him. He was then quite a different person from what he was in town. Certain sides of his character revealed themselves nowhere else. . . . But hardly had we reached the open country, than he could assure me that it would be impossible for him to live in the country again. It would be terrible for him to have to live in a village. For all his love of nature, he was always glad when we got back to the town.

As I grew to know him better, I also came to understand this apparent contradiction. He needed the town, the variety and abundance of its impressions, experiences and events; he felt there that he had his share in everything; that there was nothing in which his interest was not engaged. He needed people with their contrasting interests, their ambitions, intentions, plans and desires. Only in this problem-laden atmosphere did he feel at home. . . .

On the other hand, he needed an effective counterweight to the town, which always troubled and excited him and made constant demands on his interests and his talents. He found this in nature, which even he could not try to change and improve because its eternal laws are beyond the reach of the human will. Here he could once more find his own self, since here he was not obliged, as he was in town, eternally to be taking sides.

My friend had a special way of making nature serve him. He used to seek out a lonely spot outside the town, which he would visit again and again. Every bush and every tree was familiar to him. There was nothing to disturb his contemplative mood. Nature surrounded him like the walls of a quiet, friendly room in which he could cultivate undisturbed his passionate plans and ideas. . . .

I have often been asked . . . whether Adolf, when I knew him, had any sense of humor. One feels the lack of it, people of his entourage said. After all, he was an Austrian and should have had his share of the famous Austrian sense of humor. Certainly one's impression of Hitler, especially after a short and superficial acquaintance, was that of a deeply serious man. This enormous seriousness seemed to overshadow everything else. It was the same when he was young. He approached the problems with which he was concerned with a deadly earnestness which ill suited his sixteen or seventeen years. He was capable of loving and admiring, hating and despising, all with the greatest seriousness. But one thing he could not do was to pass over something with a smile. Even with a subject in which he did not take a personal interest, such as sport, this was, nevertheless, as a phenomenon of modern times, just as important to him as any other. He never came to the end of his problems. His profound earnestness never ceased to attack new problems, and if he did not find any in the present, he would brood at home for hours over his books and burrow into the problems of the past. This extraordinary earnestness was his most striking quality. Many other qualities which are characteristic of youth were lacking in him: a carefree letting go of himself, living only for the day, the happy attitude of "What is to be, will be." Even "going off the rails," in the coarse exuberance of youth, was alien to him. His idea, strange to say, was that these were things that did not become a young man. And because of this, humor was confined to the most intimate sphere as if it were something taboo. His humor was usually aimed at people in his immediate circle, in other words a sphere in which problems no longer existed for him. For this reason his grim and sour humor was often mixed with irony, but always an irony with friendly intent. Thus, he saw me once at a concert where I was playing the trumpet. He got enormous amusement out of imitating me and insisted that with my blown-out cheeks I looked like one of Rubens' angels.

I cannot conclude . . . without mentioning one of Hitler's qualities which, I freely admit, seems paradoxical to talk about now. Hitler was full of deep understanding and sympathy. He took a most touching interest in me. Without my telling him, he knew exactly how I felt. How often this helped me in difficult times! He always knew what I needed and what I wanted. However intensely he was occupied with himself he would always have time for the affairs of those people in whom he was interested. It was not by chance that he was the one who persuaded my father to let me study music and thereby influenced my life in a decisive way. Rather, this was the outcome of his general attitude of sharing in all the things that were of concern to me. Sometimes I had a feeling that he was living my life as well as his own.

Thus, I have drawn the portrait of the young Hitler as well as I can from memory. But for the question, then unknown and unexpressed which hung above our friendship, I have not to this day found any answer: "What were God's intentions when he created this man?"

8

Der Führer: Hitler as Seen by His Followers

LUDECKE: "ANOTHER LUTHER" (1922)[1]

Of the many qualities that have been attributed to Hitler, none is more widely agreed upon than his extraordinary power as a speaker. The virtuosity of his oratory, and its ability to move the masses has led Alan Bullock, Hitler's English biographer, to the conclusion that "Hitler was the greatest demagogue in history." In the following passage, Kurt G. W. Ludecke—an early Nazi who broke with Hitler in 1934—relates, in almost religious terms, his conversion to National Socialism as a result of a speech made by Hitler in 1922 during a right-wing nationalist rally in Bavaria.

It was a bright summer day. The Reds had tried their best to break up the Nazi columns marching through the city, comprising Storm-Troopers followed by sections of the Party. Soon the assailants were in flight, bruised and beaten, and it had been demonstrated for the first time that Nationalists as well as Reds had the right to march in formation through the streets of Munich, and that the Nazis were determined to maintain this right.

The "Patriotic Societies" had assembled without bands and without flags. But when the Nazis marched into the Koenigsplatz with banners flying, their bands playing stirring German marches, they were greeted with tremendous cheers. An excited, expectant crowd was now filling the beautiful square to the last inch and overflowing into surrounding streets. There were well over a hundred thousand.

The first speaker, little Dr. Buckeley, harangued this mass in true political fashion. At last he relinquished the platform, and Hitler faced the multitude. . . .

I was close enough to see Hitler's face, watch every change in his expression, hear every word he said.

[1] From Kurt G. W. Ludecke, *I Knew Hitler: The Story of a Nazi Who Escaped the Blood Purge* (London: Jarrolds Publishers [London] Limited; New York: Charles Scribner's Sons, 1937), pp. 12–14. Copyright © 1937 by Kurt G. W. Ludecke. Reprinted by permission of the publishers.

When the man stepped forward on the platform, there was almost no applause. He stood silent for a moment. Then he began to speak, quietly and ingratiatingly at first. Before long his voice had risen to a hoarse shriek that gave an extraordinary effect of an intensity of feeling. There were many high-pitched, rasping notes—Reventlow had told me that his throat had been affected by war-gas—but despite its strident tone, his diction had a distinctly Austrian turn, softer and pleasanter than the German.

Critically I studied this slight, pale man, his brown hair parted on one side and falling again and again over his sweating brow. Threatening and beseeching, with small, pleading hands and flaming, steel-blue eyes, he had the look of a fanatic.

Presently my critical faculty was swept away. Leaning from the tribune as if he were trying to impel his inner self into the consciousness of all these thousands, he was holding the masses, and me with them, under a hypnotic spell by the sheer force of his conviction.

He urged the revival of German honor and manhood with a blast of words that seemed to cleanse. "Bavaria is now the most German land in Germany!" he shouted, to roaring applause. Then, plunging into sarcasm, he indicted the leaders in Berlin as "November Criminals," daring to put into words thoughts that Germans were now almost afraid to think and certainly to voice.

It was clear that Hitler was feeling the exaltation of the emotional response now surging up toward him from his thousands of hearers. His voice rising to passionate climaxes, he finished his speech with an anthem of hate against the "Novemberlings" and a pledge of undying love for the Fatherland. "Germany must be free!" was his final defiant slogan. Then two last words that were like the sting of a lash: *"Deutschland Erwache!"*

Awake, Germany! There was thunderous applause. Then the masses took a solemn oath "to save Germany in Bavaria from Bolshevism."

I do not know how to describe the emotions that swept over me as I heard this man. His words were like a scourge. When he spoke of the disgrace of Germany, I felt ready to spring on any enemy. His appeal to German manhood was like a call to arms, the gospel he preached a sacred truth. He seemed another Luther. I forgot everything but the man; then, glancing round, I saw that his magnetism was holding these thousands as one.

Of course I was ripe for this experience. I was a man of thirty-two, weary of disgust and disillusionment, a wanderer seeking a cause; a patriot without a channel for his patriotism, a yearner after the heroic without a hero. The intense will of the man, the passion of his sincerity seemed to flow from him into me. I experienced an exaltation that could be likened only to religious conversion.

I felt sure that no one who had heard Hitler that afternoon could doubt that he was the man of destiny, the vitalizing force in the future of Germany. The masses who had streamed into the Koenigsplatz with a stern sense of national humiliation seemed to be going forth renewed.

The bands struck up, the thousands began to move away. I knew my search was ended. I had found myself, my leader, and my cause.

ANNA: "TRAILBREAKER TO BETTER TIMES" (1923) [2]

Unlike Ludecke's account, the next selection is not from the writings of a public figure, nor even a semipublic figure, but from the pen of an obscure person who left no noticeable impress on the course of history. We have here a letter written by a woman— an early convert to National Socialism, known to us only as "Anna"—describing her reaction to Hitler's oratory and personality as she experienced it shortly before the abortive Munich "Beer Hall Putsch" of November 1923.

Munich, 22 October 1923

My Beloved Ones:
I have learned through Hermann that Father is ardently interested in the Hitler movement; and therefore there is something I'd like to pass on to you, for during the past week I attended an evening lecture [at which Hitler was the featured speaker] and [during September] I attended the nationalist rally celebrating the release of Lieutenant Rossbach.[3] I don't want to tell you what was said by Hitler and the other officers; I assume that you will be able to read about that in the [newspaper]. I would much rather tell you about the mood, more correctly, the enthusiasm and deep conviction that dwells in all the adherents of the *völkisch*[4] movement. Above all, they consider Hitler

[2] From "Brief über einen Sprechabend mit Adolf Hitler als Redner und über die Rossbach-Kundgebung September 1923," Berlin Document Center, Hauptarchiv der NSDAP, File 706, published for the first time in Hans-Adolf Jacobsen and Werner Jochmann, eds., *Ausgewählte Dokumente zur Geschichte des Nationalsozialismus 1933–1945* (Bielefeld: Verlag Neue Gesellschaft, 1961–1966), AB, Dokument 22. X. 1923; trans. G. H. Stein. Reproduced in English translation by permission of the publisher.

[3] Gerhard Rossbach was an early Nazi who had made a reputation as leader of a *Freikorps,* an armed right-wing military band active in Germany in the years immediately following the end of World War I.

[4] The German word *völkisch* has no English equivalent. For Nazis and others who shared their basic ideology, the term stood for the union of the people with

the only man who has not yet abused their trust, and therefore they regard him as the only man that they can trust unconditionally. A Dr. (I don't remember his name) begged all the members to subordinate themselves to their Führer because he desires only what is best for them; he pointedly suggested to the older members that they ought to think back and try to recall whether Hitler had ever promised too much, whether everything had not always turned out just as he had predicted. And even though he (the speaker) often did not see eye to eye with Hitler, he told himself: our Führer is more clever and wiser than you—subordinate yourself to him. . . . Hitler spoke on this evening only to members—not to the public—and therefore the entire speech had a different tone. I have never heard any other speaker (and I have, after all, heard many) who was so able to penetrate into the soul of the individual, who spoke with such a sense of righteousness about those confused German racial comrades who even today know no Fatherland. To show them the way to the Fatherland, to teach them to love the Fatherland, is the principal, and at the same time, the most difficult task. In my opinion, there is no man on German soil that can do more to awaken in all of us this love of our homeland and loyalty to our Fatherland. His past efforts certainly have not been in vain, for the number of his followers is as great as the faith in him. Unmatched rejoicing breaks out when he enters the hall, and he has to wait a long time until the shouting dies down. . . . [At the Rossbach Rally in September] the hall was very nicely decorated with the old [Imperial] black-white-red flag, the Swastika, and the Navy Flag. The band played various marches, then came the individual units of the Fighting Union,[5] threading their way through the audience and the rows of chairs like a gray-green snake. . . . The high point of the evening was not reached until Hitler stepped up to the podium. His appearance was greeted with an endless series of "Heils," and, in a few words, he spoke from his heart into the hearts of all.

You cannot imagine how silent it becomes as soon as this man speaks; it is as if all of the thousand listeners are no longer able to breathe. When he angrily condemns the deeds of those who have ruled our people since the revolution and those who now prevent him and his followers from settling accounts with those November big-wigs cheers ring through the hall for minutes on end. There is no silence until he waves his hands repeatedly to indicate that he wants to con-

a transcendental essence, which in twentieth century *völkisch* circles was usually regarded as blood and soil. In a very general sense then, *völkisch* means racial or biological nationalism.

[5] Early in September 1923, a number of right-wing paramilitary groups joined the National Socialists in an alliance called the German Fighting Union (*Deutscher Kampfbund*) for the purpose of overthrowing the Weimar Republic and casting off the "chains of Versailles."

tinue speaking. . . . Adolf Hitler is so firmly convinced of the correctness of his nationalistic views that he automatically communicates this conviction to his listeners. God grant that, as trailbreaker to better times, he will be able to gather many more racial comrades under the Swastika. After all, every class is represented. Workers and lower-ranking civil servants, officers and storm toopers, students and old pensioners—all sit together, and all are in agreement with the great concept embodied in the person of Adolf Hitler. It is often said that where eleven Germans come together, ten political parties are represented. Here, however, I have never heard anyone say that Hitler should do this, or that he should have done that. Sometimes it almost seems to me as if Hitler used a magic charm in order to win the unconditional confidence of old and young alike. When one considers, however, that the common man, suffering from the spiritual malaise that goes hand in hand with economic misery, seeks stability and finds it in the one man who will not disappoint him, then one understands the jubilation that is evoked by his very appearance.

I think that all of you, and especially Father, now have a little insight into what I am experiencing. . . .

With best wishes to you all,
Anna

GOEBBELS: "THE COMING DICTATOR" (1925–1926) [6]

Apart from Hitler himself, Joseph Goebbels was certainly the most dynamic and intelligent of the Third Reich's principal leaders. As Gauleiter (District Leader) of Berlin and Reich Minister for Public Enlightenment and Propaganda, he was also one of the most influential members of Hitler's inner circle. But this had not always been so. In 1925, the National Socialist Party, which had already been seriously weakened by the failure of the Munich Putsch and the subsequent imprisonment of Hitler, was beset by a split in its own ranks. A north German group led by Gregor and Otto Strasser took rather seriously the anticapitalist points in the Nazi program, whereas Hitler and his Munich-based colleagues were essentially opportunists who were willing to disregard portions of the party platform in order to gain the support of industrialists and big landowners. Goebbels—then a twenty-eight-year-old footloose intellectual with a Ph.D. from Heidelberg—was a vociferous member of the Strasser-led faction.

[6] From Helmut Heiber, ed., *The Early Goebbels Diaries, 1925–1926* (New York: Frederick A. Praeger, Inc., 1962), pp. 41–42, 47–48, 50, 66–67, 76–80, 91–92, 100–1. Reprinted by permission of Frederick A. Praeger, Inc., and Weidenfeld & Nicolson, Ltd.

In the course of the internecine struggle between the two wings of the Nazi Party, Goebbels came into frequent contact with Hitler and quickly fell under his spell. By mid-1926, Goebbels had abandoned the Strassers and thrown in his lot with Hitler. Thereafter, he was one of the Führer's most devoted followers; and in 1945, he—alone among Hitler's chief lieutenants—chose to share his master's fate. Our selection consists of excerpts from Goebbels' early diary, a portion of which was salvaged from the ruins of the Propaganda Ministry in Berlin. Unlike the "official" diaries that Goebbels kept in later years, this personal record was not written with a view to subsequent publication. The following excerpts illustrate not only Hitler's seduction of the young Goebbels and the latter's growing adoration of his new master, but also the many-faceted personality of Adolf Hitler during the years in which he simultaneously consolidated his grip on the leadership of the Nazi Party and built up a national following.

October 12, 1925 [7]

Hitler does not trust me, He has abused me. How that hurts. . . . To sacrifice all and then reproaches from Hitler himself. . . . If only I could be alone with Hitler for two hours. Then everything would come right. . . .

October 14, 1925

I am finishing Hitler's book [the first volume of *Mein Kampf*— ED.]. Thrilled to bits! Who is this man? Half plebeian, half God! Really Christ, or only John? . . .

November 2, 1925

On Wednesday, when Hitler speaks at Braunschweig, I am to address an overspill meeting. I look forward to this. Perhaps I shall succeed in collaring Hitler for a while. I shall go straight to the point. I shall tell him everything that troubles my soul. Everything depends on it. . . .

November 6, 1925

In the morning to Braunschweig. . . . We drive to Hitler. He is having his meal. He jumps to his feet, there he is. Shakes my hand. Like an old friend. And those big blue eyes. Like stars. He is glad to see me. I am in heaven. . . . I drive to the meeting. And speak for two hours. Punctuated by applause. And then *Heils* and clapping. There he is. He shakes my hand. His big speech has quite finished

[7] The dates that head the entries are not necessarily the ones on which the events described actually occurred.

him. Then he makes another half-hour speech here. Full of wit, irony, humor, sarcasm, seriousness and glowing with passion. That man has got everything to be a king. A born tribune. The coming dictator.

November 23, 1925

Plauen. I arrive. Hitler is there. Great joy. He greets me like an old friend. And looks after me. How I love him! What a fellow! And he tells stories all evening. I could go on listening forever. A small meeting. He asks me to speak first. Then he speaks. How small I am! He gives me his photograph. With greetings from the Rhineland. *Heil Hitler!* . . . I want Hitler to be my friend. His photograph is on my desk. I could not bear it if I had to despair of this man. . . .

February 12, 1926

Tomorrow Bamberg. Hitler is to address the Gau leaders. I shall see Strasser a few hours earlier. We shall decide on the plan for action. . . .

February 15, 1926

Sunday morning. Strasser comes to fetch me. . . . He is hopeful. Plan for action ready. . . . Then tour of Bamberg. Charming town. Old, Jesuit. Hitler's car tears past us. A handshake. . . . Then to work. Hitler speaks for two hours. I am almost beaten. What kind of Hitler? A reactionary? Amazingly clumsy and uncertain. Russian question: altogether beside the point. Italy and Britain the natural allies. Horrible! It is our job to smash Bolshevism. Bolshevism is a Jewish creation! We must become Russia's heirs! Hundred and eighty millions!!! Compensation for princes! Law is law. Also for the princes. Question of not weakening private property (*sic*).[8] Horrible! Program will do! Happy with it. . . . A horrible night! Probably one of my greatest disappointments. I can no longer believe in Hitler absolutely. That is terrible: I have lost my inner support. I am only half myself. . . . We are socialists. We don't want to have been it in vain! . . . Then Wednesday to Strasser. Proposal: Kaufmann, Strasser, and I go to Hitler to impress on him: he must not allow those rogues down there [Munich—ED.] to tie him hand and foot. . . .

April 13, 1926

Munich. Hitler's car to meet us. To the hotel. What a grand reception. . . . Hitler had telephoned. Wants to welcome us. . . . In fifteen minutes he is there. Tall, healthy and full of life. I like him.

[8] *Sic* in original. Hitler's speech to the Gauleiters at Bamberg, the main points of which Goebbels is outlining here, placed him squarely in opposition to the position taken by the Strasser, or socialist, wing of the NSDAP to which Goebbels belonged.

He shames us with his kindness. . . . He lends us his car for the afternoon. . . . At eight p.m. by car to the Bürgerbräu. Hitler is already there. My heart beats to breaking-point. Into the hall. Roaring welcome. Packed. . . . I speak for two and a half hours. I go all out. Roaring and tumult. Hitler embraces me at the end. He has tears in his eyes. I feel something like happy. Through the pressing crowd to the car. *Heil* calls and we are off. Hitler by himself waits for me at the hotel. Then we dine together. He is host. And what a great host! . . . To the Reichsadler. Concert! Hitler is with me all the time. . . . Friday morning. . . . To the office. . . . The master comes. To his room. . . . And then a veritable hodgepodge of accusations. Preferred worthily and pleasantly. In this too Hitler is all right. . . . In the end unity. Hitler is great. He gives us all a warm handshake. Let's have done with it! In the afternoon follow-up. . . . Hitler comes. . . . He speaks for three hours. Brilliant. Could make one uncertain. . . . We are moving closer. We ask. He gives brilliant replies. I love him. . . . He has thought it all out. I am reassured all round. Taken all round he is a man. With this sparkling mind he can be my leader. I bow to his greatness, his political genius! Warm farewell. . . .

April 19, 1926

Saturday! It pours. Farewell Munich! Real leave-taking weather! There is the car. Hitler comes to fetch me. He wears a motoring outfit. . . . Off. Pouring rain. Augsburg. Breakdown. Hitler like a boy. Riotous, singing, laughing, whistling. . . . We celebrate Hitler's birthday. He is thirty-seven. Flowers surrounded by thirty-seven candles. And he talks about 9th November 1923. Adolf Hitler, I love you, because you are both great and simple. A genius. Leave-taking from him. Farewell! He waves. . . .

June 16, 1926

Hitler is the same dear comrade. You cannot help liking him as a man. And on top of it that overriding mind. You always discover something new in that self-willed head. As a speaker he has developed a wonderful harmony of gesture, histrionics and spoken word. The born whipper-up! Together with him you can conquer the world. Give him his head and he will shake the corrupt Republic to its foundations. His best epigram yesterday: "For our struggle God gave us His abundant blessing. His most beautiful gift was the hate of our enemies whom we too hate with all our heart."

June 17, 1926

Yesterday with Hitler in Cologne. Cathedral, Rhine, exhibition. He knows everything, a genius. Wonderful drive via Düsseldorf to Essen. In Essen he spoke to two thousand members. And defined the essence of German socialism. Such a fellow can turn the world inside out. That evening was a very great event. "The day will come when Hitler will lead us out of our misery!"

June 21, 1926

Yesterday Hitler talked about organization. Brilliant as always. On Saturday he and I went to . . . Düsseldorf. I again saw something new in that fabulous man and his profound mind. Then he told stories all day. Yesterday and the day before. Witty, humorous and spirited. Fiery nature. We talked about Wagner. He loves Wagner. . . .

July 23, 1926

[Obersalzberg] . . . You beautiful, beautiful mountains! We lie in the burning sun in front of the Hochlenzer. I hear a deep, resonant voice: the chief. . . . We meet like friends. Then he begins to talk. The social question: thoughts which he developed in Munich some time ago. But always new and compelling, illustrated with telling examples. Yes, you can serve under this man. The creator of the Third Reich. . . .

July 24, 1926

In the morning . . . the chief talks about race questions. It is impossible to reproduce what he said. It must be experienced. He is a genius. The natural, creative instrument of a fate determined by God. I am deeply moved. He is like a child: kind, good, merciful. Like a cat: cunning, clever, agile. Like a lion: roaring and great and gigantic. A fellow, a man. He talks about the state. In the afternoon about winning over the state and the political revolution. Thoughts which I may well have had, but never yet put into words. After supper we go on sitting in the garden . . . , and he goes on for a long time preaching about the new state and how we are going to fight for it. It sounds like prophecy. Up in the skies a white cloud takes on the shape of the swastika. There is a blinking light that cannot be a star. A sign of fate?! We go back late! The lights of Salzburg shine in the distance. I am indeed happy. This life is worth living. "My head will not roll in the sand until I have completed my mission." Those were his last words. That's what he is like! . . .

July 25, 1926

The afternoon we spend in his room and have a natter. He spoils me like a child. The kind friend and master! Outside it is pouring. And Hitler talks! In the evening: he speaks about the country's future architecture and is nothing but an architect. And he fills in the picture by describing the new German constitution: and then he is the master of statecraft! Farewell, my Obersalzberg! These days have signposted my road! A star shines leading me from deep misery! I am his to the end. My last doubts have disappeared. Germany will live! *Heil Hitler!*

SCHACHT: "HIS IDEAS WERE NOT UNREASONABLE" (1931) [9]

Although Hitler's dialectical ability was most often displayed in the beer hall and the public arena, he could perform equally well in more intimate situations and before more sophisticated audiences. Having learned relatively early in his political career that the assumption of power by legal means would require the support not only of the masses but also of the conservative establishment, Hitler worked hard to make himself Salonfähig, *acceptable to "good" society. The measure of his success is illustrated in this account by Hjalmar Schacht of his first meeting with Hitler in 1931. At the time, Schacht—having just recently completed a six-year term as President of the Reichsbank—was Germany's leading financial expert. During the Third Reich he served Hitler as both President of the Reichsbank (1933–39) and Acting Minister of Economics (1934–37).*

. . . I received an invitation to dinner from Hermann Göring and his wife . . . accompanied by a note to the effect that Adolf Hitler would be there.

Göring's dinner party took place on January 5, 1931. Besides my wife and myself there were present Fritz Thyssen [German steel magnate—ED.], Frau Karin Göring's son by her first marriage, and Dr. Goebbels. . . .

Hitler came in after dinner. He wore dark trousers and the traditional yellowish-brown jacket—the uniform of the party. His appearance was neither pretentious nor affected—there was nothing about him to indicate that he was already the leader of the second largest German party in the Reichstag. After the many rumors that we had heard about Hitler and the published criticisms we had read of him we were pleasantly impressed by the general atmosphere.

Our talk quickly turned to political and economic problems. At this first meeting I learned what all of us experienced later, that in a discussion with Hitler his associates contributed only 5 per cent; Hitler himself supplied the remaining 95 per cent of the conversation. His skill in exposition was most striking. Everything he said he stated as incontrovertible truth; nevertheless his ideas were not unreasonable.

[9] From Hjalmar Schacht, *Confessions of "The Old Wizard"* (Boston: Houghton Mifflin Company, 1956), p. 257. Reprinted by permission of the publisher.

He was obviously anxious to avoid anything that might shock us in our capacity as representatives of a more traditional society. Goebbels and Göring maintained an impressive silence throughout and did nothing to underline Hitler's arguments. Since I had not come in order to sell Hitler my political and economic opinions I contented myself with taking note of his views and intentions. The thing that impressed me most about this man was his absolute conviction of the rightness of his outlook and his determination to translate this outlook into practical action.

GÖRING: "SENT TO US BY GOD IN ORDER TO SAVE GERMANY" (1933) [10]

Veneration of the leader, the so-called "cult of the personality," is a phenomenon common to all totalitarian dictatorships. But unlike Stalin, whose charisma was a synthetic creation of the Soviet propaganda machine, or Mussolini, whose charisma was largely illusory, Hitler was a genuine charismatic leader whose irrational belief in his own divine inspiration and special mission was shared not only by his lieutenants but also by millions of his countrymen. To state this is not to deny that there existed a Hitler myth, or cult, assiduously cultivated and shrewdly manipulated to enhance the Führer's position and power. But the Hitler cult was not entirely, nor even largely, an artificial creation, for National Socialism was something more than a political movement: it was a faith, a pseudoreligion, and Adolf Hitler was its prophet. The fact is that at least a third of the German people revered Hitler long before he became Chancellor. Hermann Göring, the Third Reich's "number-two man" was perhaps the most pragmatic and least "ideological" of Hitler's lieutenants, yet he too was deeply and earnestly committed to an unreasoning belief in Hitler's superhuman powers. The next selection, from a short and boastful book that Göring authored (actually dictated) in the aftermath of the Nazi assumption of power in 1933, records his feelings about Hitler and demonstrates once again the adulation and religious devotion that he inspired in his followers. Despite the hagiographic character of the piece, Göring was perfectly sincere, a conclusion supported by both his behavior toward Hitler throughout the existence of the Third Reich and his conduct while a defendant on trial before the International Military Tribunal at Nuremberg after the war.

[10] From Hermann Göring, *Aufbau einer Nation* (Berlin: E. S. Mittler & Sohn, 1934), pp. 31, 51–52; trans. G. H. Stein.

When the need was greatest the Lord God gave the German people its savior—an unknown soldier of the World War, a man of the people, without rank or property or connections, a plain, simple man, but one with an overwhelming genius and greatness of character. From the primordial force of the people itself Adolf Hitler strode forward and took Germany's destiny into his clean, strong hands. Adolf Hitler arose and passed through all of Germany as the herald of German freedom and German justice, appealing, arousing, and inflaming the people like the incarnation of the German conscience itself. And then it seemed to all ardent, expectant Germans as if the beacon of the hidden Germany had illuminated the starless night of hopeless despair. The German heart was found again; with magic power it drew to itself and into itself the noblest German blood and poured it out again into the people [*Volk*] in countless streams of resolution and strength. . . .

Just as the Roman Catholic is convinced that the Pope is infallible in all matters of religion and morals, so we National Socialists believe with the same inner conviction that for us the Führer is infallible in all political and other matters that concern the national and social interests of the people. What is the secret of his mighty influence on his followers? Is it his goodness as a person, his strength of character, or his unique modesty? Is it perhaps his political talent for divining and foreseeing the course that events will take? Or is it his exceptional courage or his extraordinary loyalty to his followers? I believe that, whatever one singles out, one will in the end arrive at the conclusion that it is not only the sum of all these virtues but also something mystical, inexpressible, almost incomprehensible in this unique man, and he who does not feel it will not understand it. For we love Adolf Hitler, because we believe deeply and unalterably that he has been sent to us by God in order to save Germany.

And it is Germany's blessing that Hitler is that rare combination of penetratingly logical thinker, genuinely profound philosopher, and iron man of action, tenacious to the extreme. How seldom are the gifts of genius united with the will to action! In Hitler they find a perfect union.

ASSMANN: "HE MIGHT HAVE DONE MUCH GOOD FOR GERMANY" (1944) [11]

Hitler may not have been "the greatest military leader of all time" portrayed in Nazi propaganda, but he was undeniably the

[11] From Captain Heinz Assmann, former German Navy, "Some Recollections of Adolf Hitler," trans. Captain Roland E. Krause, U.S. Navy (retired), *U.S. Naval Institute Proceedings* (December 1953), pp. 1289–91, 1293–95. Copyright © 1953 U.S. Naval Institute. Reprinted from *Proceedings* by permission.

supreme war lord of Germany (and of her allies) during World War II. With the coming of the war, Hitler rapidly extended his dictatorial powers of decision into the sphere of military operations. From 1940 until the collapse of the Third Reich in 1945 he appeared in public only on rare ceremonial occasions, saw all but a handful of his political leaders only infrequently, and spent most of his time not in the Reich Chancellery but in his various military headquarters in the company of his military staff and his immediate entourage. It is therefore not surprising that some of the most informative accounts of Hitler as war lord have come from those who helped plan his campaigns and fight his war. Heinz Assmann, a naval captain, was assigned to the Armed Forces Operations Staff in 1943, and served as naval representative at the daily military conferences that occupied most of Hitler's work day during the last years of the war. Hitler's distrust of the army, particularly its leaders, did not extend to the navy; perhaps for this reason, Assmann's account, although not uncritical, lacks the waspish and falsely self-righteous tone so characteristic of similar accounts by many army generals. Assmann, writing in 1953, offers some personal recollections of Adolf Hitler in 1944.

During my duty in *Führer* headquarters in the last year and a half of the war up to April 23, 1945, I saw and spoke to Hitler daily with the exception of a period while I was in the hospital. My own opinion is that he was a genius and that he might have done much good for Germany had he not given way to demoniacal forces which eventually controlled him and plunged him and his works into destruction. When he failed in adherence to God, his prayer in his book *Mein Kampf* died unanswered; "Almighty God, bless our arms when the time comes, be righteous, just as Thou hast always been, judge for Thyself whether we have now merited freedom: Lord, bless our fight."

Hitler's genius was rooted in a psychopathic personality, I am convinced, a fact which provides a basic explanation for certain character traits, unusual ideas, emotions, passions, and reactions. His constitution was basically sound and robust; he was in no wise naturally a sick man. If he had been, he would never have been able to produce as prodigiously as he did during the twelve years of his rule. The terrible strain on his nervous system and the burden of work far beyond that to be expected of any one man, in conjunction with an unhealthy mode of living, seriously undermined his health in the course of the years, however, so that he finally could keep at his work only by using very powerful nerve and physical stimulants. Various observers noted how remarkably fast Hitler recovered from physical collapse after he had taken tablets or injections.

Hitler was perhaps not a normal type physically. Strict adherence to a vegetarian diet, abstinence from tobacco and alcoholic beverages, indicate certain peculiarities. It was these peculiarities, however, which gave him particular capacity for work. Since he made night into day and, moreover, shunned all physical exercise except for a little walking, the conditions of his life were rather unfavorable for good physical and mental condition, especially in view of the gruelling life in shelters[12] during the war. In addition there was also the irregularity in his mode of life occasioned by his responsibilities.

At the end Hitler was a physical wreck. The decline seemed to date from July 20, 1944, when the German resistance movement attempted to assassinate him; it was promoted by his illness in September, 1944, and by the improper medical treatment of Dr. Morell.[13] I am personally of the opinion that the severe political and military shocks likewise exerted decisive effect on his physical condition and that the latter declined in the same relationship as the general situation deteriorated. Stalingrad, the retreat in Russia, the loss of Africa and the Mediterranean, the failure of invasion defense, the events of the 20th of July, the growing distrust of the Army, the known, yet indeterminate, resistance movement, and finally the failure of the Ardennes offensive left deep scars on Hitler.

To one who had a fanaticism without equal, who believed in his mission and in final victory, the slowly increasing realization that our defeat was inevitable was bound to have a crushing effect. Consequently, at the end he was simply a beaten man—a physical wreck who moved with slow shuffling step, dragging his right leg, bent over with a shaking head, and a trembling hand on a limp left arm. His hand clasp was weak and soft; all his movements were that of a senile man, only his eyes retained their flickering gleam and penetrating look.

Despite this physical collapse, his energy and will power remained unbroken to the end; it was amazing for those of us who witnessed this each day. He worked under strain into the early morning hours until the last enemy planes had started on their return flight. The days were filled with continuous conferences and discussions on military, political, and economic problems. To the very end, he preached

[12] Assmann is referring to the underground bunkers in which Hitler lived and worked while he conducted military operations.

[13] Dr. Theodor Morell, Hitler's personal physician, was by all accounts a quack whose treatment of the Führer during the war years consisted largely of injections of various drugs, hormones, and vitamins.

impressively again and again to his entourage, perseverance, rigor, ruthlessness, and energy. Indicating his paralyzed arm, he stated with a sullen look: ". . . and if my whole left side were paralyzed, I would still call on the German people again and again; do not capitulate, but hold out to the end, because the consequences of an unconditional surrender would be terrible in view of the Bolshevist danger." He fought against his physical decline with unbelievable rigor and determination and rose to face the irresistible fate confronting him and his people.

He was modest and rather unassuming in his mode of life and private requirements. In the conduct of business, however, he was usually presumptuous, often dogmatic and stubborn. It was at best most difficult for him to take correction. In general he was incapable, and also unwilling, to engage in purely objective debate. He was loathe to let others take the floor, and when they did he often would not listen; he preferred to do the talking and even in a small group he was very apt to deliver an oration, endeavoring to convince the others with his forceful logic. Consequently, he did not in general participate in lengthy conversations, because they tended to turn into monologues in short order.

He frequently maintained a high standard in talks and conversations; he demonstrated extremely keen criticism and sarcasm. It was seldom that he admitted to having made a mistake; rarely, if ever, did he say, "You were right after all." He would not make such an admission on any reproach; it was necessary that he himself arrive at the conviction that he had been wrong. He admitted, for instance, that the attempt to establish a new order in the Evangelical Church by installing a Reich Bishop was one of his most serious mistakes.

One might have supposed that the growing resistance movement and the resulting assassination attempts would have induced Hitler to moderate his course; actually it had the opposite effect. The failure of his foes to eliminate him served to increase Hitler's belief in his calling, in his self-confidence, and in his overweening opinion of self. He responded with further hardness, inflexibility, much greater obstinacy, and ruthlessness. Thus he rose to demoniac heights.

I recall that Hitler sat at my bedside in the Carlshof Hospital at Rastenburg for some time a few days after the assassination attempt of July 20. He made the following remarks, among others: "There you are with serious injuries, and yet you are not the one that was to be assassinated. These gentlemen had me, and only me, in mind. But I escaped entirely. This is the fourth time in this war that my opponents have sought after my life in order to eliminate me for good. However, they did not succeed a single time despite most favorable conditions; on the contrary they suffered a renewed reverse each time, and now the Almighty has stayed their hands once again. Don't you agree that I should consider it as a nod of fate that it intends to preserve me for my assigned task? Must I not recognize therein the governance of a higher power which protects me, so that I can lead the German people to victory? Providence has frustrated all attempts against me. That can have only one historical meaning, that it has elected me to lead the German people. Thus I have been right in my course to date, with my regulations and orders, with my entire work toward the destined end and I see no occasion for deviating from this course. Fate has given me the strength to lead the German people in an incomparable ascent to a height which is unique in their history. And the Lord has blessed our arms in the war to date in such manifold ways. However, my whole fight, my successes and my work, would lose all historical meaning if fate had not intended that I should lead the German people *to victory*. Consequently, the 20th of July can only confirm my recognition that Almighty God has called me to lead the German people—not to final defeat, but to victory."

Despite the fact that Adolf Hitler's unteachability, obstinacy, and stubbornness were frequently in evidence, it would be wrong to maintain that one could not tell him anything or that he was completely unreceptive to other opinions. No doubt, it is correct to say that it was difficult to present a concept to him which deviated from his own or to help him to arrive at a reasonable, objective estimate of the situation. Much depended upon who voiced the opinion and how it was done. Hitler would at once reject advice and sagacious criticism. He was entirely inclined to receive a frank presentation of the situation, but then he wished to make the estimate of the situation himself. Mistrust was a fundamental characteristic of Adolf Hitler. Few people had his complete confidence. . . .

Those working in close association with Hitler were constantly torn between admiration, recognition, despair, disappointment, and hatred. It was often that one felt like hating him; yet one would be disarmed again on the very next day by his creative ideas, his staunch confidence in victory, his amazing knowledge, and his radiant kindness. He was very friendly and kind to his subordinates, in his concern about their health; he was attentive and sent presents or flowers when someone was sick.

We in Führer headquarters found reason to hate him for his acts of ruthlessness, hardness, injustice, and brutality which came within our purview, as for instance when he would make severe reproaches against certain army commanders or troops in a coldblooded, unjust manner, when he issued inconsiderate orders, when he made illogical criticism, when he directed the ruthless sacrifice of defense positions, fortifications, and whole divisions. . . .

It is a tragic conclusion that Hitler was in no wise possessed of the requisite military education and training for the post of Commander-in-Chief Army but fundamentally remained a military dilettante with inadequate judgment to make military decisions. . . .

So, Hitler led us on to fight to the bitter end. He repeatedly expressed the hope to us that the German people would be able to hold out to the autumn of 1945, when [a] favorable turn would necessarily ensue. He entertained certain hopes of a change in the Western Powers' attitude toward their ally, Soviet Russia, and the promise of new technical developments. The thought of giving up the fight in the West and holding only in the East was often broached to Hitler during the last months. The latter always turned it down; he contended that negotiations were impossible with one who has a knife at your throat and that such a measure could only be successful if the Western Powers tacitly agreed to cease action and not engage the defense forces in the East from the rear.

Hitler always rejected any deliberations to save his people from the last sacrifices and destruction by promptly ending the war because of the rigid adherence of the opponents to "unconditional surrender" and because of his own hopes of a turn for the better, as mentioned above. In view of his aspiration to lead his people to "unparalleled" greatness and in view of the tremendous sacrifices which had already been made—without success—Hitler was fundamentally disinclined to accept final defeat. He could only go on. I am reminded of his reply to the urgent warnings and entreaties of the aged Field Marshal von Mackensen before the war: "Perhaps you are right, Field Marshal. But I cannot do otherwise; I cannot turn back." Thus he lost all regard for the dignity of man and transgressed ruthlessly the bounds set by God. Such arrogance and utter lack of restraint inevitably had to lead to the downfall of Adolf Hitler and all his works.

RIBBENTROP: "CANNOT BE MEASURED BY ORDINARY STANDARDS" (1945) [14]

Joachim von Ribbentrop—from 1938 until the fall of the Third Reich Hitler's Foreign Minister—was by all accounts a

---

[14] From Joachim von Ribbentrop, "Niederschrift über die Persönlichkeit Adolf Hitlers," in Diether Krywalski, "Zwei Niederschriften Ribbentrops über die Persönlichkeit Adolf Hitlers und die letzten Tage in Berlin," *Geschichte in Wissenschaft und Unterricht*, XVIII, 12 (December 1967), 734–40; trans. G. H. Stein. Reprinted in English translation by permission of the Editors of *Geschichte in Wissenschaft und Unterricht*.

vain, arrogant, and unqualified amateur, who filled a largely ceremonial post with little distinction. Indeed, his major distinction may well lie in the fact that he was the only one of Hitler's principal lieutenants to be hanged at Nuremberg.[15] *The following selection is taken from a memorandum written by Ribbentrop at the request of his defense attorney, Dr. Georg Froeschmann, who subsequently donated it to the Bavarian State Archives. It is a frankly sympathetic account by a man whose greatest virtue was his slavish and unshakable loyalty to his master. Even after allowances are made for the purpose for which it was written, Ribbentrop's memorandum demonstrates, once again, the extraordinary hold that Hitler exercised over those around him.*

I saw Adolf Hitler for the first time in August 1932. . . . [His] entire personality impressed me strongly. . . . I was especially fascinated by his domineering blue eyes in his otherwise dark appearance. Even then I got the impression that this man, whose speeches I had read with so much interest, was quite an unusual phenomenon. What struck me most was his thoroughly self-contained, though not reserved, manner. Not only his thoughts and words but also the way in which he expressed them clearly distinguished him from other men; they seemed to come out of his innermost being; they were simple and clear, and therefore so convincing. Another thing that struck me was the finality with which he expressed his views. There was room for neither discussion nor contradiction. He simply stated facts that his listeners were expected to accept. He was clearly monomaniacal; a man hard to influence and not given to compromise. That was even then my impression. . . .

Although I spent much time with him, never during all those years did I get any closer to him than I did on the first day we met. He was indescribably aloof. Although millions adored him, Adolf Hitler was a lonely man. . . . He did not want to be unapproachable, but that was how nature had made him. I think he probably suffered as a result. Despite all this, however, he could be engagingly amiable, cordial, and gay. . . . When he was out to win someone over or to get something out of somebody he could be extraordinarily charming and persuasive. I have seen men with strong personalities go in to see Hitler, their hearts full, determined to tell him categorically that unless this or that were changed a catastrophe would occur, for which

---

[15] Hermann Göring, at one time the Third Reich's number-two man, was also condemned to death by hanging, but managed to commit suicide just before his scheduled execution.

they could not assume responsibility. After half an hour they would emerge, beaming and content, ready to support Adolf Hitler's point of view with the greatest conviction, although often it was the very opposite of what they had intended to tell him. . . .

Adolf Hitler could also be so extraordinarily exciting, humorous, and exuberant when he talked about his youth, his military service in the World War, and his political struggle, that everyone listening to him was captivated. And when he spoke about art and architecture, his essentially artistic nature became clearly evident . . . [and] his listeners could not help being drawn to him. . . .

To judge Hitler's personality yet another factor must be mentioned: he was hot-tempered and could not always control himself. This sometimes became apparent even during diplomatic negotiations. At [Bad] Godesberg [September 22, 1938], for example, he wanted to break off his conference with [Neville] Chamberlain [British Prime Minister] when word of the Czech mobilization arrived. His face red (a typical sign), he spontaneously leaped to his feet. So did Chamberlain. I intervened and thus saved the conference. Adolf Hitler [later] specifically thanked me. During the war [he] once told me quite frankly: "You know, Ribbentrop, at times I simply can't control myself." . . .

There can be no doubt that Hitler's whole life was devoted to only one aim: to serve the German people. . . . He lived selflessly, sacrificed his health, and to his last breath thought of nothing but the future of the nation, which he loved above all else. This guided his thoughts and his actions. To this end he made momentous decisions in foreign affairs. He believed that the future of Germany could be guaranteed only in this way. That he failed, so he told me, was fate. *Why* he failed, will be determined by historians.

It is very difficult to judge the character of a phenomenon, a genius like Adolf Hitler. He cannot be measured by ordinary standards. Most noticeable was the burning patriotism and the fanatical will with which he tried to make Germany great. He was convinced of his mission, for the fulfillment of which he believed he had been chosen by Providence. His will was inflexible and the energy with which he pursued his aims was unimaginable. Both his power of comprehension and his intelligence were astounding. He always thought in terms of great historical perspectives and drew historical parallels. Frederick the Great was often his example.

Despite all his phantasizing, however, he was enough of a realist to assess situations soberly. Yet when he had to make great decisions, he regarded himself as the executor of a fate that the Almighty had predestined for Germany. He once told me that always before great decisions (usually overnight) a kind of hypnotic certainty came over him, so that suddenly he knew precisely what he had to do in order to carry out his duty. He was completely unscrupulous in pursuit of the interests of the German people . . . and thus he felt that even violent measures were fully justified. . . .

In summary, I can only close this memorandum concerning the personality of Adolf Hitler with these words: I don't know who he was; I know only that he was great!

9

The Reich Chancellor: Hitler as Seen by Foreign Diplomats and Journalists

FRANÇOIS-PONCET: "A CHARACTER OUT OF THE PAGES OF DOSTOYEVSKY" (1933–1938) [1]

André François-Poncet, the French Ambassador in Berlin from 1931 through 1938, was one of the few foreign diplomats fluent enough in German to converse directly with Hitler without recourse to an interpreter. During his lengthy period of service in Nazi Germany, he saw Hitler frequently and had numerous direct and relatively unencumbered conversations with him. This selection from François-Poncet's memoirs describes his first (1933) and his last (1938) interviews with Hitler and offers his assessment of the Nazi leader. François-Poncet's impressions of Hitler's appearance, behavior, and personality—and his rare description of Hitler's mountain-top eyrie—add up to an extraordinarily intimate portrait of the Reich Chancellor in the heyday of his power.

On April 8 [1933] I had an interview with him at the Chancellery. . . . I was already familiar with Hitler's countenance, voice, gestures, and oratory, but I was now meeting him for the first time in diplomatic conversation. Viewing him at close range while he was relaxed, I was struck, as I was to be struck whenever I approached him later, by the vulgarity of his features and the insignificance of his face, though I realized that this very insignificance made him the representative of those masses which acclaimed him and recognized themselves in his person. Nor was I ever affected by his glance, which so many others considered magnetic but which always seemed to me

[1] From André François-Poncet, *The Fateful Years: Memoirs of a French Ambassador in Berlin, 1931–1938*, trans. J. LeClerq (New York: Harcourt, Brace & World, Inc., 1949), pp. 95, 280–82, 285–86, 289–91. Copyright © 1949 by Harcourt, Brace & World, Inc. Reprinted by permission of Harcourt, Brace & World, Inc., and MM. Flammarion et Cie. Editeurs.

to be vague, dull, and opaque, save when some violent urge possessed him and anger swept over him. Even at such moments, however, I could not help feeling that his wrath was more comical than frightening. During our conversation he behaved quite courteously, displayed no personal embarrassment, and was apparently quite at his ease, if fairly reserved and somewhat aloof. He expressed himself in downright, clear terms which bore all the earmarks of frankness. . . .

Hitler himself was bent on giving an unusual form to the farewell audience granted me on the occasion of the last political conversation I was to have with him. He summoned me neither to the Chancellery in Berlin nor to his Berghof chalet at Berchtesgaden, but to his mountain retreat, which his intimates only, and no foreigner, had ever visited. In his mind this was a rarer favor than I appreciated at the time. Later he felt particularly offended because he believed that I had failed to value his gesture and the intent that inspired it.

I was never to see him again, our interview of October 1938 being our last.

Inviting me on the evening of October 17, Hitler placed one of his personal airplanes at my disposal. I flew next day to Berchtesgaden, arrived there at about 3:00 P.M. and proceeded by automobile.

From afar the extraordinary place to which I was summoned looked like a sort of observatory or hermitage, perched at an altitude of over six thousand feet, atop the crest of a ridge of rocks. A hairpin road about ten miles long, cut boldly through the rocks, wound upward. Its daring layout honored the talents of the engineer Todt[2] and the dogged labors of the workmen who had accomplished this gigantic task within three years. The road led to the entrance of a long underground passageway dug deep into the soil and commanded by a massive double door of bronze. At the end of this corridor a roomy copper-lined elevator awaited the visitor; its shaft, hewn vertically through the rock, rose over three hundred seventy feet to the level on which the Führer had his dwelling.

I was ushered into a squat, solid building which consisted of a gallery with Roman pillars, an immense glassed-in rotunda (giant logs blazed in a huge fireplace and there was a long table with some thirty chairs around it), and several handsomely appointed rooms on the side. To look out in any direction over the endless panorama of mountains was like looking down from an airplane. In the hollow of the amphitheater lay Salzburg and its neighboring villages, dominated, as far as the eye traveled, by a horizon of chains and peaks with meadows and

[2] Fritz Todt, a Nazi since 1923, was Hitler's construction czar. He was appointed Inspector General of German highways in 1933 and directed the construction of the *Reichsautobahnen* (superhighways) and the West Wall, Germany's fortifications along the western frontier. During the war, Todt served as Minister of Armaments and Munitions until his death in a plane crash during 1942.

woods clinging to the slopes. Hitler's house gave the impression of being suspended in space; the whole view, bathed in the chiaroscuro of autumn dusk, loomed grand, savage, hallucinant. Was this the Castle of Monsalvat, peopled by the Knights of the Grail, or a Mount Athos, where the cenobite may meditate, or Antinea's palace amid the heart of the Atlas Mountains? Was it the execution of the fantastic sketches Victor Hugo had penciled in the margins of *Les Burgraves?* Was it a billionaire's folly or the hideout where brigands relaxed and heaped up their swag? Was this edifice the work of a normal mind or of one tormented by megalomania and haunted by visions of domination and solitude? Or had it been built by a man who was simply a prey to his fears? . . .

The Chancellor greeted me amiably and with courtesy. His face was pale and drawn with fatigue. This was not one of his days of excitement; rather, he was in a phase of relaxation. He led me at once to one of the bay windows of the main room, showed me the view, and enjoyed the astonishment and admiration which I did not seek to conceal. Then he expressed his regret at my forthcoming departure. We exchanged a few compliments of courtesy and a few polite phrases. At his order tea was served in one of the adjoining salons, to which Ribbentrop accompanied us while other Nazi familiars remained aloof in neighboring rooms. The servants having retired and the doors closed upon them, we began a three-party conversation, into which Ribbentrop entered rarely but always in order to repeat and to stress the Führer's remarks. . . .

For two hours Hitler allowed me to question him, answering without the slightest embarrassment, quite simply and apparently quite frankly.

The castle of Antinea was now bathed in the shadows that lay over valley and mountain. I took my leave. The Führer expressed the wish that I might subsequently return to Germany and visit him in a private capacity. Several times he took my hands in his and shook them. Emerging from the lift and from the underground, I found the car awaiting me at the door and returned via Berchtesgaden to the airport whence I flew through the darkness to Berlin.

Throughout our conversation, except for a few violent outbursts when he spoke of Britain, Hitler was calm, moderate, and conciliatory. A witness would have been justified in believing that here was a well-balanced man, filled with experience and wisdom, who desired nothing so much as to see peace reign among the nations. At certain moments he spoke of Europe and of his sentiments as a European, more genuine than those which many men advertised noisily. He spoke of the "white civilization" as of a precious common possession which must be defended. He seemed to be sincerely struck by the persistent antagonism that survived the Munich agreement and clearly revealed to him what was Britain's attitude.[3]

Manifestly the prospect of an early crisis and a general war was on his mind. I labored under no illusions about his character. I knew him to be changeable, dissimulating, contradictory, and uncertain. The same man, good-natured in appearance and sensitive to the beauties of nature, who across a tea table expressed reasonable opinions on European politics, was capable of the wildest frenzies, the most savage exaltation, and the most delirious ambition. There were days when, bending over a map of the world, he upset nations and continents, geography and history, like some demiurge in his madness. At other times he dreamed of being the hero of an eternal peace within whose framework he would raise the loftiest of monuments.

What manner of man was Hitler? . . . A Hitler cannot be confined within a simple formula. For my part I knew three facets of his personality, each corresponding to a like facet in his nature.

His first aspect was one of pallor; his jumbled complexion and vague globular eyes, lost in a dream, lent him an absent, faraway air, the troubled and troubling face of a medium or somnambulist.

The second aspect was animated, colored, swept away by passion. His nostrils would twitch, his eyes dart lightning; he was all violence, impatience of control, lust for domination, abomination of his antagonists, cynical boldness, with a fierce energy ready at no provocation to pull down the universe about his ears. Then his "storm and assault" face was the face of a lunatic.

Hitler's third aspect was that of any naïve, rustic man, dull, vulgar, easily amused, laughing boisterously as he slapped his thigh; a commonplace face without any distinguishing mark, a face like thousands of other faces spread over the face of the earth.

People who spoke with Hitler sometimes saw these three expressions successively. At the beginning of the conversation he seemed not to listen, let alone understand; he remained indifferent, amorphous. . . . Then, suddenly, as though a hand had released a lever, he would burst forth into a harangue, uttered in shrill, excited, choleric tones. His arguments, gathering speed and volume, came more abundant

---

[3] Hitler was dissimulating. Actually, it was he who was antagonistic, for, contrary to popular opinion at the time, Hitler was disappointed with the results of Munich. (The Munich Agreement of September 30, 1938, resulted in the cession to Germany of 11,000 square miles of Czech territory in which dwelt 2,800,000 Sudeten Germans and 800,000 Czechs.) What he really wanted was not so much the Sudeten areas of Czecholsovakia as the destruction of the entire Czech state, a step which would bring him materially closer to his ultimate goal of securing "living space" and an area for colonial exploitation in the Slavic east. Three days after his talk with François-Poncet, Hitler issued a top secret directive calling for military preparations to liquidate the remainder of Czechoslovakia.

and virulent, emphasized by raucous tones, by a rolling of *r*s and by the harsh accent of the Austrian mountaineer, and he roared and thundered as though addressing thousands of listeners. Here was the orator, the tribune full of *pectus*, at once chesty and throaty, the great orator of the Latin tradition who instinctively employed all the figures of rhetoric; here was the virtuoso, playing upon all the chords of eloquence, excelling in caustic irony and in invective. This apparition proved the more striking to native crowds because they were little accustomed to it, political eloquence in Germany being generally colorless and boring.

When Hitler launched into this sort of tirade or diatribe it was useless to seek to interrupt him or to protest. He would have blasted that luckless imprudent who dared to, exactly as he blasted Schuschnigg [Chancellor of Austria, 1934–38—ED.] and Hácha, the President of rump-Czechoslovakia, when they sought to object to his ideas. These "fits" might last ten minutes or a half hour or even three quarters of an hour. Then, suddenly, the flow stopped; Hitler would fall silent. He seemed exhausted; it was as though his batteries had run dry. Sinking into a sort of hebetude, he relapsed into inertia. This offered the proper opportunity to present objections, to contradict him, to drive home an opposing thesis. When in this state he ceased to grow indignant; he would hesitate, ask for time to think things over, procrastinate. If, in this instant, a man found a *mot* to touch him, or a witticism to break the strain, immediately the deep wrinkles vanished from the Führer's brow and his tenebrous face lit up in a smile.

These alternate states of excitement and depression, these fits mentioned by his familiars, ranged from the most devastating fury to the plaintive moanings of a wounded beast. Because of them, psychiatrists have considered him a "cyclothimic"; others see in him the typical paranoiac. This much is certain: he was no normal being. He was, rather, a morbid personality, a quasi-madman, a character out of the pages of Dostoyevsky, a man "possessed."

SHIRER: "LIKE A ROMAN EMPEROR" (1934)[4]

The National Socialists were masters in the art of conducting mass demonstrations. Nowhere in recorded history can one find a ceremony to match in either size or spectacle the annual Nazi party rallies held in Nuremberg during the Third Reich. "To see the films of the Nuremberg rallies even today," Alan Bullock notes, "is to be recaptured by the hyponotic effect of thousands

[4]From William L. Shirer, *Berlin Diary: The Journal of a Foreign Correspondent 1934–1941* (New York: Alfred A. Knopf, Inc., 1941), pp. 16–21, 23. Copyright © 1940, 1941 by William L. Shirer. Reprinted by permission of the author and publisher.

of men marching in perfect order, the music of massed bands, the forest of standards and flags, the vast perspectives of the stadium, the smoking torches, the dome of searchlights." For as long as eight or nine days each September, the Nazi regime sought to display both to its people and to the world the power and the unity of the new Germany. But the central attraction, the true object of these massive celebrations was in reality not Germany, nor even the Nazi party, but Adolf Hitler. William L. Shirer, author of a well-known popular history of the Third Reich, attended a number of the annual Nuremberg rallies in his capacity as a newspaper correspondent and radio commentator. The following extract from Mr. Shirer's diary records his impressions of the 1934 Nazi party rally at which he saw Hitler for the first time.

Nuremberg, September 4

Like a Roman emperor Hitler rode into this medieval town at sundown today past solid phalanxes of wildly cheering Nazis who packed the narrow streets that once saw Hans Sachs and the *Meistersinger*. Tens of thousands of Swastika flags blot out the Gothic beauties of the place, the façades of the old houses, the gabled roofs. The streets, hardly wider than alleys, are a sea of brown and black uniforms. I got my first glimpse of Hitler as he drove by our hotel, the Württemberger Hof, to his headquarters down the street at the Deutscher Hof, a favorite old hotel of his, which has been remodelled for him. He fumbled his cap with his left hand as he stood in his car acknowledging the delirious welcome with somewhat feeble Nazi salutes from his right arm. He was clad in a rather worn gaberdine trench-coat, his face had no particular expression at all—I expected it to be stronger—and for the life of me I could not quite comprehend what hidden springs he undoubtedly unloosed in the hysterical mob which was greeting him so wildly. He does not stand before the crowd with that theatrical imperiousness which I have seen Mussolini use. I was glad to see that he did not poke out his chin and throw his head back as does the Duce nor make his eyes glassy—though there *is* something glassy in his eyes, the strongest thing in his face. He almost seemed to be affecting a modesty in his bearing. I doubt if it's genuine. . . .

About ten o'clock tonight I got caught in a mob of ten thousand hysterics who jammed the moat in front of Hitler's hotel, shouting: "We want our Führer." I was a little shocked at the faces, especially those of the women, when Hitler finally appeared on the balcony for a moment. They reminded me of the crazed expressions I saw once in the back country of Louisiana on the faces of some Holy Rollers who were about to hit the trail. They looked up at him as if he were a Messiah, their faces transformed into something positively inhuman. If he had remained in sight for more than a few moments, I think many of the women would have swooned from excitement. . . .

Nuremberg, September 5

I'm beginning to comprehend, I think, some of the reasons for Hitler's astounding success. Borrowing a chapter from the Roman church, he is restoring pageantry and color and mysticism to the drab lives of twentieth-century Germans. This morning's opening meeting in the Luitpold Hall on the outskirts of Nuremberg was more than a gorgeous show; it also had something of the mysticism and religious fervor of an Easter or Christmas Mass in a great Gothic cathedral. The hall was a sea of brightly colored flags. Even Hitler's arrival was made dramatic. The band stopped playing. There was a hush over the thirty thousand people packed in the hall. Then the band struck up the *Badenweiler March,* a very catchy tune, and used only, I'm told, when Hitler makes his big entries. Hitler appeared in the back of the auditorium, and followed by his aides, Göring, Goebbels, Hess, Himmler, and the others, he strode slowly down the long center aisle while thirty thousand hands were raised in salute. It is a ritual, the old-timers say, which is always followed. Then an immense symphony orchestra played Beethoven's *Egmont* Overture. Great Klieg lights played on the stage, where Hitler sat surrounded by a hundred party officials and officers of the army and navy. Behind them the "blood flag,"the one carried down the streets of Munich in the ill-fated putsch. Behind this, four or five hundred S.A. standards. When the music was over, Rudolf Hess, Hitler's closest confidant, rose and slowly read the names of the Nazi "martyrs"—brown-shirts who had been killed in the struggle for power—a roll-call of the dead, and the thirty thousand seemed very moved.

In such an atmosphere no wonder, then, that every word dropped by Hitler seemed like an inspired Word from on high. Man's—or at least the German's—critical faculty is swept away at such moments, and every lie pronounced is accepted as high truth itself. . . .

Nuremberg, September 6

Hitler sprang his *Arbeitsdienst,* his Labor Service Corps, on the public for the first time today and it turned out to be a highly trained, semi-military group of fanatical Nazi youths. Standing there in the early morning sunlight which sparkled on their shiny spades, fifty thousand of them, with the first thousand bared above the waist, suddenly made the German spectators go mad with joy when, without warning, they broke into a perfect goose-step. Now, the goose-step has always seemed to me to be an outlandish exhibition of the human being in his most undignified and stupid state, but I felt for the first time this morning what an inner chord it strikes in the strange soul of the German people. Spontaneously they jumped up and shouted their applause. There was a ritual even for the Labor Service boys. They formed an immense *Sprechchor*—a chanting chorus—and with one voice intoned such words as these: "We want one Leader! Nothing for us! Everything for Germany! *Heil Hitler!*". . .

Nuremberg, September 7

Another great pageant tonight. Two hundred thousand party officials packed in the Zeppelin Wiese with their twenty-one thousand flags unfurled in the searchlights like a forest of weird trees. "We are strong and will get stronger," Hitler shouted at them through the microphone, his words echoing across the hushed field from the loudspeakers. And there, in the flood-lit night, jammed together like sardines, in one mass formation, the little men of Germany who have made Nazism possible achieved the highest state of being the Germanic man knows: the shedding of their individual souls and minds—with the personal responsibilities and doubts and problems—until under the mystic lights and at the sound of the magic words of the Austrian they were merged completely in the Germanic herd. Later they recovered enough—fifteen thousand of them—to stage a torch-light parade through Nuremberg's ancient streets, Hitler taking the salute in front of the station across from our hotel. . . .

Nuremberg, September 10

. . . . LATER.—After seven days of almost ceaseless goose-stepping, speech-making, and pageantry, the party rally came to an end tonight. And though dead tired and rapidly developing a bad case of crowd-phobia, I'm glad I came. You have to go through one of these to understand Hitler's hold on the people, to feel the dynamic in the movement he's unleashed and the sheer, disciplined strength the Germans possess. And now—as Hitler told the correspondents yesterday in explaining his technique—the half-million men who've been here during the week will go back to their towns and villages and preach the new gospel with new fanaticism. . . .

HALIFAX: "SARDONIC HUMOR, SCORN, SOMETHING ALMOST WISTFUL" (1937)[5]

Although the international political moves Hitler made in the years after the Nazi assumption of power were not part of a care-

[5] From Lord Halifax (Edward Frederick Lindley Wood), *Fulness of Days* (London: William Collins Sons & Co., Ltd., 1957), pp. 184–86, 188–89. Reprinted by permission of the author.

fully prepared timetable, they were in line with the long-standing aggressive aims he had outlined in Mein Kampf *and countless public statements. By 1937, Hitler's revisionist intentions began to be given clearer expression, and the British Government, now seriously concerned by the direction events were taking, resolved to make an effort to reach a comprehensive settlement with Nazi Germany. When Lord Halifax, then Lord President of the Council,[6] received an invitation from Göring to attend a hunting exhibition in Berlin, Prime Minister Chamberlain agreed that the occasion should be used to establish contact with Hitler and to explore the possibility of arriving at an understanding with the Nazi dictator. Unfortunately, nothing in Halifax's background had prepared him to deal with men like Hitler and his lieutenants. His conventional way of looking at things, his almost complete ignorance of German character and history (he had neither read* Mein Kampf *nor listened to anyone who had), and his admiration for the way in which Hitler had dealt with the German communists blinded him to the demoniac nature of the Nazi system and its leaders. As a result, Halifax seems to have been at least partially taken in by his hosts. For example, Hitler struck him "as very sincere, and as believing everything he said." He found Göring "frankly attractive: like a great schoolboy, full of life and pride in what he was doing." As for Goebbels: "I had expected to dislike him intensely—but didn't. I suppose it must be some moral defect in me, but the fact remains." [7] At all events, Halifax returned to England believing that Hitler's goals were relatively limited and therefore negotiable—a bad mistake that helped push Great Britain into a tragic policy of appeasement. A portion of Halifax's diary entry describing his visit with Hitler is reproduced below.*

November 19th. After a day in Berlin I was taken off to Berchtesgaden which we reached after a night in the special train, and were driven by what I assumed to be storm-troopers straight up to Hitler's chalet. Snow was on the ground and a path had been swept up the steep steps to the house. As I looked out of the car window, on eye

[6] One of the handful of ministerial positions that involve no departmental duties and to which the Prime Minister generally names prominent political figures whom he would like to have as advisers. Halifax later served as Secretary of State for Foreign Affairs (February 1938–December 1940).

[7] Quoted in Lord Birkenhead, *Halifax: The Life of Lord Halifax* (London: Hamish Hamilton, 1965), pp. 371, 372, and 373 respectively. This book contains portions of Halifax's diary that he omitted from his postwar memoir.

level, I saw in the middle of this swept path a pair of black trousered legs, finishing up in silk socks and pumps. I assumed this was a footman who had come down to help me out of the car and up the steps, and was proceeding in leisurely fashion to get myself out of the car when I heard [Foreign Minister] Von Neurath or somebody throwing a hoarse whisper at my ear of *'Der Führer, der Führer';* and it dawned upon me that the legs were not the legs of a footman, but of Hitler. And higher up, the trousers passed into khaki tunic with swastika armlet complete. He greeted me politely and led me up to the house and to his study, which was very overheated, but with a magnificent mountain view from immense windows.

Hitler invited me to begin our discussion, which I did by thanking him for giving me this opportunity. I hoped it might be the means of creating better understanding between our two countries. The feeling of His Majesty's Government was that it ought to be within our power, if we could once come to a fairly complete appreciation of each other's position, and if we were both prepared to work together for the cause of peace, to make a large contribution to it. Although there was much in the Nazi system that profoundly offended British opinion, I was not blind to what he (Hitler) had done for Germany, and to the achievement from his point of view of keeping Communism out of his country. If and when we were able to develop understanding, we should no doubt feel it right to bring into any conversations that we might have those with whom we had special contacts: Italy and France; and if we four could ever agree between ourselves we should have laid a very solid foundation for peace. He did not challenge this and said that formal agreement between the four Powers might not be very difficult to achieve. It would not, however, be worth much unless it took account of realities, even if unpleasant. Germany had had to recognize such a reality in the shape of Poland; we all had to recognize such a reality in acknowledging Germany to be a great Power; we had to get away from the Versailles mentality and recognize that the world could never remain *in statu quo*. To this I replied that nobody wished to treat Germany as anything but a great Power, and that nobody in their senses supposed the world could stay as it was for ever. The whole point was how changes were to be brought about. This led him to say that there were two, and only two, alternatives: the free play of forces that meant war; and settlement by reason. The world had had experience of the first: was it able to prefer the second? . . .

It is not easy to give a concise or consecutive account of a conversation lasting over three hours and one which followed no very orderly course. Hitler was on the whole quiet and restrained, except now and again when he got excited; over Russia or the Press. I can quite see why he is a popular speaker; very much alive, eyes, which I was surprised to see were blue, moving about all the time, points in the argument reinforced by sharp gestures of the hands. And the play of emotion—sardonic humor, scorn, something almost wistful—is rapid. As to the political value of the talk, I am not disposed to rate this very high. I dare say it was all to the good making contact; but I definitely got the impression that apart from colonies there was little or nothing he wanted from us, and that as regards European problems he felt time to be on his side. . . .

One had a feeling all the time that we had a totally different sense of values and were speaking in a different language. It was not only the difference between a totalitarian and democratic state. He gave me the impression of feeling that, whilst he had attained to power only after a hard struggle with present-day realities, the British Government was still living comfortably in a world of its own making, a fairy-land of strange, if respectable, illusions. It clung to shibboleths—"collective security," "general settlement," "disarmament," "non-aggression pacts"—which offered no practical prospect of a solution of Europe's difficulties. He regards the whole conception embodied in a League of States equal in their rights of sovereignty as unreal, based on no foundation of fact; and consequently does not believe that discussions between large numbers of nations, with varying interests and of quite unequal value, can lead anywhere. Hence his preference for dealing with particular problems in isolation. With this goes the distrust of democratic method, to him inefficient, blundering, paralyzed by its love of talk, and totally unsuited to the rough world, constantly changing, in which we have to live.

KIRKPATRICK: "A SPOILED, SULKY CHILD" (1937) [8]

Sir Ivone Kirkpatrick, First Secretary of the British Embassy in Berlin from 1933 until the end of 1938, accompanied Lord Halifax to Berchtesgaden to meet with Hitler. Kirkpatrick's atmospheric account of the event, which is concerned not so much with the substance of the discussions as with the behavior of the discussants, offers an unusually intimate glimpse of Hitler in a social situation.

In the evening Lord Halifax and I set out by train to Berchtesgaden to visit Hitler. It was in line with Hitler's mood at the time to plead that he could not come to Berlin, and that in consequence Lord Halifax must come to Bavaria. Nevertheless, it must be admitted

[8] From Sir Ivone Kirkpatrick, *The Inner Circle* (London: Macmillan & Co. Ltd., 1959), pp. 94–98. Reprinted by permission of The Macmillan Company of Canada, Ltd., Macmillan & Co. Ltd., and the author.

that everything was done to make the journey pleasant. Hitler put at our disposal his special train consisting of two coaches, each containing a sitting-room, three sleeping compartments and a bathroom. Lord Halifax and I occupied one coach; [Foreign Minister] Neurath, his private secretary, and the famous interpreter, Schmidt, the other. The servants on the train evidently thought that Englishmen lived on whisky, for they appeared every half-hour or so with a tray of whisky and soda, but they must have found us disappointing customers. We reached Berchtesgaden shortly after 9 o'clock in the morning and were met by tracked Mercedes cars which took us straight up to the chalet. Hitler, dressed in a brown coat, black trousers and black patent-leather shoes, met us at the top of the steps leading up to the house. The first snows had fallen and the view was enchanting; it seemed a pity to be on such an errand.

The opening of the conversation, into which Lord Halifax went alone, was distinctly sticky. Hitler was clearly in a peevish mood. . . . There was an interval for lunch, which was served in a hideous dining-room on the first floor. A long satin-wood table with pink upholstered chairs to match filled the body of the room, but we sat at a small round table placed in a bow window overlooking the valley. Hitler ate a purely vegetarian meal consisting of vegetable soup, a dish of mixed vegetables and a plate of mixed walnuts and plain chocolate. He drank a hot concoction out of a glass in a silver holder. We were given a rather indifferent meat lunch, and there was an imposing array of bottles on a side-table from which our glasses were constantly filled. The meal was served by Hitler's major-domo, Kannenberg, and three stalwart S.S. men in white mess-jackets. From a social point of view the lunch was a frost. Hitler was still in a bad temper, Neurath was ill at ease and Lord Halifax could only talk through the interpreter. I made ineffective efforts to get a conversation going, but they all collapsed pitifully under Hitler's determination not to play. Of course we broached the weather. Hitler at once closed this topic by snapping: "The weather. The weather prophets are idiots; when they say it is going to be fine it always rains and when they foretell bad weather, it's fine." We tried flying. Hitler retorted: "Only a fool will fly if he can go by train or road." The Hunting Exhibition came up. Hitler at once wrote that topic off with the remark: "I can't see what there is in shooting; you go out armed with a highly perfected modern weapon and without risk to yourself kill a defenceless animal. Of course Göring tells me that the pleasure lies not in the killing, but in the comradely expedition in the open air. Very well. I merely reply: 'If that's the case let's spare ourselves all bother and make a comradely expedition to a slaughter-house where in the greatest comradeship we can together kill a cow in the open air.'" At that he sat back with an angry gesture to indicate that he was not prepared to discuss the sport of shooting any further. The only mention of politics sprang from somebody's remark that Hess had just had a child, a bonny boy. Hitler observed that the Austrian birth-rate was declining sharply; and when I provocatively asked why, he retorted acidly that it was of course due to the miserable economic conditions created by Austria's forced separation from Germany. He did not, however, pursue the matter any more than the other topics laboriously dragged up by his guests. In short he behaved throughout like a spoiled, sulky child.

This painful ordeal came eventually to an end and we went downstairs to have coffee in the large sitting-room. Hitler instead of coffee drank a large cup of chocolate with a floating iceberg of whipped cream. The feature of this room was an enormous leaded window which could be lowered into the ground and which Hitler insisted on demonstrating to us. A couple of stalwart S.S. men doubled into the room, fixed things like motor-car starting-handles into the sockets and wound violently. The whole structure sank noiselessly into the floor, giving the room the appearance of a covered terrace. At each end of the room there was a grand piano and the intervening space was filled by clusters of a sofa, wicker upholstered chairs and low round tables. The walls were adorned with pictures from the museums, and there were two tapestries which could be removed to uncover a cinema screen and a projector. Brückner told me that the Führer saw two films every night, a feature film and a short. The selection of these programs was a ticklish business, for if Hitler did not like a film he used to clap his hands and order it to be replaced by one he did like. His favorite actress was Greta Garbo, and one of his favorite films *Lives of a Bengal Lancer,* which he saw three times. He liked this film because it depicted a handful of Britons holding a continent in thrall. That was how a superior race must behave and the film was a compulsory viewing for the S.S.

The mention of India led Hitler to air his views on British policy. He could not understand, he said, why we tolerated disorder or wasted time in parley with Congress leaders. The remedy was quite simple. "Shoot Gandhi," he said in his sharp staccato accent, "and if that does not suffice to reduce them to submission, shoot a dozen leading members of Congress; and if that does not suffice, shoot 200 and so on until order is established. You will see how quickly they will collapse as soon as you make it clear that you mean business." During this tirade Lord Halifax gazed at Hitler with a mixture of astonishment, repugnance and compassion. He indicated dissent, but it would have been waste of time to argue.

After coffee the talks were resumed and shortly after 4 o'clock we were able to go. Hitler came out quite civilly to see us off, and Hoffmann, the court photographer, was busy taking photographs. As soon as we had entered the special train it moved off. Neurath had a cup of tea with us and remarked that it was a pity the Führer had been tired and out of sorts, but that the visit had been useful; it was an excellent thing to bring Hitler in contact with the outside world. Having delivered these platitudes of doubtful sincerity Neurath went off to his saloon, leaving us alone. Lord Halifax confessed that Hitler had bewildered him; it was clear that he spoke a different language and it was doubtful whether the conversation had done more than might have been achieved by a talk between two men of different nations neither of whom could understand the language of the other. I thought this was true, but I also thought that Hitler had already reached a stage where any discussion or negotiation had become irksome. He felt he was wasting his time and showed that he resented it.

WELLES: "DIGNIFIED IN SPEECH AND MOVEMENT" (1940) [9]

Early in October 1939, Hitler, fresh from his lightning conquest of Poland, appealed to the British and French Governments to put an end to the war. But, in view of the fact that he offered neither suggestions for righting the wrongs done to Czechoslovakia and Poland nor convincing proof that he really wanted a just peace, his invitation was turned down. Since the Allies were incapable of mounting an offensive and the Germans were not yet ready to launch theirs, a period of quiet prevailed along the western front—a lull often referred to as the period of the "phony war." It was against this background that President Roosevelt, late in February 1940, sent U.S. Under Secretary of State Sumner Welles on a round of visits to the capitals of the belligerent nations to investigate the possibilities of re-establishing peace before the phony war erupted into a real one. As is now well known, no such possibilities existed. By the time Welles arrived in Berlin on March 1, the Wehrmacht stood poised and ready for an immediate all-out attack in the west. Nothing short of an abject acceptance by Great Britain and France of German hegemony in Europe could have stayed Hitler's hand. The following excerpt from the official report sent to President Roosevelt by Sumner Welles after his meeting with Hitler describes in great detail not only the Chancellor but also his Chancellery.

Berlin, Saturday, March 2, 1940

At eleven o'clock several Foreign Office officials, headed by Herr von Doernberg, came for me at my hotel to take me to my interview

[9] From the Report by U.S. Under Secretary of State Sumner Welles to President Franklin D. Roosevelt, March 2, 1940, *Foreign Relations of the United States: Diplomatic Papers 1940* (Washington, D.C.: Government Printing Office, 1959), I, 43–44.

with Hitler at the new Chancery, which had been completed last year within a period of eight months. Workmen had worked night and day in order to have it ready for the Chancellor's New Year's Day reception for the Diplomatic Corps so that they might have a taste of what the new Berlin was going to look like.

Kirk[10] accompanied me at my request. He had never before been permitted to see the Führer except at a distance.

The façade of the new building on the Wilhelmstrasse reminds me of a factory building. My car drove into a rectangular court with very high blank walls. At one end was a flight of broad steps leading into the Chancery. Monumental black nudes flanked the portico to which the steps led. The whole impression of the court was reminiscent of nothing other than a prison courtyard. A company of soldiers was drawn up on each side to give me the Nazi salute as I entered.

At the head of the steps I was greeted by the Reichsminister Meissner, the head of Hitler's Chancery. He spoke to me most cordially in English, as did all the other officials present.

We then formed a procession of some twenty couples headed by Meissner and myself, and with very slow and measured tread first traversed a tremendously long red marble hall, of which the walls and floor are both of marble; then up a flight of excessively slippery red-marble steps into a gallery which, also of red marble, has windows on one side and tapestries on the other. The gallery is lined on the tapestry side by an interminable series of sofas, each with a table and four chairs in front of them. From the gallery open off a series of drawing rooms. Finally, we deployed into one of these, and I was requested to sit down until the Chancellor was ready to receive me.

In a very few minutes Meissner came to announce that Hitler was ready to see me, and I went with Kirk into the adjoining room, a very long drawing-room furnished with comfortable upholstered sofas and chairs, and overlooking the garden of Bismarck's old residence, in which Hitler now lives.

Hitler received me near the door. He greeted me very pleasantly, but with great formality. Ribbentrop and Meissner [*Schmidt, the interpreter*] were the only two German officials present at the interview.

Hitler is taller than I had judged from his photographs. He has, in real life, none of the somewhat effeminate appearance of which he has been accused. He looked in excellent physical condition and in good training. His color was good, and while his eyes were tired, they were clear. He was dignified both in speech and movement, and there was not the slightest impression of the comic effect from moustache and hair which one sees in his caricatures. His voice in conversation is low and well modulated. It had only once, during our hour and a half's conversation, the raucous stridency which is heard in his speeches

---

[10] Alexander C. Kirk was the U.S. Chargé d'Affaires in Berlin.

—and it was only at that moment that his features lost their composure and that his eyes lost their decidely "gemütlich" look. He spoke with clarity and precision, and always in a beautiful German, of which I could follow every word.

SHIRER: "AFIRE WITH SCORN, ANGER, HATE, REVENGE, TRIUMPH" (1940) [11]

On November 11, 1918, in a small clearing in the Forest of Compiègne, the German Empire capitulated to France and her allies. Far away, in a German military hospital, an obscure twenty-nine-year-old soldier named Adolf Hitler was shocked and filled with grief. On June 21, 1940, barely a month after he had launched his great offensive in the west, Hitler came to the same little clearing in the woods of Compiègne to take his revenge. Covering the event for the Columbia Broadcasting System was William L. Shirer. His account of Hitler's triumph is our next selection.

Paris, June 21

The armistice negotiations began at three fifteen p.m. A warm June sun beat down on the great elm and pine trees, and cast pleasant shadows on the wooded avenues as Hitler, with the German plenipotentiaries at his side, appeared. He alighted from his car in front of the French monument to Alsace-Lorraine which stands at the end of an avenue about two hundred yards from the clearing where the armistice car[12] waits on exactly the same spot it occupied twenty-two years ago.

The Alsace-Lorraine statue, I noted, was covered with German war flags so that you could not see its sculptured work nor read its inscription. But I had seen it some years before—the large sword representing the sword of the Allies, and its point sticking into a large, limp eagle, representing the old Empire of the Kaiser. And the inscription underneath in French saying: "TO THE HEROIC SOLDIERS OF FRANCE . . . DEFENDERS OF THE COUNTRY AND OF RIGHT . . . GLORIOUS LIBERATORS OF ALSACE-LORRAINE."

Through my glasses I saw the Führer stop, glance at the monument,

[11] From William L. Shirer, *Berlin Diary: The Journal of a Foreign Correspondent 1934–1941* (New York: Alfred A. Knopf, Inc., 1941), pp. 420–22. Reprinted by permission of the author and publisher.

[12] The old railway coach (removed from a Paris museum) in which the French had dictated the terms of capitulation to a German delegation on November 11, 1918.

observe the Reich flags with their big Swastikas in the center. Then he strode slowly towards us, towards the little clearing in the woods. I observed his face. It was grave, solemn, yet brimming with revenge. There was also in it, as in his springy step, a note of the triumphant conqueror, the defier of the world. There was something else, difficult to describe, in his expression, a sort of scornful, inner joy at being present at this great reversal of fate—a reversal he himself had wrought.

Now he reaches the little opening in the woods. He pauses and looks slowly around. The clearing is in the form of a circle some two hundred yards in diameter and laid out like a park. Cypress trees line it all round—and behind them, the great elms and oaks of the forest. This has been one of France's national shrines for twenty-two years. From a discreet position on the perimeter of the circle we watch.

Hitler pauses, and gazes slowly around. In a group just behind him are the other German plenipotentiaries. . . . All the Germans are in uniform, Hitler in a double-breasted grey uniform, with the Iron Cross hanging from his left breast pocket. . . .

The time is now three eighteen p.m. Hitler's personal flag is run up on a small standard in the center of the opening.

Also in the center is a great granite block which stands some three feet above the ground. Hitler, followed by the others, walks slowly over to it, steps up, and reads the inscription engraved in great high letters on that block. It says: "HERE ON THE ELEVENTH OF NOVEMBER 1918 SUCCUMBED THE CRIMINAL PRIDE OF THE GERMAN EMPIRE . . . VANQUISHED BY THE FREE PEOPLES WHICH IT TRIED TO ENSLAVE."

Hitler reads it and Göring reads it. They all read it, standing there in the June sun and the silence. I look for the expression on Hitler's face. I am but fifty yards from him and see him through my glasses as though he were directly in front of me. I have seen that face many times at the great moments of his life. But today! It is afire with scorn, anger, hate, revenge, triumph. He steps off the monument and contrives to make even this gesture a masterpiece of contempt. He glances back at it, contemptuous, angry—angry, you almost feel, because he cannot wipe out the awful, provoking lettering with one sweep of his high Prussian boot.[13] He glances slowly around the clearing, and now, as his eyes meet ours, you grasp the depth of his hatred. But there is triumph there too—revengeful, triumphant hate. Suddenly, as though his face were not giving quite complete expression to his feelings, he throws his whole body into harmony with his mood. He swiftly snaps his hands on his hips, arches his shoulders, plants his feet wide apart. It is a magnificent gesture of defiance, of burning contempt for this

---

[13] In his history of Nazi Germany [*The Rise and Fall of the Third Reich* (New York: Simon and Schuster, Inc., 1960), p. 743], Shirer notes: "It was blown up three days later, at Hitler's command."

place now and all that it has stood for in the twenty-two years since it witnessed the humbling of the German Empire.

CIANO: "HE IS TIRED" (1942)[14]

The spring of 1942 saw Hitler approaching the pinnacle of his power. During the previous December he had dismissed the Commander in Chief of the Army, and had assumed the post himself. Hitler was now Head of State, Head of Government, Minister of War, Supreme Justice, Leader of the Nazi Party, Supreme Commander of the Armed Forces, and Commander in Chief of the Army. As if all this were not enough, he had his rubber-stamp Reichstag enact a law on April 26, 1942, that confirmed his authority to bypass existing legal regulations and to wield arbitrary power in every sphere. Hitler was now absolute master not only of Germany but also of a large portion of Europe—and the early part of 1942 was a period of continued advance in the east, of victory in north Africa, of quiet in the west. And yet there were some both within and without the Third Reich who sensed that the turn of the tide might not be far off. Neither Great Britain nor the Soviet Union had yet been defeated. On the contrary, during the winter of 1941–42 the Red Army had struck back and dealt the German Army a staggering blow. And the United States, despite a bad mauling at the hands of the Japanese, had thrown its enormous potential onto the scales against the Axis powers. Hitler continued to speak of certain victory, but those who saw him at close range were struck by the toll that the months of war had taken of his health and spirit. The following excerpts from the diary of Count Galeazzo Ciano, Mussolini's son-in-law and Italian Minister of Foreign Affairs, depict a Hitler considerably different from "the triumphant conqueror, the defier of the world" described by William L. Shirer less than two years earlier.

April 27, 1942

A long speech by Hitler. It is difficult to comment upon it because by now all his speeches are more or less alike. The tone is not very optimistic. More than anything else he looks to the past, how and why the Russian winter was so severe and they were yet able to overcome it. But there is not a hint of what all are waiting

[14] From Count Galeazzo Ciano, *The Ciano Diaries, 1939–1943*, ed. Hugh Wilson (New York: Doubleday & Company, Inc., 1946), pp. 476–79. Reprinted by permission of *The Chicago Daily News*.

for—the ending of the war. On the contrary, he declared that he is making every preparation to face the eventuality of another winter on the Russian front with more adequate forces. Then he asked for full power over the German people. He already exercises complete power, but by appealing for it in this way he has aroused the feeling that the internal situation in Germany needs a still more rigid control.

April 29–30, 1942

Arrival at Salzburg (the Puhl station). The usual scene: Hitler, Ribbentrop, the usual people, the usual ceremony. We are housed at the Klessheim Castle. This is a grandiose building, once owned by the prince-bishops of Salzburg, which has now become a guesthouse for the Führer. It is very luxurious and well arranged: furniture, hangings, carpets, all coming from France. Probably they did not pay too much for it.

There is much cordiality, which puts me on my guard. The courtesy of the Germans is always in inverse ratio to their good fortune. Hitler looks tired; he is strong, determined, and talkative. But he is tired. The winter months in Russia have borne heavily upon him. I see for the first time that he has many gray hairs.

Hitler talks with the Duce, I talk with Ribbentrop, but in two separate rooms, and the same record is played in both. . . . Napoleon, the Beresina, the drama of 1812, all this is brought to life in what he says. But the ice of Russia has been conquered by the genius of Hitler. . . .

America is a big bluff. This slogan is repeated by everyone, big and little, in the conference rooms and in the antechambers. In my opinion, the thought of what the Americans can and will do disturbs them all, and the Germans shut their eyes in order not to see. But this does not keep the more intelligent and the more honest from thinking about what America can do, and they feel shivers running down their spines. . . .

Hitler talks, talks, talks, talks. Mussolini suffers—he, who is in the habit of talking himself, and who, instead, practically has to keep quiet. On the second day, after lunch, when everything had been said, Hitler talked uninterruptedly for an hour and forty minutes. He omitted absolutely no argument: war and peace, religion and philosophy, art and history. Mussolini automatically looked at his wrist watch, I had my mind on my own business, and only Cavallero [Chief of the Italian General Staff—ED.] who is a phenomenon of servility, pretended he was listening in ecstasy, continually nodding his head in approval. Those, however, who dreaded the ordeal less than we did were the Germans. Poor people. They have to take it every day, and I am certain there isn't a gesture, a word, or a pause which they don't know by heart. General Jodl, after an epic struggle, finally went to sleep on the divan. Keitel [Chief of the German High Command— ED.] was reeling, but he succeeded in keeping his head up. He was too close to Hitler to let himself go as he would have liked to do.

PART THREE

HITLER IN HISTORY

> *More than two decades after the fall of the Third Reich no informed person disputes that Hitler was a man of infinite evil, a moral monster. Neither in Germany nor elsewhere has a revisionist school of recognized historians arisen to white-wash either Hitler or his regime. And yet few prominent figures in modern history are so easy to condemn but so difficult to explain. Consequently, while the historians' verdict on Hitler's deeds is virtually unanimous, his character, his personality, and his historical significance are the subject of considerable speculation and debate. In this section we present extracts from a representative group of recent assessments of Hitler. Although all these writers are quite specific in their condemnation of Hitler, they vary to some degree not only in their analysis of Hitler's personal character and abilities, but also in their evaluation of his role in some of the events of the period.*

10

Alan Bullock: "Hitler Will Have His Place in History . . . Alongside Attila the Hun"[1]

> *Alan Bullock, an English historian, in 1952 published the first complete biography of Hitler to appear in any language. Virtually all writing on Hitler during the last fifteen years has been dependent to some extent on Bullock's pioneer effort. Completely revised in 1962, this Oxford historian's work still stands not only as the most authoritative life of Hitler but also as one of the finest books ever written about the Nazi era.*

[1] From Alan Bullock, *Hitler: A Study in Tyranny*, completely revised ed. (New York: Harper & Row, Publishers, 1962), pp. 372–85 and "Epilogue." Copyright © 1962 by Alan Bullock. Reprinted by permission of Harper & Row, Publishers and Odhams Books Ltd.

*In the following selection Bullock brilliantly analyzes the charac-
ter of the Nazi dictator at the height of his power and offers his
assessment of Hitler's place in history.*

In the spring of 1938, on the eve of his greatest triumphs, Adolf
Hitler entered his fiftieth year. His physical appearance was un-
impressive, his bearing still awkward. The falling lock of hair and
the smudge of his moustache added nothing to a coarse and curiously
undistinguished face, in which the eyes alone attracted attention. In
appearance at least Hitler could claim to be a man of the people, a
plebeian through and through, with none of the physical characteristics of the racial superiority he was always invoking. The quality
which his face possessed was that of mobility, an ability to express the
most rapidly changing moods, at one moment smiling and charming, at another cold and imperious, cynical and sarcastic, or swollen
and livid with rage.

Speech was the essential medium of his power, not only over his
audiences but over his own temperament. Hitler talked incessantly,
often using words less to communicate his thoughts than to release the
hidden spring of his own and others' emotions, whipping himself and
his audience into anger or exaltation by the sound of his voice. Talk
had another function, too. "Words," he once said, "build bridges into
unexplored regions." As he talked, conviction would grow until
certainty came and the problem was solved.

Hitler always showed a distrust of argument and criticism. Unable
to argue coolly himself, since his early days in Vienna his one resort
had been to shout his opponent down. The questioning of his assumptions or of his facts rattled him and threw him out of his stride,
less because of any intellectual inferiority than because words, and
even facts, were to him not a means of rational communication and
logical analysis, but devices for manipulating emotion. The introduc-
tion of intellectual processes of criticism and analysis marked the
intrusion of hostile elements which disturbed the exercise of this
power. Hence Hitler's hatred of the intellectual. . . .

As an orator Hitler had obvious faults. The timbre of his voice ·
was harsh, very different from the beautiful quality of Goebbels's.
He spoke at too great length; was often repetitive and verbose; lacked
lucidity and frequently lost himself in cloudy phrases. These short-
comings, however, mattered little beside the extraordinary impression
of force, the immediacy of passion, the intensity of hatred, fury, and
menace conveyed by the sound of the voice alone without regard
to what he said.

One of the secrets of his mastery over a great audience was his

instinctive sensitivity to the mood of a crowd, a flair for divining the
hidden passions, resentments and longings in their minds. . . .

Hitler's power to bewitch an audience has been likened to the
occult arts of the African medicine-man or the Asiatic Shaman; others
have compared it to the sensitivity of a medium, and the magnetism
of a hypnotist.

The conversations recorded by Hermann Rauschning for the period
1932–4,[2] and by the table talk at the Führer's H.Q. for the period
1941–2, reveal Hitler in another favorite role, that of visionary and
prophet. This was the mood in which Hitler indulged, talking far
into the night, in his house on the Obersalzberg, surrounded by the
remote peaks and silent forests of the Bavarian Alps; or in the Eyrie
he had built six thousand feet up on the Kehlstein, above the Berghof,
approached only by a mountain road blasted through the rock and a
lift guarded by doors of bronze. There he would elaborate his fabulous
schemes for a vast empire embracing the Eurasian Heartland of the
geopoliticians; his plans for breeding a new élite biologically pre-
selected; his design for reducing whole nations to slavery in the foundation of his new empire. Such dreams had fascinated Hitler since he
wrote *Mein Kampf*. It was easy in the late 1920's and early 1930's to
dismiss them as the product of a disordered and over-heated imagination soaked in the political romanticism of Wagner and Houston
Stewart Chamberlain. But these were still the themes of Hitler's table
talk in 1941–2 and by then, master of the greater part of Europe and
on the eve (as he believed) of conquering Russia and the Ukraine,
Hitler had shown that he was capable of translating his fantasies into
a terrible reality. The invasion of Russia, the S.S. extermination
squads, the planned elimination of the Jewish race; the treatment of
the Poles and Russians, the Slav *Untermenschen*—these, too, were
the fruits of Hitler's imagination.

All this combines to create a picture of which the best description
is Hitler's own famous sentence: "I go the way that Providence dictates
with the assurance of a sleepwalker." The former French Ambassador
speaks of him as "a man possessed"; Hermann Rauschning writes:
'Dostoyevsky might well have invented him, with the morbid derange-
ment and the pseudo-creativeness of his hysteria"; one of the Defense
Counsel at the Nuremberg Trials, Dr. Dix, quoted a passage from
Goethe's *Dichtung und Wahrheit* describing the Demoniac and applied this very aptly to Hitler. With Hitler, indeed, one is un-
comfortably aware of never being far from the realm of the irrational.

But this is only half the truth about Hitler, for the baffling problem
about this strange figure is to determine the degree to which he was
swept along by a genuine belief in his own inspiration and the degree

[2] See Bibliographical Note, p. 174.

to which he deliberately exploited the irrational side of human nature, both in himself and others, with a shrewd calculation. For it is salutary to recall, before accepting the Hitler Myth at anything like its face value, that it was Hitler who invented the myth, assiduously cultivating and manipulating it for his own ends. So long as he did this he was brilliantly successful; it was when he began to believe in his own magic, and accept the myth of himself as true, that his flair faltered.

So much has been made of the charismatic nature of Hitler's leadership that it is easy to forget the astute and cynical politician in him. It is this mixture of calculation and fanaticism, with the difficulty of telling where one ends and the other begins, which is the peculiar characteristic of Hitler's personality: to ignore or underestimate either element is to present a distorted picture.

The link between the different sides of Hitler's character was his extraordinary capacity for self-dramatization. . . . Again and again one is struck by the way in which, having once decided rationally on a course of action, Hitler would whip himself into a passion which enabled him to bear down all opposition, and provided him with the motive power to enforce his will on others. . . .

One of Hitler's most habitual devices was to place himself on the defensive, to accuse those who opposed or obstructed him of aggression and malice, and to pass rapidly from a tone of outraged innocence to the full thunders of moral indignation. It was always the other side who were to blame, and in turn he denounced the Communists, the Jews, the Republican Government, or the Czechs, the Poles, and the Bolsheviks for their "intolerable" behavior which forced him to take drastic action in self-defense.

Hitler in a rage appeared to lose all control of himself. His face became mottled and swollen with fury, he screamed at the top of his voice, spitting out a stream of abuse, waving his arms wildly and drumming on the table or the wall with his fists. As suddenly as he had begun he would stop, smooth down his hair, straighten his collar and resume a more normal voice.

This skilful and deliberate exploitation of his own temperament extended to other moods than anger. When he wanted to persuade or win someone over he could display great charm. Until the last days of his life he retained an uncanny gift of personal magnetism which defies analysis, but which many who met him have described. This was connected with the curious power of his eyes, which are persistently said to have had some sort of hypnotic quality. Similarly, when he wanted to frighten or shock, he showed himself a master of brutal and threatening language. . . .

Yet another variation in his roles was the impression of concentrated will-power and intelligence, the leader in complete command of the situation and with a knowledge of the facts which dazzled the generals or ministers summoned to receive his orders. To sustain this part he drew on his remarkable memory, which enabled him to reel off complicated orders of battle, technical specifications and long lists of names and dates without a moment's hesitation. Hitler cultivated this gift of memory assiduously. The fact that subsequently the details and figures which he cited were often found to contain inaccuracies did not matter: it was the immediate effect at which he aimed. The swiftness of the transition from one mood to another was startling: one moment his eyes would be filled with tears and pleading, the next blazing with fury, or glazed with the faraway look of the visionary.

Hitler, in fact, was a consummate actor, with the actor's and orator's facility for absorbing himself in a role and convincing himself of the truth of what he was saying at the time he said it. In his early years he was often awkward and unconvincing, but with practice the part became second nature to him, and with the immense prestige of success behind him, and the resources of a powerful state at his command, there were few who could resist the impression of the piercing eyes, the Napoleonic pose, and the "historic" personality.

Hitler had the gift of all great politicians for grasping the possibilities of a situation more swiftly than his opponents. He saw, as no other politician did, how to play on the grievances and resentments of the German people, as later he was to play on French and British fear of war and fear of Communism. His insistence upon preserving the forms of legality in the struggle for power showed a brilliant understanding of the way to disarm opposition, just as the way in which he undermined the independence of the German Army showed his grasp of the weaknesses of the German Officer Corps.

A German word, *Fingerspitzengefühl*—"finger-tip feeling"—which was often applied to Hitler, well describes his sense of opportunity and timing. . . .

Until he was convinced that the right moment had come Hitler would find a hundred excuses for procrastination. . . . Once he had made up his mind to move, however, he would act boldly, taking considerable risks. . . .

Surprise was a favorite gambit of Hitler's, in politics, diplomacy, and war: he gauged the psychological effect of sudden, unexpected hammer-blows in paralyzing opposition. . . .

No régime in history has ever paid such careful attention to psychological factors in politics. Hitler was a master of mass emotion. To attend one of his big meetings was to go through an emotional experience, not to listen to an argument or a program. Yet nothing was left to chance on these occasions. Every device for heightening the emotional intensity, every trick of the theater was used. . . . Paradoxically, the man who was most affected by such spectacles was their originator, Hitler himself, and . . . they played an indispensable part in the process of self-intoxication.

Hitler had grasped as no one before him what could be done with a combination of propaganda and terrorism. For the complement to the attractive power of the great spectacles was the compulsive power of the Gestapo, the S.S., and the concentration camp, heightened once again by skilful propaganda. . . .

In making use of the formidable power which was thus placed in his hands Hitler had one supreme, and fortunately rare, advantage: he had neither scruples nor inhibitions. He was a man without roots, with neither home nor family; a man who admitted no loyalties, was bound by no traditions, and felt respect neither for God nor man. Throughout his career Hitler showed himself prepared to seize any advantage that was to be gained by lying, cunning, treachery, and unscrupulousness. He demanded the sacrifice of millions of German lives for the sacred cause of Germany, but in the last year of the war was ready to destroy Germany rather than surrender his power or admit defeat.

Wary and secretive, he entertained a universal distrust. He admitted no one to his counsels. He never let down his guard, or gave himself away. . . . Only the Führer kept all the threads in his hand and saw the whole design. If ever a man exercised absolute power it was Adolf Hitler. . . .

No word was more frequently on Hitler's lips than "will," and his whole career from 1919 to 1945 is a remarkable achievement of willpower.

To say that Hitler was ambitious scarcely describes the intensity of the lust for power and the craving to dominate which consumed him. It was the will to power in its crudest and purest form, not identifying itself with the triumph of a principle as with Lenin or Robespierre —for the only principle of Nazism was power and domination for its own sake—nor finding satisfaction in the fruits of power, for, by comparison with other Nazi leaders like Göring, Hitler lived an ascetic life. For a long time Hitler succeeded in identifying his own power with the recovery of Germany's old position in the world, and there were many in the 1930's who spoke of him as a fanatical patriot. But as soon as the interests of Germany began to diverge from his own, from the beginning of 1943 onwards, his patriotism was seen at its true value—Germany, like everything else in the world, was only a means, a vehicle for his own power, which he would sacrifice with the same indifference as the lives of those he sent to the Eastern Front. By its nature this was an insatiable appetite, securing only a temporary gratification by the exercise of power, then restlessly demanding an ever further extension of it.

Although, looking backwards, it is possible to detect anticipations of this monstrous will to power in Hitler's early years, it remained latent until the end of the First World War and only began to appear noticeably when he reached his thirties. From the account in *Mein Kampf* it appears that the shock of defeat and the Revolution of November 1918 produced a crisis in which hitherto dormant faculties were awakened and directed towards the goal of becoming a politician and founding a new movement. Resentment is so marked in Hitler's attitude as to suggest that it was from the earlier experiences of his Vienna and Munich days, before the war, that there sprang a compelling urge to revenge himself upon a world which had slighted and ignored him. Hatred, touchiness, vanity are characteristics upon which those who spent any time in his company constantly remark. Hatred intoxicated Hitler. . . .

No less striking was his constant need of praise. His vanity was inappeasable, and the most fulsome flattery was received as no more than his due. The atmosphere of adulation in which he lived seems to have deadened the critical faculties of all who came into it. The most banal platitudes and the most grotesque errors of taste and judgment, if uttered by the Führer, were accepted as the words of inspired genius. . . .

Cynical though he was, Hitler's cynicism stopped short of his own person: he came to believe that he was a man with a mission, marked out by Providence, and therefore exempt from the ordinary canons of human conduct.

Hitler probably held some such belief about himself from an early period. It was clear enough in the speech he made at his trial in 1924, and after he came out of prison those near him noticed that he began to hold aloof, to set a barrier between himself and his followers. After he came to power it became more noticeable. It was in March 1936, that he made the famous assertion already quoted: "I go the way that Providence dictates with the assurance of a sleep-walker." . . .

It was in this sense of mission that Hitler, a man who believed neither in God nor in conscience ("a Jewish invention, a blemish like circumcision"), found both justification and absolution. He was the Siegfried come to reawaken Germany to greatness, for whom morality, suffering and "the litany of private virtues" were irrelevant. It was by such dreams that he sustained the ruthlessness and determination of his will. So long as this sense of mission was balanced by the cynical calculations of the politician, it represented a source of strength, but success was fatal. When half Europe lay at his feet and all need of restraint was removed, Hitler abandoned himself entirely to megalomania. He became convinced of his own infallibility. But when he began to look to the image he had created to work miracles of its own accord—instead of exploiting it—his gifts deteriorated and his intuition deluded him. Ironically, failure sprang from the same capacity which brought him success, his power of self-dramatization, his ability to convince himself. His belief in his power to work miracles kept him going when the more sceptical Mussolini faltered. Hitler played out his "world-historical" role to the bitter end. But it was this same belief which curtained him in illusion and blinded him to what was actually happening, leading him into that arrogant overestimate of his own genius which brought him to defeat. The sin which Hitler committed was that which the ancient Greeks called *hybris,* the sin of overweening pride, of believing himself to be more than a man. No man was ever more surely destroyed by the image he had created than Adolf Hitler.

* * *

Many attempts have been made to explain away the importance of Hitler, from Chaplin's brilliant caricature in *The Great Dictator* to the much less convincing picture of Hitler the pawn, a front man for German capitalism. Others have argued that Hitler was nothing in himself, only a symbol of the restless ambition of the German nation to dominate Europe; a creature flung to the top by the tides of revolutionary change, or the embodiment of the collective unconscious of a people obsessed with violence and death.

These arguments seem to me to be based upon a confusion of two different questions. Obviously, Nazism was a complex phenomenon to which many factors—social, economic, historical, psychological—contributed. But whatever the explanation of this episode in European history—and it can be no simple one—that does not answer the question . . . , what was the part played by Hitler. It may be true that a mass movement, strongly nationalist, anti-Semitic, and radical, would have sprung up in Germany without Hitler. But so far as what actually happened is concerned—not what might have happened—the evidence seems to me to leave no doubt that no other man played a role in the Nazi revolution or in the history of the Third Reich remotely comparable with that of Adolf Hitler.

The conception of the Nazi Party, the propaganda with which it must appeal to the German people, and the tactics by which it would come to power—these were unquestionably Hitler's. After 1934 there were no rivals left and by 1938 he had removed the last checks on his freedom of action. Thereafter, he exercised an arbitrary rule in Germany to a degree rarely, if ever, equalled in a modern industrialized state.

At the same time, from the remilitarization of the Rhineland to the invasion of Russia, he won a series of successes in diplomacy and war which established an hegemony over the continent of Europe comparable with that of Napoleon at the height of his fame. While these could not have been won without a people and an Army willing to serve him, it was Hitler who provided the indispensable leadership, the flair for grasping opportunities, the boldness in using them. In retrospect his mistakes appear obvious, and it is easy to be complacent about the inevitability of his defeat; but it took the combined efforts of the three most powerful nations in the world to break his hold on Europe.

Luck and the disunity of his opponents will account for much of Hitler's success—as it will of Napoleon's—but not for all. He began with few advantages, a man without a name and without support other than that which he acquired for himself, not even a citizen of the country he aspired to rule. To achieve what he did Hitler needed —and possessed—talents out of the ordinary which in sum amounted to political genius, however evil its fruits.

His abilities have been sufficiently described . . . : his mastery of the irrational factors in politics, his insight into the weaknesses of his opponents, his gift for simplification, his sense of timing, his willingness to take risks. An opportunist entirely without principle, he showed both consistency and an astonishing power of will in pursuing his aims. Cynical and calculating in the exploitation of his histrionic gifts, he retained an unshaken belief in his historic role and in himself as a creature of destiny.

The fact that his career ended in failure, and that his defeat was pre-eminently due to his own mistakes, does not by itself detract from Hitler's claim to greatness. The flaw lies deeper. For these remarkable powers were combined with an ugly and strident egotism, a moral and intellectual cretinism. The passions which ruled Hitler's mind were ignoble: hatred, resentment, the lust to dominate, and, where he could not dominate, to destroy. His career did not exalt but debased the human condition, and his twelve years' dictatorship was barren of all ideas save one—the further extension of his own power and that of the nation with which he had identified himself. Even power he conceived of in the crudest terms: an endless vista of military roads, S.S. garrisons, and concentration camps to sustain the rule of the Aryan "master race" over the degraded subject peoples of his new empire in the east.

The great revolutions of the past, whatever their ultimate fate, have been identified with the release of certain powerful ideas: individual conscience, liberty, equality, national freedom, social justice. National Socialism produced nothing. Hitler constantly exalted force over the power of ideas and delighted to prove that men were governed by cupidity, fear, and their baser passions. The sole theme of the Nazi revolution was domination, dressed up as the doctrine of race, and, failing that, a vindictive destructiveness, Rauschning's *Revolution des Nihilismus.*

It is this emptiness, this lack of anything to justify the suffering he caused rather than his own monstrous and ungovernable will which makes Hitler both so repellent and so barren a figure. Hitler will have his place in history, but it will be alongside Attila the Hun, the barbarian king who was surnamed, not "the Great," but "the Scourge of God," and who boasted "in a saying," Gibbon writes, "worthy of his ferocious pride, that the grass never grew on the spot where his horse had stood."

The view has often been expressed that Hitler could only have come to power in Germany, and it is true—without falling into the same error of racialism as the Nazis—that there were certain features of German historical development, quite apart from the effects of the Defeat and the Depression, which favored the rise of such a movement.

This is not accuse the Germans of Original Sin, or to ignore the other sides of German life which were only grossly caricatured by the Nazis. But Nazism was not some terrible accident which fell upon the German people out of a blue sky. It was rooted in their history, and while it is true that a majority of the German people never voted for Hitler, it is also true that thirteen millions did. Both facts need to be remembered.

From this point of view Hitler's career may be described as a *reductio ad absurdum* of the most powerful political tradition in Germany since the Unification. This is what nationalism, militarism, authoritarianism, the worship of success and force, the exaltation of the State, and *Realpolitik* lead to, if they are projected to their logical conclusion.

There are Germans who reject such a view. They argue that what was wrong with Hitler was that he lacked the necessary skill, that he was a bungler. If only he had listened to the generals—or Schacht—or the career diplomats—if only he had not attacked Russia, and so on. There is some point, they feel, at which he went wrong. They refuse to see that it was the ends themselves, not simply the means, which were wrong: the pursuit of unlimited power, the scorn for justice or any restraint on power; the exaltation of will over reason and conscience; the assertion of an arrogant supremacy, the contempt for others' rights. As at least one German historian, Professor Meinecke, has recognized,[3] the catastrophe to which Hitler led Germany points to the need to re-examine the aims as well as the methods of German policy as far back as Bismarck.

[3] This is a reference to Friedrich Meinecke (1862–1954) and his book, *The German Catastrophe*, trans. S. B. Fay (Cambridge, Mass.: Harvard University Press, 1950; Boston: Beacon Press Paperback, 1963).

The Germans, however, were not the only people who preferred in the 1930's not to know what was happening and refused to call evil things by their true names. The British and French at Munich; the Italians, Germany's partners in the Pact of Steel; the Poles, who stabbed the Czechs in the back over Teschen; the Russians, who signed the Nazi-Soviet Pact to partition Poland, all thought they could buy Hitler off, or use him to their own selfish advantage. They did not succeed, any more than the German Right or the German Army. In the bitterness of war and occupation they were forced to learn the truth of the words of John Donne which Ernest Hemingway set at the beginning of his novel of the Spanish Civil War:

> No man is an Iland, intire of it selfe; every man is a peece of the Continent, a part of the maine; If a clod bee washed away by the Sea, Europe is the lesse, as well as if a Promontorie were, as well as if a Mannor of thy friends or of thine own were; Any man's death diminishes me, because I am involved in Mankinde; And therefore never send to know for whom the bell tolls; It tolls for thee.

Hitler, indeed, was a European, no less than a German phenomenon. The conditions and the state of mind which he exploited, the *malaise* of which he was the symptom, were not confined to one country, although they were more strongly marked in Germany than anywhere else. Hitler's idiom was German, but the thoughts and emotions to which he gave expression have a more universal currency.

Hitler recognized this relationship with Europe perfectly clearly. He was in revolt against "the System" not just in Germany but in Europe, against the liberal bourgeois order, symbolized for him in the Vienna which had once rejected him. To destroy this was his mission, the mission in which he never ceased to believe; and in this, the most deeply felt of his purposes, he did not fail. Europe may rise again, but the old Europe of the years between 1789, the year of the French Revolution, and 1939, the year of Hitler's War, has gone for ever—and the last figure in its history is that of Adolf Hitler, the architect of its ruin. *"Si monumentum requiris, circumspice"*—"If you seek his monument, look around."

11

Ernst Nolte: "Lord and Master of His Troubled Era"—A Psychological Portrait[1]

Whether or not Hitler was abnormal or mentally ill in a clinical sense is a matter of dispute. Beyond question, however, his emotional make-up contained elements that exceeded the bounds of what is commonly called "normal." Ernst Nolte, a German philosopher-turned-historian, is the author of an ambitious study of fascism in which he presents a provocative, if somewhat tentative, psychological portrait of Adolf Hitler.

[In Hitler] certain dominant traits came to the fore which, although they cannot immediately be dubbed "abnormal," did approach the abnormal and are best described in psychopathological terms. . . .

The fact that, according to August Kubizek, the friend of his youth, Hitler's favorite stories were legends of German heroes, that he steeped himself in the world of those ancient times and identified himself with their heroes, was no doubt something he had in common with innumerable boys of his age. The fact that he designed a magnificent house in the Renaissance style for the woman he silently adored from afar merely put him on a level with a smaller group of young men. But that he should plan, down to the last detail, a luxurious apartment for himself and his friend in the firm hope of winning a lottery, that he should mentally engage an "exceptionally refined elderly lady" as receptionist and tutor for the two art students, that after the disillusionment of the lottery drawing he should passionately and in all seriousness inveigh against the lottery in particular and the world in general—this must have removed him some considerable distance from the majority of even the most fanciful of his age group.

[1] From Ernst Nolte, *Three Faces of Fascism: Action Française, Italian Fascism, National Socialism,* trans. Leila Vennewitz (New York: Holt, Rinehart & Winston, Inc., 1966), pp. 288–94. First published in Germany under the title: *Der Faschismus in seiner Epoche: Die Action Française, Der italienische Faschismus, Der Nationalsozialismus* (Munich: R. Piper & Co. Verlag, 1963). Translation © 1965 by R. Piper & Co. Verlag. Reprinted by permission of Holt, Rinehart & Winston, Inc., and Weidenfeld & Nicolson, Ltd.

Moreover, this extraordinary capacity for wishful thinking, this min-gling of reality and dream, did not diminish with time. Scarcely had one of his companions in a Vienna men's hostel described certain tech-nical plans, of direct concern to him as a future engineer, than Hitler already saw himself part owner of the firm "Greiner & Hitler, Airplane Construction." In *Hitler's Table Talk* (published in America as *Hit-ler's Secret Conversations*), Hitler speaks of the poverty of that period of his life. "But in my imagination I dwelled in palaces." It was dur-ing that time, he said, that he drew up the first plans for the remodel-ing of Berlin.

There are many witnesses to the fact that during his time of strug-gle he was already living in the Third Reich, untouched by doubts of any kind, impervious to counsels of moderation, devoid of any desire for sober assessment and calculation. . . .

When he was in the throes of remodeling Berlin and Linz, his plans were far from exhausted. The new Reich Chancellery had to be so vast that all would recognize it immediately as the seat of the "master of the world," and by comparison St. Peter's would seem a mere toy. No turn of events in the war could shake the power of this desire, this vision, nor was its force of conviction affected by the fact that this dream was just as divorced from reality as it had been during his youth.

In January, 1945, the *Gauleiter* of Danzig came to Hitler, disheart-ened and full of defiant resolve to confront Hitler with the whole truth about the desperate situation of his city. He left the room, ac-cording to the secretary, a changed man, miraculously cheered and encouraged: the Führer had promised him relief. There was no relief anywhere in sight, but Hitler saw it in his mind's eye and was able to convince a man with perfect vision that he was blind.

As late as March, 1945, his secretary saw him standing interminably in front of the wooden model of the future city of Linz. He was still dreaming the dreams of his youth.

The dominant trait in Hitler's personality was infantilism. It ex-plains the most prominent as well as the strangest of his characteristics and actions. The frequently awesome consistency of his thoughts and behavior must be seen in conjunction with the stupendous force of his rage, which reduced field marshals to trembling nonentities. If at the age of fifty he built the Danube bridge in Linz down to the last detail exactly as he had designed it at the age of fifteen before the eyes of his astonished boyhood friend, this was not a mark of con-sistency in a mature man, one who has learned and pondered, criticized and been criticized, but the stubbornness of the child who is aware of nothing except himself and his mental image and to whom time means nothing because childishness has not been broken and forced into the sober give-and-take of the adult world. Hitler's rage was the uncontrollable fury of the child who bangs the chair because the chair refuses to do as it is told; his dreaded harshness, which nonchalantly sent millions of people to their death, was much closer to the rambling imaginings of a boy than to the iron grasp of a man, and is therefore intimately and typically related to his profound aversion to the cruelty of hunting, vivisection, and the consumption of meat generally.

And how close to the sinister is the grotesque! The first thing Hitler did after being released from the Landsberg prison was to buy a Mercedes for twenty-six thousand marks—the car he had been dreaming of while serving his sentence. Until 1933 he insisted on passing every car on the road. In Vienna alone he had heard *Tristan and Isolde* between thirty and forty times, and had time as chancellor to see six performances of *The Merry Widow* in as many months. Nor was this all. According to Otto Dietrich he reread all Karl May's boys' adventure books during 1933 and 1934, and this is perfectly credible since in *Hitler's Table Talk* he bestowed high praise on this author and credited him with no less than opening his eyes to the world.[2] It is in the conversations related in *Hitler's Table Talk* that he treated his listeners to such frequent and vindictive schoolboy reminiscences that it seems as if this man never emerged from his boyhood and completely lacked the experience of time and its broadening, reconciling powers.

The monomaniacal element in Hitler's nature is obviously closely related to his infantilism. It is based largely on his elemental urge toward tangibility, intelligibility, simplicity. In *Mein Kampf* he expressed the maxim that the masses should never be shown more than *one* enemy. He was himself the most loyal exponent of this precept, and not from motives of tactical calculation alone. He never allowed himself to face more than one enemy at a time; on this enemy he concentrated all the hatred of which he was so inordinately capable, and it was this that enabled him during this period to show the other enemies a reassuring and "subjectively" sincere face. During the crisis in Czechoslovakia he even forgot the Jews over Beneš. His enemy was always concrete and personal, never merely the expression but also the cause of an obscure or complex event. The Weimar system was caused by the "November criminals," the predicament of the Germans in Austria by the Hapsburgs, capitalism and bolshevism equally by the Jews.

A good example of the emergence and function of the clearly defined hate figure, which took the place of the causal connection he really had in mind, is to be found in *Mein Kampf*. Here Hitler draws a vivid picture of the miseries of proletarian existence as he came to know it in Vienna—deserted, frustrated, devoid of hope. This descrip-

[2] Karl May, a German author, wrote juvenile adventure books about the American west—which he had never visited.

tion seems to lead inevitably to an obvious conclusion: that these people, if they were not wholly insensible, were bound to be led with compelling logic to the socialist doctrine, to their "lack of patriotism," their hatred of religion, their merciless indictment of the ruling class. It should, however, have also led to a self-critical insight: that the only reason he remained so aloof from the collective emotions of these masses was because he had enjoyed a different upbringing, middle-class and provincial, because despite his poverty he never really worked, and because he was not married. Nothing of the kind! When he was watching spellbound one day as the long column of demonstrating workers wound its way through the streets, his first query was about the "wirepullers." His voracity for reading, his allegedly thorough study of Marxist theories, did not spur him on to cast his gaze beyond the frontier and realize that such demonstrations were taking place in every city in Europe, or to take note of the "rabble-rousing" articles of a certain Mussolini, which he would doubtless have regarded as "spiritual vitriol" like those in the *Arbeiterzeitung*.

What Hitler discovered was the many Jewish names among the leaders of Austrian Marxism, and now the scales fell from his eyes—at last he saw who it was who, beside the Hapsburgs, wanted to wipe out the German element in Austria. Now he began to preach his conclusions to his first audiences; now he was no longer speaking, as until recently he had spoken to Kubizek, to hear the sound of his own voice: he wanted to convince. But he did not have much success. The management of the men's hostel looked on him as an insufferable politicizer, and for most of his fellow inmates he was a "reactionary swine." He got beaten up by workers, and in conversations with Jews and Social Democrats he was evidently often the loser, being no match for their diabolical glibness and dialectic. This made the image of the archenemy appear all the more vivid to him, all the more firmly entrenched. Thirty years later the most experienced statesmen took him for a confidence-inspiring statesman after meeting him personally; hard-bitten soldiers found he was a man they could talk to; educated supporters saw in him the people's social leader. Hitler himself, however, made the following observations in the presence of the generals and party leaders around his table: though Dietrich Eckart had considered that from many aspects Streicher was a fool, it was impossible to conquer the masses without such people, . . . though Streicher[3] was criticized for his paper, *Der Stürmer*; in actual fact Streicher idealized the Jew. The Jew was far more ignoble, unruly, and diabolical than Streicher had depicted him.

Hitler rose from the gutter to be the master of Europe. There is no doubt that he learned an enormous amount. In the flexible outer layer of his personality he could be all things to all men: a statesman

---

[3] Julius Streicher, *Gauleiter* of Franconia, was the publisher of *Der Stürmer*, a semipornographic, virulently anti-Semitic hate sheet.

to the statesmen, a commander to the generals, a charmer to women, a father to the people. But in the hard monomaniacal core of his being he did not change one iota from Vienna to Rastenburg.[4]

Yet if his people had found that he intended after the war to prohibit smoking and make the world of the future vegetarian it is probable that even the SS would have rebelled. There are thousands of monomaniacal and infantile types in every large community, but they seldom play a role other than among their own kind. These two traits do not explain how Hitler was able to rise to power.

August Kubizek tells a strange story which there is little reason to doubt and which sheds as much light on the moment when Hitler decided to enter politics as on the basis and prospects of that decision. After a performance of *Rienzi* in Linz, Kubizek relates, Hitler had taken him up to a nearby hill and talked to him with shining eyes and trembling voice of the mandate he would one day receive from his people to lead them out of servitude to the heights of liberty. It seemed as if another self were speaking from Hitler's lips, as if he himself were looking on at what was happening in numb astonishment. Here the infantile basis is once again unmistakable. The identification with the hero of the dramatic opera bore him aloft, erupted from him like a separate being. There were many subsequent occasions testifying to this very process. When Hitler chatted, his manner of talking was often unbearably flat; when he described something, it was dull; when he theorized, it was stilted; when he started up a hymn of hate, repulsive. But time and again his speeches contained passages of irresistible force and compelling conviction, such as no other speaker of his time was capable of producing. These are always the places where his "faith" finds expression, and it was obviously this faith which induced that emotion among the masses to which even the most hostile observer testified. But at no time do these passages reveal anything new, never do they make the listener reflect or exert his critical faculty: all they ever do is conjure up magically before his eyes that which already existed in him as vague feeling, inarticulate longing. . . .

His behavior at a rally has often been described: how, uncertain at first, he would rely on the trivial, then get the feel of the atmosphere for several minutes, slowly establish contact, score a bull's eye, with the right phrase, gather momentum with the applause, finally burst out with words which seemed positively to erupt through him, and at the end, in the midst of thunderous cheering, shout a vow to heaven, or amid breathless silence, bring forth a solemn Amen. And after the speech he was as wet as if he had taken a steambath and had lost as much weight as if he had been through a week's strict training.

He told every rally what it wanted to hear—yet what he voiced was

---

[4] The military headquarters in East Prussia at which Hitler spent most of his time during the later war years.

not the trivial interests and desires of the day but the great universal, obvious hopes: that Germany should once again become what it had been, that the economy should function, that the farmer should get his rights, likewise the townsman, the worker, and the employer, that they should forget their differences and become one in the most important thing of all—their love for Germany. He never embarked on discussion, he permitted no heckling, he never dealt with any of the day-to-day problems of politics. When he knew that a rally was in a critical mood and wanted information instead of *Weltanschauung*, he was capable of calling off his speech at the last moment.

There should be no doubt as to the mediumistic trait in Hitler. He was the medium who communicated to the masses their own, deeply buried spirit. It was because of this, not because of his monomaniacal obsession, that a third of his people loved him long before he became chancellor, long before he was their victorious supreme commander. But mediumistic popular idols are usually simpletons fit for ecstasy rather than fulfillment. In the turmoil of postwar Germany it would have been *impossible* to love Hitler had not monomaniacal obsession driven the man on and infantile wishful thinking carried him beyond the workaday world with its problems and conflicts. Singly, any one of these three characteristics would have made Hitler a freak and a fool; combined, they raised him for a brief time to be lord and master of his troubled era.

A psychological portrait of Hitler such as this must, however, give rise to doubts in more ways than one. Does the portrait not approach that overpolemical and oversimplified talk of the "madman" or the "criminal"? There is no intention of claiming that this represents a clinical diagnosis. It is not even the purpose of this analysis to define and categorize Hitler as an "infantile mediumistic monomaniac." What has been discussed is merely the existence of infantile, mediumistic, and monomaniacal traits. They are not intended to exhaust the nature of the man Hitler, nor do they of themselves belong to the field of the medically abnormal. Rather do they represent individually an indispensable ingredient of the exceptional. There can be few artists without a streak of infantilism, few ideological politicians without a monomaniacal element in their make-up. It is not so much the potency of each element singly as the combination of all three which gives Hitler his unique face. Whether this combination is pathological in the clinical sense is very doubtful, but there can be no doubt that it excludes historical greatness in the traditional sense.

A second objection is that the psychological description prevents the sociological typification which from the point of view of history is so much more productive. Many attempts have been made to understand Hitler as typical of the angry petit bourgeois. The snag in this interpretation is that it cannot stand without a psychologizing adjective and almost always suggests a goal which is obviously psychological as well as polemical. What this theory tries to express is that Hitler was "actually only a petit bourgeois," in other words, something puny and contemptible. But it is precisely from the psychological standpoint that the petit bourgeois can best be defined as the normal image of the "adult": Hitler was exactly the reverse. What is correct, however, is that, from the sociological standpoint, bourgeois elements may be present in an entirely nonbourgeois psychological form. It remains to be shown how very petit bourgeois was Hitler's immediate reaction to Marxism. However, it was only by means of that "form" which cannot be deduced by sociological methods that his first reaction underwent its momentous transformation.

The third objection is the most serious. The historical phenomenon of National Socialism might be considered overparticularized if it is based solely on the unusual, not to say abnormal, personality of one man. Does not this interpretation in the final analysis even approach that all too transparent apologia which tries to see in Hitler, and only in him, the "*causa efficiens* of the whole sequence of events"? But this is not necessarily logical. It is only from one aspect that the infantile person is more remote from the world than other people; from another aspect he is much closer to it. For he does not dredge up the stuff of his dreams and longings out of nothing; on the contrary, he compresses the world of his more normal fellow men, sometimes by intensifying, sometimes by contrasting. From the complexity of life, monomaniacal natures often wrest an abstruse characteristic, quite frequently a comical aspect, but at times a really essential element. However, the mediumistic trait guarantees that nothing peripheral is compressed, nothing trivial monomaniacally grasped. It is not that a nature of this kind particularizes the historical, but that this nature is itself brought into focus by the historical. Although far from being a true mirror of the times—indeed, it is more of a monstrous distortion—nothing goes into it that is pure invention; and what does go into it arises from certain traits of its own. Hitler sometimes compared himself to a magnet which attracted all that was brave and heroic; it would probably be more accurate to say that certain extreme characteristics of the era attracted this nature like magnets, to become in that personality even more extreme and visible. . . . In this sense Hitler's nature may be called a historical substance.

12

A. J. P. Taylor: "The End-Product of a Civilization of Clever Talk"[1]

In 1961, A. J. P. Taylor, one of Great Britain's lead-
ing historians, published a diplomatic history of the inter-war
years entitled The Origins of the Second World War. *The ap-*
pearance of the book provoked a bitter intellectual and political
controversy, for Taylor's central thesis was that the war of 1939
was the result not of Hitler's design but of blunders committed
by both sides. Moreover, Taylor's portrayal of Hitler as a "tradi-
tional" German statesman no different in either methods or ideas
from those that preceded him was widely regarded as both a
whitewashing of Hitler and an apologia for the Nazi regime.
In actual fact, Taylor—despite his flawed and perverse book—is
neither pro-Hitler nor pro-Nazi. He is, however, the nearest thing
to a revisionist of the orthodox view of Hitler that reputable his-
torical scholarship has yet produced. In Origins, *Taylor under-*
standably concentrates on Hitler as a diplomat, and he has little
to say about the Führer's character or domestic policy. In a more
recent work, an interpretive history of Europe between 1914 and
1945, Taylor provides a brief and somewhat flippant, but more
rounded assessment of Hitler. In the following excerpt from this
book, it will be seen that Taylor differs from his Oxford col-
league, Alan Bullock, in the emphasis he places on Hitler's lack
of uniqueness. He regards Hitler not so much as a political genius
or a latter-day Attila the Hun as a creation of German history
and a reflection of his time.

Most societies have an underworld of crackpots and layabouts.
German National Socialism was transformed into a mighty force by
a single man, its Leader, Adolf Hitler. He was the Unknown Soldier,
the little man of Chaplin's inspiration, come to life and turned sour.
His mind was a junk-store of tired, second-hand ideas, which he re-

[1] From A. J. P. Taylor, *From Sarajevo to Potsdam* (London: Thames and Hudson
International, Ltd., 1966; New York: Harcourt, Brace & World, Inc., 1966), pp. 131–
37. Copyright © 1966 by Thames and Hudson International, Ltd. Reprinted by
permission of the publishers.

vived by his intense belief in them. He picked up and intensified a doctrine, common at the time, that Germany had been betrayed, when on the point of victory, by the "November criminals"—that is, by the Social Democrats and others who had concluded the armistice. Hence there followed a simple political deduction: if the democratic politicians and the democratic system were overthrown, Germany would again become great and powerful. Revolutionaries have always promised great things. None did so more plausibly than Hitler, or with such primitive means.

In domestic affairs, Hitler had no program except action, and this was mostly destructive. In foreign affairs also his program was destructive: an end to the international system created by the peacemakers of 1919. This was no mere revision of grievances and defects. Europe, which existed on the basis that Germany had lost the war, was to be rearranged on the basis that she had won. Hitler claimed further to have a creative purpose in his plans of conquest. The Germans were to find in eastern Europe the living space which the Anglo-Saxon peoples had found in the New World. A German equivalent of the United States would appear in the Ukraine. "Living space" was a phrase which Hitler had learned from geopolitics. It had no firm significance: Germany did not suffer from over-population. In any case, according to Hitler himself, the main purpose of living space in the Ukraine was to enable Germany to withstand blockade in a future war against Great Britain and France, even though, in his usual contradictory way, he postulated that such a war was unnecessary.

All this rigmarole amounted to little more than a determination to restore and to perpetuate Germany's victories in the First World War. The German General Staff and Bethmann Hollweg, the German Chancellor, had then pursued living space in the east with all Hitler's ambition, even if without the geopolitical trimmings. Indeed, Hitler was more moderate than his predecessors, in that he did not aspire to colonies overseas nor to territorial gains in western Europe—though naturally his modesty diminished when the chance of such gains actually matured. Living space itself was the invention of a British geopolitician, Sir Halford Mackinder. Hitler's enthusiasm for the German race echoed the pseudo-scientific racialism common in the later nineteenth century, and was no sillier than E. A. Freeman, Kipling, and Joesph Chamberlain on the Anglo-Saxons or than almost any Frenchman on "la grande nation."

Hitler's strongest fanaticism was for anti-Semitism, and this, too, had a long, though no doubt disreputable, intellectual history. Many countries, in their time, had expelled the Jews, as Germany was to do under Hitler; the Inquisition had burned Jews, as again Germany was to do. Racialists in France had deplored the admixture of Jewish blood. In the early twentieth century, Radical Roman Catholics such as Belloc and Chesterton had discovered that the Jews were corrupting British politics. Every fantasy in Hitler's system of ideas had forerunners and parallels elsewhere; the only difference was that Hitler took his ideas literally, and anti-Semitism most literally of all. Where others talked of eliminating Jewish influence from political or cultural life, without any clear idea of what they meant, Hitler saw the answer in precise terms of physical destruction. The First World War had taught people that it was righteous to kill others by the million for the sake of the nation. Hitler carried the doctrine further and held that it was righteous to kill others for the sake of any idea which came into his head. He was the end-product of a civilization of clever talk and helped to shake that civilization by taking the talk seriously.

Few except himself took Hitler seriously in his early days. He arrived too late to profit from the immediate confusions after the First World War. In 1923 he attempted to seize power in Munich on a ticket which combined anti-Communism and extreme nationalism. The attempt failed, and Hitler was imprisoned, under agreeable circumstances. When he emerged from prison, Germany was prosperous, and the Nazis in their brown uniforms were no more than a minor nuisance, irresponsible youngsters playing at politics. There was no social peril from which Hitler could save Germany, as Mussolini had claimed to save Italy. The Communists were an exhausted, harmless force and, while most Germans agreed with Hitler's denunciations of the peace settlement, they also thought that revision could wait for a future generation. Only the Great Depression put the wind into Hitler's sails. Every other party was obviously helpless against it. Hitler held out the promise that he would do something effective, though neither he nor anyone else knew what. Support for the National Socialist Party grew at every general election, of which Germany had many. The more youthful unemployed were glad to find occupation, and even some maintenance, as storm troopers. It was the Salvation Army all over again, this time promising Heaven on earth.

Even so, the existing political order lurched on until 1933. Great Britain, not Germany, was the center of interest in the first years of the Depression. A political upheaval there in 1931 threatened to destroy the Labor Party, actually destroyed the Liberal Party, and ended the traditional institutions of the gold standard and Free Trade. The year 1931 would do very well as the end of the long Liberal era, were it not that the supposedly new political forces in Great Britain proved to be almost as free-wheeling as the old Liberals. Still, Great Britain seemed to be leading the way towards managed currency and a closed economic system. In Germany, there was only the dreary round of deflation, imposed by emergency decree, which the Reichstag would neither oppose nor support. German governments operated in the void.

Hitler and the Nazis did not conquer power; they were intrigued into power by some particularly frivolous members of the old governing class, who imagined that they could take Hitler prisoner. At the end of January 1933, Hitler became Chancellor. Within a month he had destroyed the safeguards of the democratic constitution and was on the way to shaking off all other hindrances to his dictatorship. This was a dictatorship of a peculiar sort: a dictatorship of the masses over themselves. Though the National Socialists did not win a majority of votes at any free general election, they won more votes than any other German party had ever done. A few months after coming to power, they received practically all the votes recorded—an achievement which cannot be credited solely to terrorism, still less to fraud. No dictatorship has been so ardently desired or so firmly supported by so many people as Hitler's was in Germany. Demagogues and revolutionaries had always invoked the masses against the established order. Hitler was the first to whose call the masses responded: the most demagogic, if not the most democratic, statesman there has ever been.

Hitler and the Nazis present the historian with an almost insoluble problem. They are too loathsome to be treated easily with detachment. Criminals, barbarians, or—at the most charitable—madmen, seem the only appropriate descriptions. Yet all such phrases cause misunderstanding. Hitler was not a barbarian like Attila, breaking into a civilized Europe. He, his ideas, and his system were all products of European civilization, however unwelcome this now appears. Some observers explained Hitler by the brutality and militarism of the Germans; and many Germans were brutal and militaristic. Other observers regarded Hitler as a last desperate throw by capitalism; and many German capitalists expected to benefit from Hitler's destruction of the trade unions. A rather shaky, discontented society was pulled into order by the confident promises of a man who believed passionately in himself. Probably no one will make sense of German Fascism in our lifetime. No doubt most Germans did not appreciate at first what they were in for. No doubt many were pulled regretfully along. However, the most evil system of modern times was also the most popular, and it is silly to claim otherwise.

People in other countries were also to make out later that they had been deceived by Hitler and had failed to appreciate his true character. This is a pretence. Hitler was on the whole a frank statesman; the trouble was that others did not believe what he said. When he announced that he proposed to make Germany again the greatest power in Europe, this was taken as the ordinary sort of boasting which any statesman might use when he first came to high office. Besides, the political order in Europe had a single unfailing remedy for unruly demagogues, and this was to tame them by responsibility. This remedy was applied to Hitler, first by the governing classes in Germany and then by the rulers of other countries. Surely he would one day be bewitched by the glitter of respectability. Instead, Hitler exploited the concessions made to him by others and grew more confident with each easy success.

13

Helmut Heiber: "Prisoner of His Own Delusions"[1]

For years after the war, the German people were noticeably reluctant to reflect seriously on the things that happened during Hitler's time. By the late 1950's, however, the trial by German authorities of some former SS mass-murderers, coupled with a flurry of minor but highly publicized anti-Semitic incidents led a growing number of Germans to question the wisdom of their self-imposed amnesia. The young, particularly, began asking questions. The effect was twofold: steps were taken to introduce twentieth-century German history (with particular emphasis on the Weimar Republic and the Third Reich) into the curriculum of elementary and secondary schools; and the number of articles, books, films, plays, and television programs dealing with the Hitlerian period increased sharply. Among the first books to appear in the wake of these developments was Helmut Heiber's brief biography of Adolf Hitler. Heiber—like Ernst Nolte, one of the younger generation of German historians— synthesized the salient facts and interpretations from the more important works then available to him. The result is a sensible, balanced life of Hitler that varies little in its major conclusions from the much more comprehensive biography by Alan Bullock. Nevertheless, Heiber's assessment of Hitler, a major portion of which is reproduced below, is of special interest because, intended primarily for a German audience, it discusses the positive as well as the negative aspects of Hitler's reign.

Step by step the way led to the highest pinnacle; much force, much deception, great persuasive art were necessary, many successes whipped up the waves which Hitler, whom Otto Strasser has called the "cork of the revolution," was riding— and yet all this would have been impossible if he had not known how to win over the masses. It

[1] From Helmut Heiber, *Adolf Hitler: A Short Biography*, trans. L. Wilson (London: Oswald Wolff [Publishers] Ltd., 1961), pp. 96–97, 107–10, 112–23, 127–28, 141–45. First published by Colloquium Verlag Otto H. Hess, Berlin-Dahlem, 1960. Reprinted by permission of Oswald Wolff [Publishers] Ltd.

was not only his voice (which sounded harsher and rustier from year to year), not merely the compelling sweep of his gestures nor the magic gaze of those famous eyes which left people spellbound, it was rather the phenomenon of Hitler himself. The man who had fought his way to the top from nothing, who was so obviously of the same stuff as everyone else, whose commonplace features every block supervisor knew how to imitate, who satisfied a craving for frothy heroism as well as a demand for self-satisfaction, who managed the cult of the Grimly Beautiful as skilfully as he was able to provide fresh nourishment for traditions which had withered in the rational constitutionalism of Weimar: this man was as the people were and he wanted the same things, at any rate, they believed they wanted. In him they saw a mirror of themselves. . . .

This is not the place to trace the development of the SS-State which finally towards the end kept 500,000 people "busy" in twenty concentration camps with 165 adjoining work-camps, quite apart from the millions of Jews, Poles, Soviet prisoners of war and others who passed through the camps, died in the gas chambers, were destroyed as the human guinea-pigs of perverted "scientists" or who perished through overwork. Here we must confine ourselves to Hitler's part in the excesses of the Nazi State. It is not infrequently said in Germany: "Yes, the Führer must have known of the *existence* of the concentration camps and after all in themselves they were quite a reasonable and necessary thing—but all the degeneracy, all the cruelty, *that* belongs to the SS account, of *that* he knew nothing." Or: "Certainly, the Führer was against the Jews (and that was completely justified), but their mass destruction, that was the work of Himmler[2] alone." But was it Himmler, or was it not rather Hitler . . . ? The whole conception of the plan [Himmler] carried out came from Hitler personally. His numerous utterances including the quite irrational statements in his testament, the whole structure and principle of the Nazi State and finally Himmler's own subservient mentality leave no doubt of this, even though Hitler apparently avoided putting his instructions in writing, or rather had no need to do so. . . .

Knowing neither scruples nor inhibition, since he had seen through the conscience as a "Jewish invention" and all that is noble in man as mere humanitarian clap-trap, he believed himself entrusted by Providence with a mission which absolved him from the rules of common morality. His only conception of the law, moreover, was that it must serve the people, in other words, himself. It was—as he said—a means to domination, the codified exercise of authority. . . .

Effective, concentrated, even brilliant as it was in individual details and hectic, slipshod, slovenly as a whole, the Nazi State mirrored the

---

[2] Heinrich Himmler was Reich Leader of the SS and Chief of the German Police.

personality of its creator. For behind the façade of the Prussian cult of duty and Prussian phraseology, the bohemian from the Munich coffee houses had remained true to himself in his style of living. Only in the early months, when Hindenburg still lived in the same house and before the novelty and amusement of his new position had worn off, did Hitler behave like a normal head of government, seating himself punctually at 10 a.m. at his desk and taking a childish pride in showing his visitors a loaded out-tray. But that did not last long, and soon it was not he who adapted himself to the apparatus of government, but vice versa. As though he still lodged in a Viennese back-alley and had nothing to do but kill time, he would emerge from his bedroom towards noon, receive from amongst the waiting dignitaries whoever he felt inclined to talk to and at equally eccentric times lunch and dine with those whose uncritical admiration or intellectual inferiority he could rely on—although he himself ate very moderately and almost entirely on a vegetarian diet, was a non-smoker and, from 1924 onwards, drank no alcohol. Hitler really came to life in the evenings when, in apparent dread of being alone, he would entertain his exhausted entourage until the early hours of the morning with monologues on every possible and impossible subject.

In his daily routine of a man who even in his youth had become "sick with yawning" at the thought of "sitting one day in an office" official business . . . was done in the spare moments, in standing or in walking, between the door, as it were, and the hinge. Cabinet meetings became ever more rare—the last took place in 1937—and indeed they were no longer necessary in the Nazi State. Draft laws were dealt with in rotation and the rest was regulated by "Führer's orders" which could be obtained in the most curious fashion. For it was not necessary for them to be signed and sealed: a chance remark prompted by the mood of the moment was entirely adequate. What Hitler said was done—and the favorites were always to hand to note down his spontaneous brain-waves and pass them on as "Führer's orders" and "irrevocable decisions." . . .

That nevertheless the system functioned on the whole, though with audible grinding in the gears, and despite subsequent assertions to the contrary would probably have continued to function for further decades was due, beside the efficiency of the civil service, to Hitler's intuitive *Fingerspitzengefühl* or "finger-tip feeling" for practicable solutions. "Hitler was a genius of inventiveness," writes Schacht. "He often found surprisingly simple solutions to problems which had seemed to others insoluble." But this political ability, though certainly brilliant, was bound to lead to disaster when it induced in Hitler a conviction studiously cultivated by a swarm of flatterers that he was infallible and no longer needed advice. "With the certainty of a sleep-walker I follow the path which Providence prescribes for me," announced the seer in 1936. But anyone not prepared to swallow this dogma without contradiction became at least a potential enemy—the wicked bourgeois intellectuals, for instance, whom Hitler never trusted or understood and none of whom he included in his close circle. In the not unjustified fear that people might laugh at him behind his back, the Lord over Life and Death harbored to the end the resentment of "the eternal fourth-form boy" who had failed to gain his certificate and who—as he once expressed it—had climbed into the Paternoster from the other side.

But in the masses, so Hitler believed, the instinct was still alive which gives birth to faith. And so through the new faith which he exuded he had "welded together" this people that had once threatened to break apart, he had "bound them" to himself "by oath" after the rationally constructed Weimar State had torn its citizens from their old temples and failed to offer them a stabilizing focus for their feelings. Thus in the last resort the German masses served merely as a vehicle for Hitler's thirst for power, as the basis of a pyramid whose purpose consisted in its topmost stone; and in moments of excitement during the second half of the war Hitler made no attempt to conceal the fact. As a rule, however, he took good care not to parade his contempt.

Books entitled *Hitler as Few of Us Know Him, Hitler in His Spare Time, Hitler in His Mountains, Young People with Hitler,* etcetera, portrayed him as a story-book hero with the common touch. The Führer's interests, it was said, were quite simply universal ("no field of knowledge is strange to him"). Large numbers of fine photographs by Heinrich Hoffmann ("who sees the Führer for us") showed Hitler fondling blonde, bright-eyed children (his favorite, a particularly fine "Nordic" type was later discovered to be half Jewish and her pictures had to be withdrawn), Hitler talking to workers, Hitler clasping the hand—preferably both hands—of veterans, Hitler with peasants, Hitler with the inevitable old grannies, Hitler with chimney sweepers, Hitler with dogs, Hitler with Strength-through-Joy holiday-makers—smiling, always smiling, with a smile so hearty that even the uncreasable faces of his bodyguards could not restrain a smirk.

Of course, it was not this circus alone which did the trick. And even the persuasive arts and hypnoses of Goebbels's propaganda cookhouse, even the tentacles of Himmler's octopoid police which gripped every sphere of human existence would not have sufficed to produce that trusting "yes" with which the mass of the people affirmed the Nazi State if Hitler had not been able to draw on that enormous capital of confidence and devotion which his supporters gave him and which inevitably proved contagious. Where would he have been without those large numbers of honest and upright National Socialists who went to work in good faith and with their best will! . . .

In addition, the new régime was able to show impressive achievements in certain striking spheres, for it was typical of the Third Reich that in broad deserts of positively fantastic incapacity could be found not a few cases of outstanding efficiency—Speer's[3] technocrats, for instance, or Goebbels's young men were first-class in their field and performed excellent work. If, at the same time, Hitler's instructions were of a positive kind, results might be achieved of an intensity impossible in a democratic State. For the masses the most impressive must have been those spectacular measures which Hitler carried through in the field of social policy.

The innovations with which he contrasted his "Socialism of deeds" with a "Socialism of phrases" were of a very wide variety. Marriage-loans facilitated the founding of families; the protection of expectant mothers, post-natal care, holidays for children in the country (370,-000 in the first year alone), as well as the organization "Mother and Child" with its crèches and day-nurseries contributed to the further encouragement and easement of family life. A "Homestead Project" was entrusted with settlement plans intended to relieve the mournful monotony of tenement housing. The "Winter Help Work" with its powerful slogan "No one shall go hungry and cold" harnessed practically the whole nation and did an enormous amount to relieve the oppressive want in the early years. No less than 354 million marks were collected in the winter of 1933–1934 and though the "voluntary" subscriptions were semi-compulsory through the institution of lists and other devices this was not an important factor at the time. Finally, the "Strength-through-Joy" movement became for many the symbol of a progressive social policy designed to benefit the workers.

Nor was this all. There were further projects: the Volkswagen, or People's Car—not yet, but soon to be on the market—an undertaking carried out with Hitler's active participation and still making profits decades later when in other spheres there was little enough left of the Third Reich. Then there was the institution called "Beauty of Work" with its somewhat comically named subsidiaries, "Good Light," "Healthy Air," "Green into the Factories" and others, which compelled those managements anxious to enjoy the honor and advantages of a "Model concern" to redesign those primitive workshops which had tenaciously survived from an earlier age. There was a "Popular Education Work" and an "Office for Spare-time Activities" intended to abolish the exclusive character of culture and finally there were the famous Strength-through-Joy holidays. For a total charge of thirty-two marks which covered everything including entertainment the Berlin worker, for instance, could spent eight days on the Baltic and in the

[3] Albert Speer, an architect, was Inspector General of Construction; during the war he succeeded Fritz Todt as Inspector General of Highways and Minister for Armaments and Munitions.

less expensive resorts a whole week for as little as ten to fifteen marks. Higher-placed employees paid a supplement. This "Socialism of deeds" showed its flag abroad, as well: a total of nine ships were bought or chartered and two further liners specially built for cruises to the Mediterranean, to Norway and to Madeira which at that time became almost a synonym for the *Kraft durch Freude* [Strength-through-Joy—ED.] movement. And this was no mere façade for a handful of key-workers and Party activists: from 1934 to 1937, twenty-two million people enjoyed these holidays and even in 1939, the year when war broke out, the movement transported six million people through Germany and 150,000 overseas.

All this was a considerable achievement, let alone for a man who had risen from nothing and wasted his own youth so disastrously, and it should not be overlooked in an assessment of Hitler as a phenomenon. Certainly, other motives were involved than the pleasantly sounding names revealed. The encouragement of the family was intended to raise the birth-rate (and rise it did, from 971,000 births in Germany proper in 1933 to 1,413,000 in 1939) and this with the object of supplying Hitler with a labor-force, soldiers and settlers for his expansionist program. Social improvements were to placate the workers and in fact their cost represented a miserably small proportion of the rocketing industrial profits. The Strength-through-Joy operation was intended to absorb the excess purchasing power created by rearmament and economic autarky and finally the "Winter Help" drive financed armament projects which had nothing remotely to do with the objects advertised on the collecting boxes. Thus Hitler's social services were undoubtedly ambiguous and equivocal, quite apart from the suggestive propaganda effect which emerged when, on the prescribed Sundays, the whole nation was spooning up its one-course meal—a living symbol of that chimera, the "folk community" (*Volksgemeinschaft*) which, with the shameless exploitation of unlimited idealism was in the last resort only intended to supply an amorphous and pliant mass for the sinister purposes of an unscrupulous power politican.

The autobahns [superhighways—ED.] as well, of course, served this double function. One of Hitler's favorite projects, they provided a communication network for military purposes, but they also provided work and pointed the way to a technical future which at that time only few people were able to imagine. Here, thanks to Hitler's perhaps greatest talent, an intuitive understanding of technical problems based on genuine interest, an unparalleled result was achieved. . . .

All this must, as we have said, be taken into account and it is pointless to pass it over in silence or dismiss it with condescending remarks, for thereby a distorted picture would be created of a police State ruled exclusively by terror and fear. Certainly, that is one side of the picture, but not the decisive one, for no régime, even the most disreputable, can succeed in ruling solely at the point of the bayonet. Thus we can properly note the positive sides of the Hitler régime as well, bearing only in mind that every political system represents a whole. It is simply impossible to fabricate a theoretically ideal State from desirable features selected from widely differing political systems—philosophers have occasionally tried to do so, but in practice have always miserably failed. Whoever, therefore, in our case insists on having the Strength-through-Joy cruises, the autobahns, the maternity services, the "folk community," etcetera—and all that on this scale, at this tempo and this intensity—*must* also be prepared to accept the dark side. A State in which one man alone gives the orders will in many spheres achieve a much higher level of efficiency than a State in which everything has first to pass innumerable authorities and be thrashed out in public. Much that is good and useful undoubtedly gets lost in this process. But though they may frustrate positive achievement, both factors afford the greatest possible security against the damage that inevitably arises in an autocracy from an enlargement of the mistakes and weaknesses of the autocrat. Dictatorship and many "isms" would not be so bad if man were not so evil. And if these do change the world, no one has so far been able to change man, however loudly and repeatedly the claim may be raised to have done so.

Often, the darker side of the picture is easy to detect. Thus to the very end, Hitler indeed succeeded in maintaining a stable level of prices through his price-stop policy, but the wage-level also remained unchanged and what organized body of workers would have accepted that at a time when profits were rising continually! "Reasonable" arguments could, perhaps, even be adduced for so sinister a project as the compulsory sterilization of persons suffering from hereditary disease, but if this was allowed, who might not be sterilized or even put to death through euthanasia, *where* was the limit? No doubt, again, a series of Draconic laws rapidly restored internal security: no doubt the car-trap thieves, for instance, were quickly driven from the roads. And who, in war-time, would have dared to lay out his valuables in the cellar, what woman would have ventured on to the streets in the black-out, what would have become of the private property recovered from bombed buildings if on Hitler's order anyone stealing even a galvanized bucket did not automatically lose his head? Certainly, all this could be accounted a gain compared with the desolate conditions that often prevailed elsewhere. But . . . to send a man to the scaffold for a miserable bucket represented a blow to all natural feelings of justice. A man who could do that could also do other things. And so we are left here with the same picture: if one insists on these positive advantages, if one approves the measures that confer them, one must also desire all that was odious in the régime: tortures, concentration camps, legalized murder. To be certain that it is only the milkman when the door-bell rings at six o'clock in the morning involves accepting the darker sides of the picture as well.

Further, we should not overlook the fact that many of the so-called merits of Hitler's Reich were illusory. Who today praises the monumental pseudo-classic buildings with which Hitler, with his unfortunate life-long obsession for architecture, disfigured Munich and Berlin? Who delights in the huge naturalistic pictures to which he gave pride of place in his "House of German Art"? Or who today hazards the assertion that, in shining contrast to the bogs of corruption which democracies must continually drain, there was no corruption in Nazi Germany? Certainly, many people, including leading ones, preserved their honesty, but where the second man in the State [Göring—ED.] was himself corruption in the flesh the racketeering and graft were widespread.

All this represents, of course, wisdom after the event. At the time many people were taken in by the shoddy façade, and not only Germans, but hard-headed foreign politicians. . . .

And yet as we have seen, not everything brought into being by this gigantic will-power, dominated as it was by passion and resentment, was a mere façade. Far the most striking successes seeming to outweigh all criticism of the régime were those achieved by Hitler in the two spheres which had formed the core of the Nazi agitation against the Weimar Republic and at that time were uppermost in the public mind: the abolition of unemployment and the abrogation of the Versailles Treaty. . . .

Hitler mounted a radical attack on unemployment by the ruthless creation of work and currency, not calculating the operation as a business enterprise or a matter of raising capital, but basing it on an increase in purchasing power of the working population. The construction of the autobahns, armament production, the reconstruction of dwelling houses put the economy into gear, while development programs for the railways and posts were introduced and the marriage loans already mentioned drew women from the factories and increased the demand for household articles. The inflationary symptoms inseparable from such a policy were on the one hand made temporarily invisible through Schacht's famous trick whereby cash was replaced by "public works bills" made eligible for rediscount by the Reichsbank and on the other hand the new régime was undeniably supported by such a wave of public confidence that it could risk an extension of credit without having to fear an inflationist panic.

Thus unemployment figures sank rapidly during the first years of the Third Reich. . . . But although the complete removal of unemployment had eventually to be paid for with all the unspeakable suffering of the war and the post-war period, with countless millions of casualties and the destruction of the Reich, it was at first a success which weighed enormously in Hitler's favor and further consolidated his prestige. And the harvest he reaped in the field of foreign affairs was also a rich one—to start with, at any rate. . . .

It is curious that there is no novel and no play that starts with the assumption of Hitler's death on, say, 8th October, 1938. What a subject-matter that would be, for *who* would then have died: the liberator from the horrors of unemployment, the creator of the community of the German people, the destroyer of the chains of Versailles, the architect of Greater Germany, in short, Adolf Hitler the Great, one of the outstanding figures in German history! And whatever the policy of his successors, they would either, it would have been said, wisely and circumspectly have followed the path which he had traced for them or with insane megalomania squandered the inheritance of the Genius. But Hitler did not die in 1938. The "Providence" that he was always invoking decreed that he should pursue the basic aims and tendencies of his policy, his *Weltanschauung,* to their absurd conclusion. All this cost Europe 36 million dead and it cost German history a hero who might otherwise possibly have been accounted its greatest statesman.

But though not the greatest, was Hitler a statesman at all? To ask the question is to answer it in the negative. Hitler was an extremely skilful party leader, a crafty demagogue, an inspiring speaker, and . . . something [must] even be said for him as a military leader. But he was never a statesman. In his comprehensive biography Alan Bullock has, admittedly, brought out some of Hitler's positive abilities: his mastery of the irrational factors in politics, his insight into the weaknesses of his opponents, his gift for simplification, his sense of timing, his willingness to take risks. But in this last point lay that baneful quality which neutralized all his other gifts.

The true statesman will always understand how to suit his means and his stake to the goal at which he aims; the true statesman would never dare assert that he has "crossed out the word 'impossible' from the vocabulary." But to Hitler this was no mere phrase. Gambler that he was, he not only seemed to be, but was in fact prepared to stake everything on one card and to risk his all in each new round of the game. He conducted politics according to the rules of the American duel, lighting the fuse of a powder-barrel and waiting for his opponents to lose their nerve first and run away. For a long time, these tactics succeeded, because statesmen accustomed to weighing cost and risk were naturally at a disadvantage when confronted with this gambler. But sooner or later the time was bound to come when they preferred a terrible end to endless terror.

This was the case in 1939. It is therefore wrong to speak of a "change" in Hitler. At that time, neither he nor his policy changed in the least and if it is thought possible to draw a line between the "reasonable" and the "megalomaniac" Hitler, that is simply due to the fact that his first short-term aims removed genuine injustices and could be so presented that they found general understanding and agreement. But a few brief glances at the unread Hitler-book [*Mein Kampf*—ED.] with the sale of millions shows that behind all the deceptive talk there was always the same inordinate will to power. So the turn of the year 1938–1939 merely represents the dividing line beyond which for the world at large Hitler's policy crossed from the sphere of the tolerable to that of the intolerable. . . .

The "final solution" whose chief engineer Heydrich[4] received his instructions direct from Hitler crowned the satanic work when war and its accompanying circumstances created the conditions for its completion. The imagination of the men behind these evil deeds was that of huntsmen obsessed with the racio-biological task of rearing a racial élite on the one hand and, on the other, of rooting out "pests" —a measure of hygiene, as they called it. Through this policy the number of victims grew to such proportions that even today it still seems a problem worthy of discussion whether there were two, four or six million—as though that were a moral question and not merely a matter of organization and technique.

The correct figure is probably between four and five millions, but even if there were "only" one million victims, or "only" 500,000, and even if at some other time and place in history six million people had been destroyed in some gigantic pogrom: what was new and terrible in Hitler's action lay in the cool, mathematical calculation with which it was carried out. It is therefore wrong to speak of a "reversion to barbarism," for what occurred in Nazi Germany was done coldly and with deliberation in the name, though very largely without the knowledge, of a nation with pretensions to be called cultured and would have been impossible in this form among some Balkan mountain people or a tribe of South American Indians.

Unfortunately the Nuremberg Trials staged by the victors confused the issue by heaping together with these excesses which go beyond all bounds of human imagination or thought many of those unethical actions which tend to occur all over the world in wartime or in international affairs and which were horrifying in Hitler's Reich only by their extent or their repetition. Here people were destroyed not be-

---

[4] Reinhard Heydrich was, until his assassination by Czech resistance fighters in 1942, Himmler's right-hand man and Chief of the Main Office of Reich Security, the organization charged with over-all responsibility for the extermination of the European Jews.

cause of their real, alleged or even possible deeds, but for what they were: they were Jews and therefore in the eyes of their executioners a kind of vermin. And this merely in order to satisfy the diabolical hatred of one man, of Hitler who had become the prisoner of his own delusions. . . .

14

H. R. Trevor-Roper: "The Most Formidable Among the 'Terrible Simplifiers' of History"[1]

H. R. Trevor-Roper, Regius Professor of Modern History at Oxford University, combines two unlikely fields of professional interest: his principal historical specialty is the ecclesiastical and literary history of the seventeenth century, but he is also one of the foremost authorities on Nazi Germany. His professional interest in the Third Reich began at the end of World War II when he was assigned by British Intelligence authorities to the task of reconstructing the last days of Hitler's life and the circumstances of his death. The results of Trevor-Roper's official investigation were published in 1947 under the title of The Last Days of Hitler. *Now in its third edition, the book remains the standard work on the subject. In the past two decades, Trevor-Roper has stepped out of the early modern period often enough to contribute a small shelf full of articles, essays, reviews, and editions to the literature of the Hitlerian era. One of these contributions—a long, brilliant essay entitled "The Mind of Adolf Hitler"—is the source of our next selection. The brief excerpt printed below sums up Trevor-Roper's general assessment of Hitler's intellect.*

Who was Hitler? The history of his political career is abundantly documented and we cannot escape from its terrible effects. A whole generation may well be named in history after him and we shall speak of the Age of Hitler as we speak of the Age of Napoleon or the Age of Charlemagne. And yet, for all the harsh obviousness of its imprint on the world, how elusive his character remains! What he did is clear;

---

[1] From H. R. Trevor-Roper, "The Mind of Adolf Hitler," an introductory essay to *Hitler's Secret Conversations, 1941–1944*, trans. N. Cameron and R. H. Stevens (New York: Farrar, Straus and Young, Inc., 1953), pp. vii–viii, xxiv, xxvii–xxviii, xxxii. Reprinted by permission of Farrar, Straus & Giroux, Inc., Weidenfeld & Nicolson, Ltd., and H. R. Trevor-Roper.

every detail of his political activity is now—thanks to a seizure and exploitation of documents unparalleled in history—historically established; his daily life and personal behavior have been examined and exposed. But still, when asked not what he did but how he did it, or rather how he was able to do it, historians evade the question, sliding away behind implausible answers. To the Marxists—most old-fashioned of all—he was simply a pawn, the creature of a dying capitalism in its last stages. Others have seen him as a charlatan profiting by a series of accidents, a consummate actor and hypocrite, a sly, cheating peasant, or a hypnotist who seduced the wits of men by a sorcerer's charms. Even Sir Lewis Namier endorses the account of him given by a disgusted German official as a mere illiterate, illogical, unsystematic bluffer and smatterer. Even Mr. Bullock seems content to regard him as a diabolical adventurer animated solely by an unlimited lust for personal power. And yet, we may object, could a mere adventurer, a shifty, scatterbrained charlatan, have done what Hitler did, who, starting from nothing, a solitary plebeian in a great cosmopolitan city, survived and commanded all the dark forces he had mobilized and, by commanding them, nearly conquered the whole world? So we ask, but we seldom receive an answer: the historians have turned away, and like antique heroes we only know that we have been talking with the immortals from the fact that they are no longer there.

Now this problem, I think, is a real problem, and it is worth while to emphasize rather than to evade it. Let us consider for a moment Hitler's achievement. The son of a petty official in rural Austria, himself of meager education and no fixed background, by all accounts a shiftless, feckless, unemployable neurotic living from hand to mouth in the slums of Vienna, he appeared in Germany, as a foreigner, and, in the years of its most abject condition, declared that the German people could, by its own efforts, and against the wishes of its victors, not only recover its lost provinces, but add to them, and conquer and dominate the whole of Europe. Further, he declared that he personally could achieve this miracle. Twenty years later he had so nearly succeeded that the rest of the world thought it another miracle when he was at last resisted.

To historians there are no miracles. Whatever has happened they explain and it becomes to them, in retrospect, inevitable. But it is salutary sometimes to see events from their starting-point, not from their conclusion, and to judge thereby the prospect, not the issue, of success. Only thus can we appreciate the character of those who foresaw them. We rightly regard it as one sign of the greatness of Mr. Churchill that, from 1933, he appreciated, as few others did, the real danger of a new German Empire. We should, I think, recognize it as one sign of the genius of Hitler that he, twelve years earlier, when it seemed far more improbable, appreciated the hope of such an empire and believed—correctly as it proved—both that it could be built and that he, though then a solitary demobilized corporal, could be its builder. I have labored this point because I wish to maintain—contrary, as it appears, to all received opinion—that Hitler had a mind. It seems to me that whereas a mere visionary might, in 1920, have dreamed of such a revolution, and whereas a mere adventurer might, in the 1930's, have exploited such a revolution (as Napoleon exploited the French revolution which others had made), any man who both envisaged and himself created both a revolution as a means to empire and an empire after revolution, and who, in failure and imprisonment, published in advance a complete blueprint of his intended achievement, in no significant point different from its ultimate actual form, simply cannot be regarded as either a mere visionary or a mere adventurer. He was a systematic thinker and his mind is, to the historian, as important a problem as the mind of Bismarck or Lenin. . . .

For Hitler's miraculous career is not to be explained by the mere enumeration of his actions, or the registration of his personal behavior: it is to be explained, if at all, by the mental power which, at some time of his life, he directed to the basic questions of history and politics, revolution and ideology, strategy and power. It was because his views on these subjects were so compulsive that he was able to draw around him, as willing accomplices, not only that nucleus of devoted and fanatical revolutionaries who provided him with his *élite*, but also those millions of ordinary Germans who, recognizing in him the prophet and executor of their half-formulated and since disowned ambitions, followed him readily, even gladly, even to the end, in his monstrous attempt to impose on the world a barbarian German domination. . . .

No account or analysis of [Hitler's mind] can be complete without reference to the yawning emptiness which, on certain sides, bounded its hard, clear, monolithic structure. For if we know some of the books that Hitler read, and the subjects which he studied, and from which he built his monstrous, but, to many Germans, compelling philosophy, equally we know—and it is almost as important—some of the books which he did not read, some of the subjects which never engaged his otherwise roving, predatory, gluttonous mind. "A man," said Bishop Berkeley, "who hath not much meditated upon God, the human mind and the *summum bonum*, may possibly make a thriving earthworm, but will most indubitably make a sorry patriot and a sorry statesman." Hitler was a patriot and a statesman of this sorry kind. He never meditated on these things. No word he ever uttered even so much as touched the human spirit. His views on art were worthless. He did not know the meaning of humanity. Weakness he despised, and pity (being sympathy with weakness) he despised also. It was *Humanitätsduselei*, humanitarian stupidity. And if he despised physical weakness he also, in others, hated moral strength. What he admired in Stalin was only the craft, the cruelty and the success which he discovered in that rival revolutionary career; the British refusal to be defeated simply drove him into paroxysms of petulant hatred. Only his own strength, his own will, his own faith had for him any merit: the qualities themselves, to him, were valueless. Love meant nothing to him—it was simply a competition in which the Most Nazi of he-Germans deserved the most conventionally well-proportioned of she-Germans, and there is something repulsive in his conception of it, not cynical, nor coarse, but simply mean, mechanical, inhuman. Children were to him merely the continually replaceable (and therefore continually dispensable) material of conquest and colonization. He had views indeed on nature and often spoke of his "communion" with it, but it was a hideous nature, the devouring nature whose cruelty justified his own: not a sociable pagan Nature of nymph-haunted woods and populated streams, but a romantic Wagnerian nature of horrid Alps in whose intoxicating solitude he could best hatch his own equally violent and implacable interventions. And as for the purpose of human life, that futile quest which nevertheless is an index of humanity, it was for him merely that Germans should be the masters of the world. . . .

His ultimate conception of German culture . . . was simply a question of more cakes for Germans and less for non-Germans. He was a complete and rigid materialist, without sympathy or even tolerance for those immaterial hopes or fears or imaginations or illusions which, however absurdly, cast a faint ennobling gleam on the actions of mankind. To Hitler all this immaterial world was simply *Mumpitz*. Moral values—the whole scale of better or worse—since they depend on immaterial criteria, simply did not exist for him . . . , the most formidable among the "terrible simplifiers" of history, the most systematic, the most historical, the most philosophical, and yet the coarsest, cruellest, least magnanimous conqueror the world has ever known.

Afterword
Hitler: The Unexplained
Phenomenon

The facts of Adolf Hitler's life are already so well known that it is doubtful that further scrutiny of its details will alter significantly our present conception of his role in history. But, at best, these facts do justice only to the external scale of his career. As the man and his era recede into the past the time has come to shift our focus from the collection of facts to the analysis of human action, from the "how" to the "why." For if we seek to make the past intelligible we cannot escape the effort to understand.

To call for further efforts in new directions is not to depreciate the immense and often brilliant contribution of those scholars who have built the solid foundation on which all future research in the field must be based. But it is not enough to know, as Alan Bullock tells us, that Hitler was a political genius, a gifted demagogue, an unprincipled opportunist, a self-convinced prophet, a latter-day Attila the Hun whose driving force was an unlimited lust for personal power. Nor have we arrived at understanding with H. R. Trevor-Roper's view that Hitler was, in addition to most of what Bullock has said, a man of great, if vulgar, mental power, a monstrous intellectual giant whose compulsive mental efforts not only systematized but also actualized one of the most barbaric ideologies of all time. And even Ernst Nolte's tentative psychological portrait barely hints at the all-important link between private motivations and public acts, between Hitler's personal psychology and the psychological desires and fears of so many Germans.

What seems to be the insuperable difficulty incurred by the existing biographical accounts is to explain both why Hitler thought and acted as he did and why millions of Germans found in his frightful ideology a new faith. Now everything inclines us to believe that Hitler's life mirrored many of the psychological, sociological, and cultural factors that became the basic forces of the movement he led. It follows from this that future biographers of Hitler, if they aspire to more than storytelling, will have to come to grips with the same fundamental questions faced by students of the larger problem of German National Socialism. To suggest answers that can contribute significantly to our comprehension, they will have to follow the trend toward the adoption of newer concepts, sharper analytical tools, and a wider outlook. In short, biographers of Hitler will have to borrow more heavily than they have the techniques and insights gained from diversified fields of study.

The application of some of the newer concepts of depth psychology, for example, may shed more light on the connection between Hitler's political appeal and the irrational fears, the unconscious antagonisms, the corrosive discontent that gripped those Germans who welcomed him as a savior. A start has already been made. Viewed from one modern psychoanalytical perspective,[1] Hitler's rise to greatness can be interpreted as the story of an individual striving to find his own identity, his sense of purpose and place in society. In seeking to solve his inner problem, he develops a political ideology that is at once the expression of a personal need and a blow against the existing system. In striking out against his environment he begins to win first an audience, then a following; for there are others who feel uncertain about the time, who are alienated from the society in which they live, who are suffering a loss of identity. In short, this approach (barely sketched here) suggests that Hitler, in seeking to find himself and to give meaning to his own existence, gave a sense of identity and meaning to many Germans at a particular juncture in history. Much certainly remains to be done along these lines, but the speculative richness of this conceptual framework is obvious. And it may well be an important line of advance for future biographers of Hitler.

There are of course many other fruitful ways to study Hitler and his movement; and we have only begun to sound their potentialities. Hitler's ideology was emotionally and psychologically directed, but psychological interpretations alone are not enough. If we are to deal understandingly with these problems (which is the most we can expect, for such problems are never solved), we will need all the knowledge we can get from the combined insights of political science, psychology, economics, sociology, and the various fields of history. In conclusion, we must realize that many of the old assumptions, established presuppositions, and conventional categories of explanation cannot help us to understand Adolf Hitler and National Socialism. Regardless of where they originate, we need a fresh store of ideas and professional perspectives to cope with what is after all a relatively fresh set of historical problems.

---

[1] That projected by the psychoanalyst and part-time historian Erik H. Erikson, most notably in his book *Young Man Luther: A Study in Psychoanalysis and History* (New York: W. W. Norton & Company, Inc., 1958). Some of Erikson's concepts have found their way into the biographical essay at the beginning of this volume.

Bibliographical Note

The historical literature on Hitler is vast. Fortunately for those who do not read German a considerable portion of it has been published in English. This note confines itself to some of the principal works in that category. Students interested in doing serious research on Hitler are advised to consult the *Biographischer Katalog* from the Library of the *Institut für Zeitgeschichte* in Munich (Boston: G. K. Hall & Co., 1968). Listings of current articles and books may be found in the following two quarterly journals: *Vierteljahrshefte für Zeitgeschichte* (Stuttgart) and *Journal of Contemporary History* (London).

The most important part of the Hitler literature is what he himself wrote and said. The best English-language edition of *Mein Kampf*, although it is not free of error, is that translated by Ralph Manheim (Boston: Houghton Mifflin Company, 1943). Hitler's second book (third if the two volumes of *Mein Kampf* are counted separately)—written in 1928, discovered in 1958, and published in English under the title of *Hitler's Secret Book* (New York: Grove Press, Inc., 1961)—is essentially an elaboration of the ideas on foreign policy outlined in his first book. There is nothing even approaching a complete collection of Hitler's speeches in English. However, representative passages from his public speeches between 1922 and 1939, arranged by subject, have been translated in Norman H. Baynes, ed., *The Speeches of Adolf Hitler, April 1922–August 1939*, 2 vols. (London: Oxford University Press, 1942). Two other collections of speeches—shorter, but each useful in its own way—are: Gordon W. Prange, ed., *Hitler's Words, 1923–1943* (Washington: American Council on Public Affairs, 1944) and Raoul de Roussy de Sales, *My New Order* (New York: Reynal & Company, Inc., 1941). Hermann Rauschning's *The Voice of Destruction* (New York: G. P. Putnam's Sons, 1940), though not a verbatim record, gives the sense of Hitler's conversations with the author during the period 1932–1934. Far more reliable and revealing is the record (stenographically set down, but subsequently edited by Hitler's personal secretary, Martin Bormann) of Hitler's informal table-talk with intimate associates and guests during the war, published in English as *Hitler's Secret Conversations, 1941–1944* (New York: Farrar, Straus and Young, Inc., 1953). For a modest but representative selection from the stenographic transcripts of Hitler's daily military conferences held between December 1942 and March 1945, see Felix Gilbert, ed., *Hitler Directs His War* (New York: Oxford University Press, 1950). Another slim volume, *The Testament of Adolf Hitler* (London: Cassell and Company, Ltd., 1961), contains statements made by Hitler to Martin Bormann during the last three months of his life.

Still the best general biography of Hitler in any language is Alan

Bullock, *Hitler: A Study in Tyranny*, completely rev. ed. (New York: Harper & Row, Publishers, 1962), which also offers a reliable historical survey of the entire Nazi era. A brief, objective account of Hitler's life by a German historian is Helmut Heiber, *Adolf Hitler: A Short Biography* (London: Oswald Wolff [Publishers] Ltd., 1961). Of the numerous early biographies of Hitler only one has withstood the test of time: Konrad Heiden's *Der Fuehrer: Hitler's Rise to Power* (Boston: Houghton Mifflin Company, 1944), which—though it carries the story only through mid-1934—has not yet been entirely surpassed for the period it covers. Three of the five essays that constitute James H. Mc-Randle's *The Track of the Wolf: Essays on National Socialism and Its Leader, Adolf Hitler* (Evanston, Ill.: Northwestern University Press, 1965) focus on the Führer; together they add up to an incisive and often provocative psychic biography that is a useful supplement to Bullock's comprehensive work. A readable biographical essay is the profile of Hitler's life and career in Joachim J. Fest, *Portrait of the Third Reich* (New York: Pantheon Books, Inc., 1968), a translation of a well-received German book originally published in 1963.

Only in the last decade or so has any substantial light been shed on Hitler's early years. August Kubizek's intimate recollections of the adolescent Hitler during the years 1904 to 1908, *The Young Hitler I Knew* (Boston: Houghton Mifflin Company, 1955), should be supplemented with the more comprehensive and objective book by Franz Jetzinger, *Hitler's Youth* (London: Hutchinson & Co. [Publishers], Ltd., 1958). Also of interest in this connection is William A. Jenks, *Vienna and the Young Hitler* (New York: Columbia University Press, 1960), which—its title notwithstanding—deals not so much with the young Hitler as with the cultural and political atmosphere in Vienna during the years he lived there. Despite the virtues of the three foregoing books, the most thorough and scholarly investigation of Hitler's antecedents and early life available in English is Bradley F. Smith, *Adolf Hitler: His Family, Childhood, and Youth* (Stanford: Hoover Institution on War, Revolution & Peace, 1967), which not only synthesizes most of the relevant published material but also draws on unpublished material from various Nazi archives.

In addition to those reminiscences that have been excerpted in Part Two, the following memoirs make a contribution to Hitler's biography. Like most of their genre, however, they must be handled with care. *By Germans who served Hitler:* Karl Doenitz, *Memoirs: Ten Years and Twenty Days* (Cleveland: World Publishing Company, 1959); Ernst Hanfstaengl, *Hitler: The Missing Years* (London: Eyre & Spottiswoode [Publishers], Ltd., 1957); Erich von Manstein, *Lost Victories* (Chicago: Henry Regnery Co., 1958); Heinz Guderian, *Panzer Leader* (New York: E. P. Dutton & Co., Inc., 1952); Franz von Papen, *Memoirs* (New York: E. P. Dutton & Co., Inc., 1953); Serge Lang and Ernst von Schenck, eds., *Memoirs of Alfred Rosenberg* (Chicago: Ziff-Davis, 1949); Wilhelm Keitel, *The Memoirs of Field-Marshal Keitel* (New York: Stein & Day Publishers, 1966); Walter Warlimont, *Inside Hitler's Headquarters, 1939–45* (New York: Frederick A. Praeger, Inc., 1964); Otto Dietrich, *Hitler* (Chicago: Henry Regnery Co., 1955); Franz Halder, *Hitler as Warlord* (London: Putnam, Coulton, 1950); Heinrich Hoffmann, *Hitler Was My Friend* (London: Burke, 1955); Fritz Thyssen, *I Paid Hitler* (New York: Farrar & Rinehart, Inc., 1941); Joachim von Ribbentrop, *The Ribbentrop Memoirs* (London: Weidenfeld & Nicolson, Ltd., 1954); Otto Strasser, *Hitler and I* (Boston: Houghton Mifflin Company, 1940); Erich Raeder, *My Life* (Annapolis: United States Naval Institute, 1960); Paul Schmidt, *Hitler's Interpreter* (New York: The Macmillan Company, 1951). *By foreign diplomats and journalists who observed Hitler:* Nevile Henderson, *Failure of a Mission: Berlin 1937–1939* (New York: G. P. Putnam's Sons, 1940); G. Ward Price, *I Know These Dictators* (New York: Holt, Rinehart & Winston, Inc., 1938); Kurt von Schuschnigg, *Austrian Requiem* (New York: G. P. Putnam's Sons, 1946). To this list should be added the following diaries and letter collections: Louis P. Lochner, ed., *The Goebbels Diaries, 1942–43* (Garden City, N.Y.: Doubleday & Company, Inc., 1948); William E. Dodd, Jr. and Martha Dodd, eds., *Ambassador Dodd's Diary, 1933–1938* (New York: Harcourt, Brace & World, Inc., 1941); H. R. Trevor-Roper, ed., *The Bormann Letters* (London: Weidenfeld & Nicolson, Ltd., 1954). Some of Hitler's lieutenants on trial before the International Military Tribunal in Nuremberg reveal their innermost thoughts about their former Führer to a prison psychologist in G. M. Gilbert, *Nuremberg Diary* (New York: Farrar, Straus and Young, Inc., 1947).

Much of importance to an understanding of Hitler's life and career is contained in specialized works on the cultural, political, economic, social, and military history of his time. The cultural and intellectual currents on which National Socialism battened are treated in George L. Mosse's sweeping *The Crisis of German Ideology: Intellectual Origins of the Third Reich* (New York: Grosset & Dunlap, Inc., 1964) and Fritz Stern's penetrating *The Politics of Cultural Despair: A Study in the Rise of the Germanic Ideology* (Berkeley: University of California Press, 1961). Now available in English, Ralf Dahrendorf's brilliant and readable *Society and Democracy in Germany* (Garden City, N.Y.: Doubleday & Company, Inc., 1967) sheds new light on the failure of liberalism in Germany, one of whose consequences was the rise of Hitler; he also has some provocative things to say about Hitler's social revolution.

Ernst Nolte's massive *Three Faces of Fascism* (New York: Holt, Rinehart & Winston, Inc., 1966) not only includes some astute interpretations of Hitler and his movement but also places National Socialism within the larger framework of the irrational right-radical movements of our time. Nolte's article, "Germany," in Hans Rogger and Eugen Weber, eds., *The European Right: A Historical Profile* (Berkeley: University of California Press, 1966) is worth reading, though it is no substitute for the relevant portions of his larger work. A slim volume that approaches the same problem from a somewhat different perspective and along a broader front is John Weiss, *The Fascist Tradition* (New York: Harper & Row, Publishers, 1967). A considerable portion of F. L. Carsten's *The Rise of Fascism* (Berkeley: University of California Press, 1967) is devoted to a survey of Hitler's rise to power.

Neither the growth of the Nazi Party between 1919 and 1933 nor the seizure of power in 1933–1934 is at present well served in English. On the former, see Reginald Phelps's article, "Hitler and the Deutsche Arbeiterpartei" in the *American Historical Review*, LXVIII, No. 4 (July 1963), 974–86, as well as two recent articles by Dietrich O. Orlow, "The Organizational History and Structure of the NSDAP, 1919–23" in the *Journal of Modern History*, XXXVII, No. 2 (June 1965), 208–26 and "The Conversion of Myths into Political Power: The Case of the Nazi Party, 1925–1926" in the *American Historical Review*, LXXII, No. 3 (April 1967), 906–24. On the Nazi seizure of power we have only the essays by Karl Dietrich Bracher and Helmut Krausnick in *The Path to Dictatorship, 1918–1933: Ten Essays by German Scholars* (Garden City, N.Y.: Doubleday & Company, Inc., 1966) and William Sheridan Allen's *The Nazi Seizure of Power: The Experience of a Single German Town, 1930–1935* (Chicago: Quandrangle Books, Inc., 1965), a brilliant microcosmic study whose limits are clearly stated in its subtitle. However, more will soon be available. A detailed survey of the Nazi revolution through the summer of 1935 is promised in the forthcoming book by Eliot B. Wheaton, *Prelude to Calamity: The Nazi Revolution and Its Origins* (Garden City, N.Y.: Doubleday & Company, Inc., 1968). And the standard study of all aspects—political, constitutional, social, economic, diplomatic, military, institutional, and cultural—of the Nazi consolidation of power during the crucial first two years of Hitler's reign, the monumental work by Karl Dietrich Bracher, Wolfgang Sauer, and Gerhard Schulz, *Die nationalsozialistiche Machtergreifung: Studien zur Errichtung des totalitären Herrschaftssystems in Deutschland 1933–1934*, 2nd ed. (Cologne: Westdeutscher Verlag, 1962) will be published in English translation by Yale University Press in the not too distant future.

Two books that shed light on the nature of Hitler's appeal to the average German are Theodore Abel, *The Nazi Movement* (New York: Atherton Press, 1965; originally published by Prentice-Hall, Inc. in 1938 under the title *Why Hitler Came into Power*) and Milton Mayer, *They Thought They Were Free: The Germans 1933–45* (Chicago: Chicago University Press, 1955). The nature of Hitler's social appeal and the extent to which he fulfilled the expectations of his various supporters are impressively dealt with in David Schoenbaum, *Hitler's Social Revolution: Class and Status in Nazi Germany, 1933–1939* (Garden City, N.Y.: Doubleday & Company, Inc., 1966), which also provides a partial corrective to Franz Neumann's pioneering—and still useful—*Behemoth: The Structure and Practice of National Socialism, 1933–1944* (New York: Oxford University Press, 1944). The process by which the German press became a pliable instrument in Hitler's hands is described in Oron J. Hale's detailed and scholarly study of the *Captive Press in the Third Reich* (Princeton: Princeton University Press, 1964), while Hamilton T. Burden's *The Nuremberg Party Rallies: 1923–39* (New York: Frederick A. Praeger, Inc., 1967) vividly describes Hitler's use of the awesome, semireligious ceremonies held annually on "Party Day" to impress the masses. Some sense of what it was like to live under Hitler can be gauged from the documentary collection prepared by George L. Mosse, ed., *Nazi Culture: Intellectual, Cultural, and Social Life in the Third Reich* (New York: Grosset & Dunlap, Inc., 1966).

The relationship between Hitler and the German Army is well treated in the following works: J. W. Wheeler-Bennett, *The Nemesis of Power: The German Army in Politics, 1918–1945,* 2nd ed. (New York: St. Martin's Press, Inc., 1964); Telford Taylor, *Sword and Swastika: Generals and Nazis in the Third Reich* (New York: Simon & Schuster, Inc., 1952); and Robert J. O'Neill, *The German Army and the Nazi Party 1933–1939* (London: Cassell & Company, Ltd., 1966). The Führer and his private army, or praetorian guard, are discussed in George H. Stein, *The Waffen SS: Hitler's Elite Guard at War, 1939–1945* (Ithaca: Cornell University Press, 1966). On Hitler's foreign policy and his warlike intentions, see the brief but incisive book by E. M. Robertson, *Hitler's Pre-War Policy and Military Plans, 1933–1939* (London: Longmans, Green & Company, Ltd., 1963). A. J. P. Taylor's mischievous and misleading *The Origins of the Second World War* (New York: Atheneum Publishers, 1962) should be read in conjunction with the following correctives: H. R. Trevor-Roper, "A. J. P. Taylor, Hitler and the War" in *Encounter,* XVII, No. 1 (July 1961), 88–96; Robert Spencer, "War Unpremeditated?" in the *Canadian Historical Review,* XLIII, No. 2 (June 1962), 136–44; and T. W. Mason, "Some Origins of the Second World War" in *Past and Present,* No. 29 (December 1964), pp. 67–87. Alan S. Milward's *The German Economy at War* (London: The Athlone Press of the University of London, 1965) not only implicitly rejects Taylor's contention that Germany's failure to mobilize her economy for total war in the thirties meant that Hitler's intentions were peaceful, but also discusses the extent to which Hitler himself took a hand in economic matters. The war Hitler envisaged is revealed in the documentary collection by H. R. Trevor-Roper, ed., *Blitzkrieg to Defeat: Hitler's War Directives, 1939–1945* (New York: Holt, Rinehart & Winston, Inc., 1965). Additional perspectives on Hitler as warlord are offered in the memoirs of his military leaders (Keitel, Warlimont, Halder, Manstein, Doenitz, and Guderian) cited above. Hitler's relationship with his two principal wartime allies is covered in Johanna Menzel Meskill, *Hitler and Japan: The Hollow Alliance* (New York: Atherton Press, 1966), a slim volume, and F. W. Deakin, *The Brutal Friendship: Mussolini, Hitler, and the Fall of Italian Fascism* (New York: Harper & Row, Publishers, 1962), a massive volume; the size of the respective books reflects the extent of the relationships.

The attempt to assassinate Hitler in 1944 is recounted with verve and precision in Constantine FitzGibbon, *20 July* (New York: W. W. Norton & Company, Inc., 1956). A useful documentary collection on the bomb plot published in English translation by the Press and Information Office of the Federal German Government is Erich Zimmermann and Hans-Adolf Jacobsen, eds., *Germans Against Hitler: July 20, 1944* (Bonn: Berto-Verlag, 1960). The basic account of the last days of Hitler's life, as well as the circumstances surrounding his death, is still H. R. Trevor-Roper's *The Last Days of Hitler,* 3rd ed. (New York: Collier Books, 1962), which was first published in 1947. Reuben Ainsztein's article, "How Hitler Died: The Soviet Version," in *International Affairs*, XLIII, No. 2 (April 1967), 307–18 adds a few interesting, though not fully confirmed, details drawn from Russian sources (e.g., the badly burned corpses of Hitler and his wife were found and identified by the Russians, and Hitler took his own life not with a pistol but with poison).

Index

Thinking About Cities